WHERE THE
RIVER BURNED

David Stradling
and Richard Stradling

WHERE THE RIVER BURNED

Carl Stokes and the

Struggle to Save Cleveland

Cornell University Press

Ithaca and London

Map design on endpapers by Jenn Hales.

First published 2015 by Cornell University Press

Printed in the United States of America

Library of Congress Cataloging-in-Publication Data

Stradling, David, author.
   Where the river burned : Carl Stokes and the struggle to save Cleveland /
David Stradling and Richard Stradling.
       pages cm
   Includes bibliographical references and index.
   ISBN 978-0-8014-5361-8 (cloth : alkaline paper)
   1. Cleveland (Ohio)—Politics and government—20th century.
2. Cleveland (Ohio)—Environmental conditions. 3. Urban renewal—
Environmental aspects—Ohio—Cleveland. 4. City planning—
Environmental aspects—Ohio—Cleveland. 5. Community development—
Environmental aspects—Ohio—Cleveland. 6. Stokes, Carl. I. Stradling,
Richard, author. II. Title.
   F499.C657S77 2015
   977.1'32—dc23   2014031091

Cornell University Press strives to use environmentally responsible
suppliers and materials to the fullest extent possible in the publishing
of its books. Such materials include vegetable-based, low-VOC inks
and acid-free papers that are recycled, totally chlorine-free, or partly
composed of nonwood fibers. For further information, visit our website
at www.cornellpress.cornell.edu.

Cloth printing   10 9 8 7 6 5 4 3 2 1

For
Jodie, Sarah, and Nina
and
Leanne, Sydney, and Ben

Contents

Preface

Our story begins with a river catching fire in June 1969. The Cuyahoga, prone to oil slicks and accumulating debris and, it turns out, to catching fire, burned for about half an hour on a Sunday morning. Two days after the fire, the *Plain Dealer* newspaper ran an editorial under the headline, "Cleveland: Where the River Burns," foreshadowing what would happen over the next couple of years. More and more Americans came to associate Cleveland, a once wealthy and mighty industrial city, with the environmental crisis and rapid urban decline. The burning river ran through the stories and the jokes Americans told about the "mistake on the lake."

The fire became notorious but not well understood. Over the last few decades, all kinds of people—politicians, scholars, journalists, and average Clevelanders—have told the story of the fire, usually quickly and with little detail, but always with the conclusion that this little fire had a big impact. To this day, the Cuyahoga fire plays a prominent role in the story many Clevelanders tell about their city. It also plays a prominent role in the story environmentalists tell about polluted America, about devastated industrial landscapes in the pre-regulatory era. In some versions of this story, the fire led directly to the Clean Water Act in 1972; in others it was simply a watershed moment, when Americans began to realize just how polluted their environment had become.

Since almost no one has even attempted to explain why this event took on so much meaning, we set out to write a history of the Cuyahoga, leading up to its burning and then following the role of the fire through the passage of the Clean Water Act and perhaps beyond, to the river's eventual (and partial) cleansing and Cleveland's eventual (and partial) rebirth. In essence, we set out to write a biography of the Cuyahoga, one that centered on the river's long and troubled relationship with the industrial city it helped create. Along the way, we made several discoveries that spoiled this plan.

When the river caught fire that June, most Clevelanders seemed not to care a great deal, the *Plain Dealer* editorial notwithstanding. A minor blaze—no one hurt, only a couple of railroad trestles damaged, no photos, no film—it wasn't a big story at the time, certainly not a national one. Cleveland's two daily papers, the *Cleveland Press* and the *Plain Dealer*, published photos of the damaged trestles the following day, but coverage of the fire was thin and matter-of-fact. Far too many problems plagued the city for residents to get hung up on a little fire that damaged two railroad bridges that most people never saw and couldn't find on a map. And as many Clevelanders surely knew, the Cuyahoga had caught fire numerous times before. So locals understood that the '69 fire didn't represent the culmination of an abusive relationship between a city and its environment. It was simply another sad chapter in the long story of a terribly polluted river. And the river was just one of many places in Cleveland that had been shaped or sacrificed to meet the needs of industry and commerce. Indeed, most locals were more concerned about polluted Lake Erie, with its closed beaches and declining fisheries, and air pollution, which enveloped central city neighborhoods and even threatened distant suburbs. Also, because so many American waters were appallingly polluted, Congress didn't talk much about the Cuyahoga as it debated and passed the Clean Water Act. Dwelling on one foul river simply wasn't necessary.

Since the river fire wasn't Cleveland's central concern in 1969, we decided our work couldn't remain so narrowly focused. So our project evolved, inspired mostly by Carl Stokes, the mayor of Cleveland at the time of the fire. Raised by a single mother in a Cleveland public housing complex, Stokes overcame his childhood poverty and, after a rapid rise in local politics, became the first black mayor of a major American city. He took office in November 1967, at an inauspicious moment in Cleveland's history. Circumstances forced Mayor Stokes to put out many fires, as it were, in a city that was rusting, decaying, and burning its way through what he called a "crisis in the urban environment." Stokes's expansive agenda—controlling water and air pollution, building public housing, improving public safety and public health, desegregating and improving schools, enlivening downtown with economic development—has inspired a broader agenda for our work. Stokes understood that the environmental crisis existed well beyond the river, even beyond the sootfall from the industrial smoke plumes. Stokes realized that the environmental crisis was inseparable from the broader decay of his city.

The story of the struggle to stem Cleveland's decline informs our thinking on many critical topics, including the civil rights movement, civil unrest, suburbanization, industrial pollution, environmental activism, liberal reform, and the urban crisis broadly conceived. This story offers a critique of postwar liberalism, which encouraged activist government at the local and federal levels but did nothing to address the inequalities of investment across the metropolis that ensured the creation of concentrated poverty and central city decay. The story also reveals the limits of the environmental movement, which for lack of vision or energy accepted the continued decline of American cities even as policy changes brought improvements elsewhere. And as we watch Stokes work to remake Cleveland, to build a more livable city, we learn a great deal about why the urban crisis deepened even as government increased efforts to find solutions. Because each of these storylines is so useful, we decided not to press just one theme throughout the book.

Still, one argument draws the many threads of this story together. As cities worked to solve basic environmental problems, especially to curb air and water pollution, ecological thinking spread rapidly. This thinking encouraged the breaking down of barriers, a heightened awareness of the connectedness of places and people, and an understanding of the connections between environmental and social problems. By the late 1960s, urban politicians, including Carl Stokes, recognized that just as municipal boundaries could not delimit environmental problems, they could not contain fundamental social problems either, including the persistence of poverty in an increasingly wealthy nation. But political boundaries—and the boundaries of race and class which they often amplified—could prevent the implementation of successful solutions to pressing problems. In the end, the persistence of racial and political boundaries prevented the development of fuller solutions to the crisis in the urban environment.

This story concerns the physical city, but people are at its heart. Stokes was hardly the only person to recognize the crisis in the urban environment, and he didn't work to solve Cleveland's problems by himself. He filled his administration with a diverse group of talented, but ultimately overmatched, men and women. Among them was Bailus Walker, who came from Dayton to run a rat control program and improve environmental health in the city. Cleveland native Ben Stefanski, a young and inexperienced administrator, became the director of public utilities and handled the city's effort to control water pollution. Many other Clevelanders outside the administration were just as dedicated to solving Cleveland's problems, including the *Cleveland Press*'s Betty Klaric, one of the nation's first environmental beat reporters, and David

Blaushild, a Chevrolet dealer from suburban Shaker Heights who became one of the region's most effective environmental activists. Politicians outside the administration, including Louis Stokes, the mayor's brother and a congressman from the city's East Side, also played pivotal roles in the effort to solve the city's problems.

We interviewed several of these figures, getting their sense of this moment in Cleveland's history and of the specific events that are described in this book. While these people and many others appear in *Where the River Burned*, at the center is Carl Stokes, a man who attracted national, even international, attention as he served his city but who has gathered too little recognition since he left office. Unfortunately, Stokes died in 1996, before we began this project, but he left behind an expansive archive of his mayoral papers, held at the Western Reserve Historical Society. Those papers were essential to the construction of this book.

These two different kinds of sources—interviews and archives—speak to our different approaches as authors. David is an academic historian, and Richard is a long-time journalist. Indeed, Richard was drawn to the Cuyahoga fire in 1998 as a journalism graduate student at Ohio State University, where he assessed the shifting press coverage of the many Cuyahoga fires. David joined the project, believing that Richard had uncovered an underexplored and important story in urban and environmental history, his two areas of concern. Although we came to this project with different professional backgrounds, we have similar relationships with Cleveland. We grew up (brothers) in Cleveland's Ohio antipode—Cincinnati. As children, we knew Cleveland mostly in contrast to our home: it was northeast to our southwest, a lake city rather than a river city. Cleveland made steel; Cincinnati made soap. It was solidly Democratic, and Cincinnati leaned Republican. In Cleveland they eat pierogies and corned beef, while in Cincinnati we eat chili and goetta. In other words, in economy, history, and culture, these two Ohio metropolises are very different kinds of cities. Despite this, some similarities are unmistakable. Most important, both places experienced the urban crisis; both struggled with job loss, racism, white flight, and a deteriorating core, all this mostly in our lifetimes. It is this mix of the familiar and the foreign that has kept us fascinated with Cleveland over the last fifteen years, as we made dozens of trips to explore the city through interviews, in the archives, and, most enjoyably, on foot, as we walked through the neighborhoods about which we have written.

This book is based largely on the documents created by the Stokes administration and on the myriad other primary sources that concern Cleveland in this era. But we would not have been able to construct this narrative without the guidance of the rich literature written by generations of scholars. To improve readability we confine our discussion of secondary works to the bibliographical essay. Of course, knowledgeable readers will surely recognize the contributions of dozens of scholars throughout the book.

A quick word on terminology: we decided to use the term "riots" to describe the outbursts of civil disorder in the 1960s. Some historians prefer broader terms, such as "uprising," or even "rebellion," both of which place the disorder in the broader context of the black freedom struggle. The African American uprising of the 1960s consisted of much more than periodic street action, however, and so we use "riots" to refer to the discrete violent events of the Long Hot Summers, to distinguish those events from the broader struggle and from the persistent civic disorder in impoverished African American neighborhoods. This brings us to another politically loaded term: "ghetto." We use this word to describe Hough and surrounding neighborhoods largely because it reflects the language and interpretation of the day. As Kenneth B. Clark so powerfully described in *Dark Ghetto* (1965), impoverished African Americans were trapped by more than just poverty in their degraded neighborhoods.

Finally, we should offer an explanation about a word we do *not* use: "environmentalist." Although what follows is very much a story about the rise of the environmental movement, this book does not trace the growing influence of environmental interest groups. Nearly everyone who appears in this book expressed concern about Cleveland's environment, but very few of them would have self-identified as an environmentalist. This includes Carl Stokes. Since our intention is to show how widespread environmental concern had become, how broadly ecological thinking had pervaded American culture, we spend little time describing the actions of national environmental organizations, such as the Izaak Walton League and the Sierra Club, both of which were active in Cleveland in this era. Nor do we stress the role of local environmental groups, such as the Air Conservation Committee. By analyzing the broader political discourse, we find a pervasive environmentalism in the rhetoric of many Clevelanders—politicians, the media, schoolchildren, citizens.

In the many years we've been working on this book, we have received considerable help and accumulated many debts. Richard began researching the Cuyahoga River under the guidance of Jim Neff, former director of the Kiplinger Program in Public Affairs Journalism at Ohio State University. Many people aided our work by agreeing to be interviewed, including Betty

Klaric, Ben Stefanski, Bailus Walker, Louis Stokes, David Zwick, Steve Tuckerman, and Patrick Conway. Dave Wollman and Donald R. Inman, of the Beaver County Industrial Museum, shared their collection of Jones & Laughlin materials. David received research help from University of Cincinnati students Daniel Baum, who researched Tremont, and Ryan Nagel, who helped with mapping and census data. We will never forget the kindness of Anita Weaver, who gave David a tour and an impromptu oral history of the Liberty Hill Baptist Church.

Most of the research for this book took place in a handful of libraries. The Ohio Historical Society holds important government documents, and we thank its professional staff. At Case Western Reserve University's Special Collections, Eleanor Blackman was equally helpful. Meghan Hays helped us locate useful materials in the Shaker Heights Library. We had helpful conversations with Paul Nelson, historian at the Western Reserve Fire Museum, which holds documents from the fire department. Conversations with Bill Barrow at Cleveland State University Special Collections helped us find useful resources at his institution and at others around the city. Later Bill was instrumental in our acquisition of images.

We owe special gratitude to everyone who makes research at the Western Reserve Historical Society a joy, especially Ann Sindelar, Vikki Catozza, and George Cooper. They provide an invaluable service to the people of Cleveland and to scholars from around the world.

Our work was much improved by close readings by the urban historian Mark Souther, the environmental historian Adam Rome, the *Boston Globe* editor Felice Belman, and an anonymous reader for Cornell University Press. This work also benefited from David's participation in a river-themed conference at the Rachel Carson Center, Ludwig Maximilians University, Munich.

At Cornell University Press, Michael McGandy worked with us from nearly the beginning, offering encouragement and consistently good advice as we framed the book and expert editing once words were on the page. Thanks to Max Richman and Ange Romeo-Hall for shepherding the book through production, and to Kim Vivier, our expert copyeditor. We owe special thanks to Jenn Hales for her wonderful stylized map of Cleveland, and to William Keegan for his map of metropolitan Cleveland circa 1970.

Through the years we have benefited from the encouragement and friendship of a group of fine Cleveland scholars, including Todd Michney, Mark Tebeau, Dan Kerr, and Norm Krumholz. At the University of Cincinnati, David has been surrounded by supportive colleagues, including Michael Griffith, Arnie Miller, Jana Braziel, Jeff Timberlake, and participants in the Kunz

Urban and Race workshop. In the Department of History, Maura O'Connor, Mark Raider, Willard Sunderland, and David Ciarlo (now at the University of Colorado) were especially generous with their support, as were three department emeriti: John Brackett, Roger Daniels, and Zane Miller. Former students Aaron Cowan, Rob Gioielli, David Merkowitz, Feay Coleman, and Charlie Lester, and current doctoral students Brittany Cowgill, Alyssa McClanahan, Nate McGee, and Angela Stiefbold, have all helped create a lively intellectual community. Substantial financial support for this book came from the Taft Research Center, without which humanities research would be nearly impossible at the University of Cincinnati.

Finally, we are grateful to our families—Jodie, Sarah, and Nina; Leanne, Sydney, and Ben—for their patience and support. This book is dedicated to them.

WHERE THE
RIVER BURNED

Introduction

THE CRISIS IN THE
URBAN ENVIRONMENT

Mayor Carl Stokes lived in a handsome Tudor house on Larchmere Boulevard on Cleveland's far East Side. Out his window, across the wide street and its grassy, landscaped median, was Shaker Heights, the rapidly integrating suburb with stunning stone and brick homes set on pleasant, carefully planned streets shaded by towering trees. The police car parked in front of the mayor's house may have seemed out of place in this tranquil neighborhood, but violence was not so far away, and a black politician could not be too cautious in the late 1960s. Although it was just four miles from the public housing project where he grew up, Stokes's home was well removed from the city's core, sitting up on the Allegheny Plateau beside the gracious eastern suburbs. Indeed, the location of Stokes's home revealed a remarkable journey from impoverished childhood to political power.

Driven to work by his bodyguard, a Cleveland police officer, Stokes came down Woodland Avenue, a long, straight thoroughfare that descended from the heights. Before he headed down the hill, the mayor was greeted by a grand view of his city—all its promise and problems laid out before him. The vista centered on Terminal Tower, the city's highest skyscraper, a slender beauty, the symbol of Cleveland's early success and rapid rise. The terminal was built by the partnership that created Shaker Heights to serve the commuter rail line that connected the two, and at this great distance, up on the bluff, Terminal Tower's role in the city was especially clear—for *distance* was surely the point. The terminal complex, completed in 1930, and the Shaker Heights Rapid Transit helped a burgeoning middle class to be *of* the city but not *in* it, to enjoy its great benefits and avoid its troubles, to bypass the neighborhoods traversed by Woodland and the other avenues that fanned across the East Side.

Coming down the hill, Stokes could catch a glimpse of the forty-story Erieview Tower, completed in 1964, rising from downtown's expansive urban renewal project. Erieview's dark glass edifice—and the long-stalled renewal of the acres around it—represented Cleveland's great hope for a modern downtown. When the winds were right, Stokes might have been distracted by the streaks of coal smoke running from the tall stacks of Municipal Light, the large, city-owned power plant on the lake farther to the east. In the other direction, south of downtown, the stacks of the massive steel mills sent out a greater cloud of smoke and steam, a gray shroud that hung over the unseen Cuyahoga River, tucked in its valley, out of sight. Clevelanders knew how to find the river, should they need to do so: head for the smoke.

Much closer to Stokes as he commuted to work were the troubled neighborhoods through which Woodland passed, including Woodhill Homes, a public housing project near the base of the hill. On June 9, 1969, a young white man, Donald Waight, was murdered near Woodhill by a group of African Americans whom he had been harassing in a misguided and unsuccessful attempt to defend his neighborhood from racial transition. Waight was the fourth Clevelander to be killed in a twenty-four-hour period, and the 127th of the year. Violence had become a hallmark of Cleveland's crisis, and of the urban crisis around the nation. Stokes didn't need any physical reminders of this struggle, but he had them anyway, and not just here.

As Stokes traveled farther, Woodland Avenue took him through Central, the neighborhood in which he grew up and where he had ample opportunity to stop his car and chat with friends and strangers, to smile and connect, to play the politician, which he did so well. Central was a neighborhood degraded so long that on some streets vacant lots outnumbered the remaining buildings. In bursts of arson and demolition, Central was disappearing—its people and its structures. To reach City Hall, Stokes passed by the downtown campus of Cuyahoga Community College, opened in 1966, and then under the Innerbelt Freeway, part of Interstate 90, and into the southern section of downtown. Here his driver had options, including East 9th, a wide, two-way street that cut due north through the Erieview renewal area to City Hall, which sat on the northern edge of downtown, just above the harbor and the great, dying Lake Erie. Here Stokes had a daily reminder that the urban crisis didn't end at the city's edge; it flowed out into the lake. No barriers, man-made or natural, contained the polluted city.

Completed in 1916, City Hall is a beautiful beaux arts box, a near twin of the nearby Cuyahoga County Courthouse. Both were built as part of Daniel Burnham's 1903 Group Plan for downtown Cleveland. Sitting in the mayoral office, Stokes could overlook the central feature of that plan, a grassy mall that stretched south toward the beaux arts federal building. Beyond, Stokes had a clear view of Terminal Tower, less obscured here by the city's smog. It was a grand view, created as the city's fortunes waxed fifty years earlier. From here, literally in his seat of power, Stokes could reflect on the trajectory of his city and perhaps think it more hopeful than his daily commute would suggest.

Cleveland's industrial East Side and downtown may seem like an odd setting for a study of environmental policy and the growing influence of ecological thought in American culture, but the city's struggles in the late 1960s help us think about the environmental movement in a new, more inclusive way. Beyond the burning river, which not every city had, Cleveland's deepening urban crisis was typical of the nation's deindustrializing, heavily polluted cities. In Cleveland, we find themes and struggles found in Detroit, Newark, St. Louis, Philadelphia, Chicago, and dozens of other cities. By the late 1960s, all these cities were facing concurrent environmental and urban crises, and they battled heightened problems with diminished resources. In Cleveland, the polluted and burning Cuyahoga put an exclamation point on these confluent crises, but what makes this city especially interesting is Carl Stokes, a black mayor in a white city, forced to consider issues related to race at every turn. His political skill was considerable, although that didn't make him universally liked. His administration was active and its policies progressive, although that didn't necessarily make them effective. What made the Stokes administration revolutionary was his perspective. Never had a black man raised in poverty grown up to run a major industrial city. When he talked of inadequate housing, rats, and poor city services, he did so with an authority that no other mayor had. Stokes's background allowed him to see the city more completely than any of his predecessors; he perceived so clearly the boundaries that ran through his community, the barriers that held Cleveland back.

THE AMERICAN CITY IS OBSOLESCENT

In June 1968, a little more than half a year into his administration, Stokes, already a popular speaker at the national level, addressed the Capital Press Club at the Shoreham Hotel in Washington, D.C. Founded in 1944 by a group of prominent African American journalists, the club worked to promote black participation in media. Stokes chose this forum to describe the plight of blacks in Cleveland. He opened: "I have been told that the approved way to talk about the city, any big city, these days is to speak solemnly, ominously, and fearfully about their problems. One cannot be expected to rate as an expert on the city unless one foresees its doom." He listed problems that were by then a drumbeat: "spreading slums, increasing crime, declining tax duplicate, [rising] infant mortality and illiteracy rates, air and water pollution, and the mounting tensions between the races." In sum these constituted, in Stokes's phrase, "urban crises."[1]

Despite all this, Stokes tried to keep a positive attitude, as a mayor and as a speaker. The problems, as diverse as they were serious, were solvable. "Permit me then to say," he continued, "that as a Negro, and as the mayor of a metropolitan complex, no one knows better than I that there are no easy answers to the problems of the Negro or to the problems of our cities. Except that I am sure that one will not be solved without a solution to the other." Perhaps most remarkable here is not Stokes's understanding that the problem of race was connected to the problems of the city, but his description of his own post: "mayor of a metropolitan complex." This he was not. He was mayor of Cleveland, a city embedded in that metropolitan complex. The distinction would become clearer to him as he struggled to solve problems that traversed the boundaries of his authority. Beyond the complexities of regional governance, Stokes understood that metropolitan Cleveland would need major federal investment to solve its problems. His big take-home message, reported in the *New York Times* the next day, was that proposed federal budget cuts would be devastating to cities in crisis. "Never before have our big cities needed so urgently the massive assistance of the federal government, assistance that only the federal government can provide."

Later in the speech, Stokes revealed that his perspective on the city's future derived in part from an understanding of its past. "In Cleveland, as in other cities, we have passed through three eras in the last 100 years: the agricultural era of pre-1900; the manufacturing era of the first half of this century; and the post-manufacturing era now coming to the fore," he said, asserting that urban America had begun a fundamental transition. "Cleveland is still strongly involved and tied to the manufacturing era and is only just beginning to understand and grasp the potentials of the post-manufacturing period." Stokes called the emerging postindustrial period "the Human Resources Era" to emphasize the importance of education and the development of marketable business skills. At the end of his speech, taking advantage of his lectern's location in the nation's capital, Stokes endorsed the candidacy of Vice President Hubert Humphrey, "the man I see as the next President of the United States." In that instance, at least, Stokes's vision of the future was not so clear.

Like all great industrial cities, Cleveland was built through a rapid accumulation of capital, the influx of profit converted into greater productive capacity, new buildings, infrastructure, and cultural institutions. Some of the nation's great industrial firms arose in Cleveland, including Standard Oil, American Ship Building, the Sherwin-Williams Paint Company, and Republic Steel—innovative companies that helped shape the nation's economy. The city grew quickly, and despite the wealth and employment, there were also many complaints about noise, smoke, and the chaos wrought of poor planning. Still, Cleveland's boosters spent decades pointing to the city's spectacular growth and its significant contributions to industrial America. Ironically, it was the city's even more spectacular decline that finally attracted the nation's gaze. Cleveland was built in a hurry but was dismantled even more quickly.

During the seventy years from the beginning of the Civil War to the onset of the Great Depression, Cleveland added more than 850,000 residents while it built a complex economy around oil refining, chemical manufacturing, and steel production. Factories, warehousing, and docks dominated the waterfront; railroads pushed through neighborhoods and gained access to the riverside and lakeshore; densely packed, poorly built housing clustered around industrial zones; wastes poured into waterways and the air overhead. The city and individual businesses reshaped the river, dredging, widening, straightening, and holding it back, all in the effort to make it more useful for industry by allowing the passage of ore boats upstream to the southern flats, where great steel mills produced the raw materials that attracted even more factories to the region. The federal government built an extensive breakwater in Lake Erie to protect Cleveland Harbor, and dredge spoils and urban waste, including garbage, provided the fill that gave the city more flat lakeside land. In other words, industrial capitalism didn't just manufacture widgets in Cleveland; it manufactured Cleveland. The total environment was put to work for profit.

All this was permitted and encouraged by a policy environment that privileged economic growth over all else. Regulation was modest, ineffective, or unenforced. Industries simply passed along the cost of water and air pollution to their neighbors. Cleveland, like municipal governments throughout industrializing America, demanded little of employers, keeping taxes low while providing potable water, paved roads, and unfettered access to publicly owned waterways and waterfronts. Through the nineteenth century and into the twentieth, housing was essentially unregulated and then poorly regulated, and therefore cheap and often dangerous and unhealthy. Since taxes were low, government services were meager. Public health suffered, and recreational opportunities were limited. In sum, through the boom decades, government provided little more than cheerleading for major industries. All this meant that Cleveland, like all industrial cities in this era, was a good place to find work but a poor place to live.

In the late 1940s, threats to the industrial regime began to accumulate. The Great Depression had caused a decade-long hiatus in the building of homes and businesses, and new wartime factories appeared disproportionately on the outskirts of the metropolis. After the war, state and local governments planned the construction of highways that would speed decentralization by enabling longer commutes. Prescient scholars and politicians began to express concern for the dense industrial city, for urban life as Americans had created it. One of these observers was Mabel Walker, an urban economist who had written the definitive study on blight in the 1930s with a special eye toward the tax consequences of decay in the central city. In the spring of 1947, Walker gave a speech in New York to the Municipal Finance Officers Association titled "The American City Is Obsolescent," in which she used census numbers to describe shrinking central cities. "I think the simplest and briefest explanation of the population trend," she said, "is that people did not come to the city in the first place because they liked living in the city, but because the city offered them a means of livelihood." Now that residential and employment opportunities were decentralizing, she argued, planners and politicians should not work against the will of the people but instead "make way for the fluid city of tomorrow." Although Walker did not imagine just how far the decentralization would proceed, at least not in this speech, she concluded that the "creaking old structure must be readjusted to modern needs." The city would have to be rebuilt.[2]

Walker was most concerned about the effects of automobiles and trucks, and in her conception transportation drove change in the metamorphosing city. But automobility didn't account for all of urban America's new fluidity; capital, labor, sites of production—every aspect of the industrial city became unmoored, no longer beholden to the old economic geography. At the same time, white urbanites fled desegregating neighborhoods in central cities, preferring to move to white suburbs than to share their communities and schools with African Americans. In other words, broader changes were at work in industrial cities, as fundamental economic shifts compounded the consequences of the centrifugal forces pulling urbanites toward the edges. Still, Walker described perfectly the severity of the situation: "A new type of city adapted to present and future needs is struggling to evolve, but it is held back by the dead carcass of the past."

This book describes Cleveland's struggle to remake itself, the struggle against the carcass of its past. Encased in its industrial shell, Cleveland found the transformation into a fluid city more difficult than many places, but its story speaks to the urban crisis as it ran through many American cities. As manufacturing growth slowed and employment shrank, cities found themselves engaged in a new competition for capital investment. Service industries, including banking, insurance, education, and health care, took on greater importance; government services also became more important. An increasingly large group of people who had options in their lives, the middle class, demanded better recreational opportunities, better schools, safer streets, cleaner air, and cleaner water. They rejected the carcass of the industrial city and demanded a city that served them better. Cleveland's halting, painful, and incomplete transition from industrial city to service city required massive investments in the urban landscape. Cleveland, like other industrial cities, slowly reclaimed its waterfront, reduced pollution, and improved housing. Citizens demanded these changes, forcing government—local, state, and national—to create policies that would aid the transition toward the service city.

The continued political power of industry impeded the development and enforcement of environmental policies that might have speeded the transition, but even with rapid changes in regulatory policy, the industrial city would not have easily or quickly morphed into a successful service city. Waterfronts, so long given over to industry and commerce, would need reworking, becoming parks or prime residential space. Empty warehouses and abandoned industrial plants would have to be repurposed or torn down. Cheaply built and under-regulated housing would have to be replaced. Citizens would have to imagine new uses for rail lines, usually as recreational spaces—linear parks. New employers, in medicine, higher education, insurance, finance, and other service industries, would need new facilities and space to grow. The modernization of American cities required imagination and political will, but the actual renewal was largely physical. In the service city era, residents would not tolerate polluted waterways, perpetually foul air, and inadequate parks and playgrounds. Successful service cities would have to be good places to work *and* live.

CAN CLEVELAND ESCAPE BURNING?

The 1950 census found nearly 915,000 residents in Cleveland, its high-water mark. The city lost a modest number of residents in the 1950s, as new housing enticed Clevelanders into the suburbs. In the 1960s, Cleveland lost more than

125,000 residents, shrinking by 14 percent. In the next decade, the population loss accelerated; nearly 180,000 fewer people called Cleveland home by 1980, by which time the metropolitan region had stopped growing as well. In the course of twenty years, Cleveland lost roughly 35 percent of its population, falling below 575,000. Cleveland was not alone. Some small industrial cities, such as Gary, Indiana, hemorrhaged residents, and even large, economically complex cities such as Chicago saw declines. Since population loss served as a marker of urban decline, you didn't need to walk through city neighborhoods to understand that Cleveland and other industrial cities were in trouble in the late 1960s. But if you did explore the city, the depths of the problems became clearer, especially on Cleveland's East Side, where the Hough neighborhood, the site of the city's first major race riot in 1966, was losing a staggering 50,000 residents over the course of twenty years, shrinking by two-thirds—a decline that represented an incredible disinvestment in and abandonment of the inner city.

In 1967, a year after the Hough riot and a year before the city's second major riot, the Glenville Shootout, left seven people dead and caused extensive damage to the expanding East Side ghetto, a *Saturday Evening Post* headline asked, "Can Cleveland Escape Burning?" In the lengthy exposé that followed, John Skow described Cleveland's ghetto and the city's growing economic malaise. As the summer heated up, Skow talked to people in Hough and about Hough. He reported, "It is hard to find a city resident who believes Cleveland will go unburned through the summer." Cleveland's problems went well beyond Hough, of course. People were already calling it "the mistake on the lake," Skow said, also noting that Lake Erie was fouled with pollution, a problem that many Clevelanders had also recognized as a mistake. In this way, Skow captured the connections between the urban and environmental crises: the urban environment had been devastated—both its natural features and its neighborhoods. And over the next two summers both would burn.[3]

Many of the nation's largest cities found themselves confronting similar decline, even while embedded in the world's most successful economy. The United States added nearly thirty million people to its population, expanding by nearly 20 percent in the 1960s. At the same time, gross national product nearly doubled and per capita income surged. The United States was in the midst of its longest economic expansion to date; it was far and away the world's great economic power. This juxtaposition makes the American urban crisis a world-historical event. Never before had a nation thrived—grown in population and in wealth—while its major cities decayed. Even before the decline became precipitous, some scholars, journalists, and policy makers began to wonder what had gone wrong. What was causing the failure of urban America?

There was no shortage of possible culprits, but most observers blamed suburbanization in some way. Jobs moved to the periphery, attracted by cheap land, lower taxes, and access to highways. People moved out too, repulsed by dirty and increasingly dangerous neighborhoods and attracted by new housing set in spacious communities served by good schools. The city bore the burdens of racism and segregation, which combined to keep black residents poor and confined, powerless to improve their neighborhoods and subject to the brunt of urban violence, while whites fled to more prosperous communities. Despite the development of government programs designed to alleviate urban poverty, state and federal policies in critical areas such as transportation and taxation sped the decentralization of metropolitan areas by putting cities at a competitive disadvantage against their own suburbs.

By the 1960s, urban politicians understood that suburban growth came at the expense of central cities. Stokes was especially blunt about the problem in a speech to the City Club of Cleveland in the summer of 1970. "The cost of local government falls much more heavily on those who live in Cleveland proper than on suburbanites in this country," he said, adding that because the city paid much more for police, fire protection, and recreation, "Cleveland subsidizes its much wealthier suburban neighbors." The imbalance was compounded as falling populations and property values caused a decline in the municipal tax base. Federal aid programs could not compensate for shrinking resources in Cleveland, and as Stokes argued repeatedly, the state sent too little money to its cities. Noting the anti-urban bias of state legislators, Stokes claimed, "Ohio has practiced a rural and suburban philosophy that ignores big central city problems because those who run the state win their positions by soliciting the solid backing of farmers and small town residents."[4]

In the standard accounts of the urban crisis, the physically deteriorating city serves largely as setting or symbol. But the urban environment was not just a setting for Cleveland's decline; it was a central factor. As investment slowed, the rot, brought on by age, weather, pollution, and wear, greatly outpaced improvements. On street after street, clapboard houses slowly fell apart or were quickly engulfed in flames. Urban decay was real; it was physical, not metaphorical. Although Clevelanders had long pointed to the city's flaws—the river was too crooked, transportation too limited, air too foul, water too murky, housing too shoddy—no one could have guessed how rapidly decay would set in once people started flowing out. In 1969, as he struggled with a litany of urban ills, Stokes appropriately labeled Cleveland's predicament a "crisis in the urban environment."[5]

EVERYTHING IS CONNECTED TO EVERYTHING ELSE

Hardened by four years in office and liberated by his decision not to seek reelection, Stokes became even more candid during his public appearances in the waning months of his administration. He was particularly blunt in a 1971 speech delivered to the Colorado Municipal League conference in Colorado Springs titled "Issues and Prospects in a Regional City." Retaining his positive outlook on the future of American cities and emphasizing that the doomsayers were wrong, Stokes argued that cities could be rebuilt to out-compete suburbs. "I say this because I sincerely believe that life in the central cities' inner neighborhoods, so much closer to the downtown center of excitement and activities and to its heritage of cultural, social and educational institutions, can be so superior to life in the generally lifeless, monotonous, sterile average suburb." But, sounding very much like Mabel Walker twenty years earlier, Stokes added, "It is, I am certain, patently clear to everyone in this audience that the central cities of our metropolitan areas are physically and functionally obsolete." This obsolescence necessitated substantial investments in cities—their schools, hospitals, and services; metropolitan regions needed more rational development of transportation, water supplies, and sewers. "The inescapable conclusion," Stokes said, "must be that reconstruction of the central cities is essential and that such reconstruction must be undertaken on a scale which would permit them to be rebuilt for a rich variety of uses and for as economically and socially heterogeneous a population as possible." Stokes recommended a new tax system, less reliant on property taxes, combined with state restrictions on suburban development as first steps toward a recalibration of metropolitan growth. These would be difficult steps, however, as Stokes well knew, because metropolitan governance was terribly fragmented. "The difficulty arises from the fact that the rich neighborhoods, entrenched behind their individual municipal boundaries, are thereby isolated from any responsibility for the support of those portions of the regional city which constitute the poor neighborhoods."[6]

Stokes's call for better governance of the "regional city" was part of a national conversation concerning how best to manage the sprawling metropolis. Postwar suburbanization led to an intensification of this conversation, but attempts to redefine the city dated to the early twentieth century. The phrase "Greater Cleveland" became popular in the 1920s, as Clevelanders recognized that the municipal boundary no longer contained the city. In 1949, the federal government defined the Cleveland Standard Metropolitan Area as Cuyahoga and Lake counties, suggesting that the city had sprawled to the east. In 1959, the federal definition became the Standard Metropolitan Statistical Area and now included Geauga and Medina counties. But federal definitions of the metropolis excluded other, integral parts of Greater Cleveland, including heavily populated Lorain County to the west, and Summit County, which contains Akron, to the south. Regardless of how one defined metropolitan or Greater Cleveland, however, no one governed it, as such, since governmental power remained at the municipal or county level.

Even before Stokes called for better governance, Cleveland saw several attempts to overcome the problems of the fractured metropolis. Before the end of World War II, the city established the Metropolitan Cleveland Development Council in the hopes of solving regional problems, especially those related to transportation. Cuyahoga County replaced that short-lived, city-led organization with the Regional Planning Commission in 1947. Soon even the county boundary was too tight. In 1962, the state of Ohio created a seven-county region for cooperative transportation planning to meet a requirement for federal funding. Still, planning organizations held little power, and governmental authority remained diffuse. In 1970, Cuyahoga County alone contained 57 municipalities, some of them growing rapidly, including Beachwood and Brook Park, while others were declining, such as Cleveland, Shaker Heights, and Cleveland Heights. These places had different pasts and envisioned very different futures, ensuring conflicts of interest that made municipal-level governance inefficient. As Stokes well understood, municipal lines were not the only boundaries that held Cleveland back. Even within the city, boundaries divided residents, white from black, prosperous from impoverished. As Skow reported in 1967, "the city has degenerated into a loose and rancorous federation of walled villages," as white ethnics, most notably Italian Americans, defended their neighborhoods from black encroachment.

Although largely inspired by shifting demographic and economic realities, the conversation about redefining the city also reflected the growing influence of ecological thought in American culture. Ecology taught that all boundaries are porous. Indeed, the first law of ecology, as described by Barry Commoner in 1971, is "Everything is connected to everything else." Ecological thought had influenced thinking about cities since the 1920s, but mostly through metaphor, as urban scholars compared cities to organisms that had life cycles and were capable of catching diseases. Increasingly in the postwar era, observers argued that human systems weren't *like* natural systems but were in fact *part*

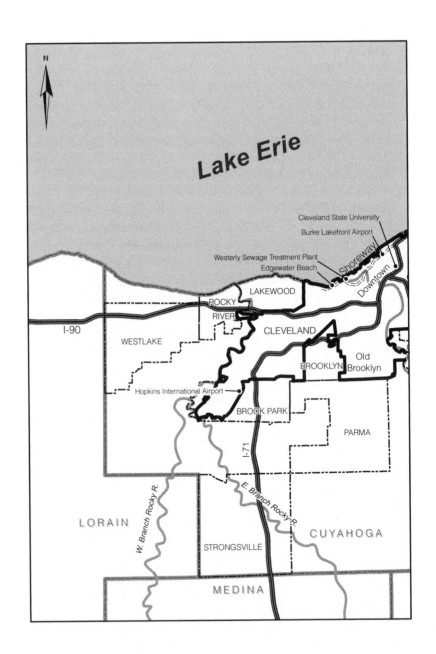

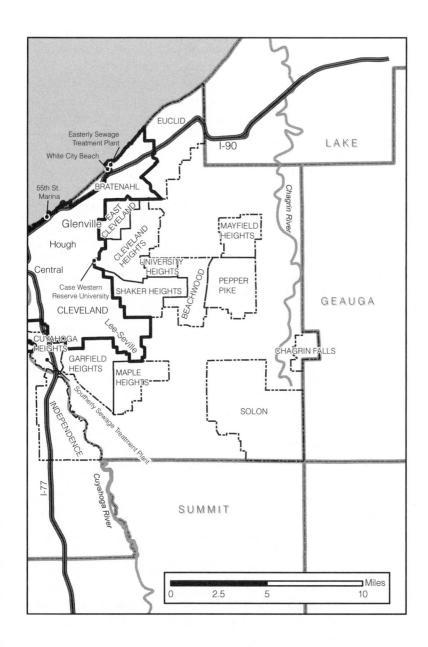

LAKE

EUCLID

I-90

Easterly Sewage
Treatment Plant

White City Beach

55th St.
Marina

BRATENAHL

Glenville

EAST
CLEVELAND

CLEVELAND
HEIGHTS

Hough

UNIVERSITY
HEIGHTS

MAYFIELD
HEIGHTS

Central

Case Western
Reserve University

SHAKER HEIGHTS

BEACHWOOD

PEPPER
PIKE

CLEVELAND

Lee-Seville

GEAUGA

CUYAHOGA
HEIGHTS

GARFIELD
HEIGHTS

Chagrin River

CHAGRIN FALLS

MAPLE
HEIGHTS

INDEPENDENCE

Southerly Sewage Treatment Plant

SOLON

I-77

Cuyahoga River

SUMMIT

Miles

0   2.5   5   10

of them. This became especially clear as cities addressed fundamental environmental problems, such as treating sewage and supplying water. Solutions required consideration of the entire environment, not just streams, rivers, lakes, pipes, and treatment plants but also agricultural land and housing developments. Planners came to realize that watersheds marked the proper boundaries for water resource management, not municipal lines.

Ecological thinking, emphasizing connections rather than boundaries, only gradually influenced urban policy, and many of the actions taken to save Cleveland in the years around 1970 seem modest or misguided to us today. Many Americans held tight to their modern philosophy, which sorted and divided the world: man and nature; city and suburb; black and white. That these divisions continue to run through contemporary Cleveland, and contemporary America, reflects the lasting influence of modern thinking. Stokes struggled to break down barriers in Cleveland. He prioritized erasing those that separated citizens by race and class, but the movement for social equality, like the effort to solve the problems of the city, including those of the urban environment, affirmed the primary lesson of ecology: everything is connected to everything else.

THE POLLUTED STATES OF AMERICA

In April 1970, in the weeks surrounding the first Earth Day, thousands of Cleveland residents, many of them children, signed petitions demanding government action to curb pollution. Many of the petitions circulated through the blue-collar neighborhoods of South Broadway and Union Miles, densely packed with clapboard homes, interspersed with factories that lined the Erie, New York Central, and Pennsylvania railroad corridors, all of which passed through the industrial South Side. Most of the petitions circulated through neighborhood schools: Fullerton Elementary, South High, Holy Name Elementary, and many others. "We the future voters of the United States demand the enforcement of existing air and water pollution laws," one petition read, "and the creation of new enforceable laws dealing with cleansing our air and water for the protection of the people's health and welfare." Another petition, carried street by street, sought the signatures of neighborhood adults. It read, "We the electorate of the polluted states of America, in order to form a more perfect country, demand clean air, clean water, and clean land. To secure the blessings of a pure environment for ourselves and our children we do present this petition." Those who circulated the petitions, hundreds of mimeographed sheets altogether, presented them to Mayor Stokes.[7]

Although the size of this protest was unusual, there was nothing new in urban residents demanding a cleaner environment. In 1970, however, residents had good reason to expect action. Stokes had come to power at liberalism's high tide. In the nation's capital, Lyndon Johnson's activist administration had passed civil rights legislation and declared war on poverty. A wide range of reforms addressed the urban crisis. From Model Cities to Head Start, federal programs poured money into troubled neighborhoods in the hope of improving job training, early childhood education, housing, and employment opportunities. Although these initiatives made a difference in the lives of individuals, nothing stemmed the crisis, which only deepened as government intervention increased. Still, Stokes maintained an activist stance, demanding federal aid at every opportunity and siding with citizens who insisted on improved air quality, a cleaner lake, and better housing.

Stokes hoped to do more while in office, but as long as jobs and capital continued to flow out of the city, all he could realistically expect was to shape the decline. He served for four years, having gained reelection once, and then decided to move on, to New York, where he became a newscaster. Even before he left office, Stokes received considerable blame for Cleveland's continued decline, especially after the second of the city's major race riots, the Glenville Shootout in July 1968. And like many transitioning cities, Cleveland couldn't support as many residents as it had as an industrial city. The service economy couldn't absorb the excess labor created as manufacturing receded. Great advances in the transition to a service city, during the Stokes administration and after, could not halt the population decline. Improved air quality, cleaner beaches, more plentiful open space, new office towers, and expanding college campuses all helped Cleveland become a better place to be, but fewer and fewer people chose to live there. In other words, successful physical transformations didn't translate into demographic growth, and this lag suggested to critics that policies focused on physical improvements didn't work. We argue otherwise. No doubt Stokes made missteps and his administration had its shortcomings, but the story that follows is not one of wasted opportunities and mismanagement. Rather, it is the story of a politician and his administration struggling to shape the future of a city in transition.

As Richard Nixon entered the White House in early 1969, and national politics began its long conservative drift, more than one observer noted that liberalism had been broken on the shoals of the urban crisis. But in one area of urban concern—the environment—liberal policies persisted and even expanded in the Nixon years and eventually proved effective. Tighter regulation of pollution, investments in sewage treatment plants, and the construction of new recreational spaces were all necessary steps in the creation of a new type of city. Although we often forget how much environmental policy is also urban policy, it should be clear that environmental regulation made American cities more livable. Johnson's War on Poverty and Nixon's War on Pollution were in many ways two campaigns in the same war—the liberal state's attempt to refashion American urban life. Demanded by residents of metropolitan America, new government policies and programs worked to turn degraded industrial cities into livable service cities.

A variety of factors contributed to the development of the environmental movement, including the growing awareness of ecological science, even among average citizens. The rise of liberal politics, heightened women's political activism, and the developing counterculture all contributed to environmentalism's growing influence, too. Suburbanization helped drive some aspects of the environmental movement—concern for protecting open space particularly. As it evolved in the 1960s, environmental activism addressed a diverse agenda, including the preservation of wilderness, an aspect of the movement that achieved remarkable success. Scholars have tended to connect the growing demand for environmental quality to the nation's growing wealth, but the stories in this book—of the burning river, the dying lake, the fouled air, and decaying neighborhoods—do not describe a wealthy society gradually improving its environment. This was a landscape in crisis, a crisis fed by decline more than growth, and as Cleveland's story makes clear, in addition to working to preserve wilderness and protect suburbia's natural amenities, the environmental movement worked to halt the decay of cities. The concern for urban places, including long-industrialized landscapes, explains why Cleveland's burning river evolved into one of the founding myths of the environmental movement, and why the Cuyahoga still attracts so much attention today.

Now, as most American cities have turned the corner and begun to recover from the crisis in the urban environment, historical perspective allows a fuller analysis of what was happening in the 1960s and 1970s. It is clear that the long transition from industrial city to service city was more disruptive than anyone anticipated. By the 1980s, high unemployment, race riots, homelessness, drug-related violence, and blighted neighborhoods had all become markers of urban America, especially in the deindustrializing cities of the Midwest. But just as the decline began to feel permanent, cities began to recover—not all of them and not all at once, but Chicago, New York, Pittsburgh, Milwaukee, and others stabilized and in some cases recovered economically and demographically. Today, explaining the recovery of American cities is the new scholarly focus. From our perspective, Chicago's construction of Millennium Park, which replaced the intrusive Illinois Central rail yards, and Manhattan's incredibly successful High Line Park, created from a long-abandoned elevated freight rail line, do not mark the beginning of a new middle-class urbanity but are the culmination of a long, concerted effort to remake the urban landscape.

Describing the transition between types of urban regimes is especially relevant today. We have entered a new era of transition, from the service city to the sustainable city, in which the community must attend to ecological health as well as environmental amenities. The reality of climate change has encouraged communities to diminish their ecological footprints, minimizing reliance on fossil fuels and carbon-intensive agriculture, a process that may become more urgent in the near future. The transition from livable service cities to lasting sustainable cities promises to be just as disruptive as the one described in *Where the River Burned*, and it will undoubtedly create a new urban crisis. Some cities will make good policy choices, preparing for a warmer climate, stronger storms, higher sea levels, and droughts. Surely those policies will matter. But some cities are simply better positioned for a warmer world, just as some cities were better positioned to become successful service cities. Cleveland, finally finding its legs in the service economy, is hard at work remaking itself again as a sustainable city.

The nonlinear narrative that follows pivots around two months: June 1969, the month the Cuyahoga caught fire, and April 1970, which included the first Earth Day. By reaching back periodically for historical context, *Where the River Burned* tells the longer story of how the city fell into crisis and how Clevelanders mapped a way out. The story opens on Earth Day, when letters and petitions sent to Mayor Stokes described two environmental crises—one suburban and one urban. This exploration of Earth Day introduces many of the pressing environmental issues and more fully introduces Stokes. The story then falls back to June of the previous year, following the mayor as he makes a series of public appearances. First, Stokes introduces a rat control program to be managed by Bailus Walker. Much of this story takes place in Hough, the rapidly deteriorating neighborhood that took on special meaning in the urban crisis. Here we see a city divided by the invisible wall of the ghetto, the most powerful and persistent boundary in Cleveland. The story then moves downtown, using the celebration of the new Central Bank tower to describe the great economic and symbolic importance of the central business district. Downtown redevelopment may seem rather removed from the urban crisis, especially as it played out in Hough just a few miles away, but urban planning and urban renewal were critical to both of these places, and vital to the broader story we tell. Four days after celebrating the development downtown, Stokes attended the opening of the 55th Street Marina, part of Cleveland's effort to reconnect with Lake Erie, which was so polluted that the city had to take extraordinary measures to permit swimming. Even as the city attempted to solve its water pollution problem, it addressed air pollution, especially from the Municipal Light plant and the steel mills. In the summer of 1969, Cleveland struggled to write an effective air pollution code while working-class neighborhoods around the mills continued to empty out.

The pivotal event in June 1969 was the Cuyahoga fire, of course. The river had burned many times before, but newspaper coverage of these earlier fires had focused exclusively on their economic consequences. Only after the 1969 fire did Clevelanders, and others, begin to dwell on the broader ecological implications of the burning river. Then the narrative returns to Earth Day 1970, describing events in the city that week and looking into the 1970s, as the environmental crisis was eased through regulation but the urban crisis only deepened with continued flight of people and capital from the city. We bring the story into the present at the end, to describe Cleveland as it exists today in the midst of a new transition—the attempt to build a more sustainable city.

1 What Will Become of Cleveland?

On April 22, 1970, schoolchildren from around metropolitan Cleveland sat in their classrooms and wrote to Mayor Carl Stokes. Over the next few days, hundreds of letters poured into City Hall, where staffers read, sorted, and distributed them for responses. On some, they circled key words (pollution, in particular), and on others they scrawled numbers at the top, probably indicating which form letter should be sent out in reply. Many of the children asked for information about the city's environmental policies; others asked for a photo of the mayor, who was, after all, quite famous. Despite the diversity of the letters sent on the first Earth Day—some came from the city, others from the suburbs; some from young children, others from teenagers—altogether they described an environmental crisis in remarkably familiar terms, and they tended to discuss what had become distressingly familiar topics. They described a city in which heavy air pollution threatened lives—children's lives—and water pollution fouled Lake Erie's beaches and killed its fish. For these children, the terrible pollution raised questions about the future of Cleveland and its residents, and even of the nation as a whole.

Most of the letters were short and to the point. For instance, all students in one second-grade class wrote the identical letter, which reads in its entirety: "We do not like dirty air. We want our air to be clean so we can be healthy. Please make our air clean." Although they were practicing penmanship as much as participatory democracy, these students' letters took on special meaning because they came from the Hodge School, on the East Side, just four blocks from the Cleveland Electric Illuminating Company's massive, coal-burning, smoky lakeshore power plant. These kids had good reason to worry about their own health, even in second grade. At other elementary schools, children wrote their letters on oversized paper with space at the top for drawings. Here the youngest students exerted some freedom of expression, and many made liberal use of black crayons; dark smoke curled out of factories and trailed behind airplanes. Some imagined solutions, including a great lid that could be lowered onto polluting factories, trapping the smoke—a poignant mix of childish fantasy and dead seriousness.[1]

The brainchild of Gaylord Nelson, Democratic senator from Wisconsin, Earth Day was a national event featuring teach-ins on college campuses, at schools, and in public parks. There were lectures, demonstrations, and opportunities to clean up green spaces, waterways, and schoolyards. An estimated twenty million Americans participated in Earth Day in some way or another, and the event became a watershed for the environmental movement, which was growing rapidly. A great range of environmental issues gained attention during Earth Day, but air and water pollution were the most important nearly everywhere, including Cleveland, where despite the fact that Mayor Stokes declined to participate personally, citizen involvement in what the city called

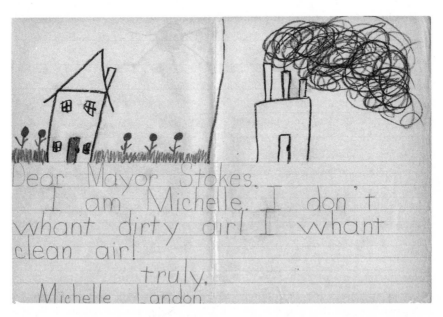

Figure 1. Many of the suburban children who wrote to Mayor Stokes complained about pollution as an urban phenomenon. The first-grader Michelle Landon used green and black crayons to contrast her beautiful middle-class home in Lyndhurst with the heavily polluted environment of Cleveland. Carl Stokes Papers, container 75, folder 1435, Western Reserve Historical Society. Used with permission.

"Environmental Crisis Week" was extraordinary. Residents of metropolitan Cleveland had long been acutely aware of their city's pollution problems, but in case someone had missed the other clues—the smoke shroud, the fouled beaches, the burning river—on April 20, Monday-morning commuters on Interstate 71 were greeted by a banner hanging from the W. 25th Street overpass: "Welcome to the 5th Dirtiest City."[2]

The Earth Day letters reveal how well educated students had become on environmental issues. Fifteen-year-old Andrea Rady wanted Stokes to know that she and other students at suburban Westlake High School had "conducted several studies on the pollution problem in Cleveland." Her letter discussed pollution broadly, but it mentioned just one example of the problem: the Municipal Light plant, a smoky, coal-fired power station on the city's East Side lakeshore, not far from the Illuminating Company's plant. As Rady put it, the plant was "both an eyesore and a health hazard to anyone coming within 1 mile of it." Rather than fault Muny Light itself, Rady blamed the pollution on Stokes. "For the past four years, you and your officials have been arguing over petty legalities while pollution continues to strangle our city. To my knowledge, several solutions have been proposed, but none have gotten past *your* desk." Rady's portrayal of Stokes as the impediment to progress wasn't accurate, but Muny Light was owned and operated by the city, and so she was right to claim that Cleveland officials deserved special blame for the plant's smokiness. The pollution from Muny Light had earned attention from the press for nearly a decade, and the Stokes administration had been working on solutions. We might wonder, though, why Rady decided to single out the Muny plant. After all, she was not among the Clevelanders who lived within a mile of the plant, and given that she resided in a middle-class suburb to the west of the city, she wasn't likely to come within a mile of it regularly either.[3]

Many students complained about Muny Light on Earth Day. Rady's classmate Robert Tasse wrote Stokes with the understanding that the mayor was "not responsible for everything that goes on" in Cleveland, but he hoped to encourage action, as so many writers did. He asked Stokes to "pressure some (if not all) of the growing industries in Cleveland, like Republic Steel, Muny Light Plant and Edgewater Park"—a remarkable list, mostly because it didn't include any actual "growing industries." Despite a series of capital investments in new facilities in the postwar decades, Republic Steel hadn't grown in years. Perhaps Tasse inferred that the mill complex along the river was growing because of the constant media attention to its incredibly smoky stacks and its heavy contribution to water pollution in the Cuyahoga. Edgewater Park was just that—a park along Lake Erie west of the mouth of the Cuyahoga and, perhaps more important, adjacent to the Westerly Sewage Treatment Plant. Edgewater included a beach that in recent years had featured signs warning against swimming due to high coliform bacteria counts. During the summer before Earth Day, the beach had gained significant press attention as the Stokes administration attempted to clean the shore and nearby waters, at least enough to allow safe swimming at the park. Like Edgewater Beach, the Municipal Light plant was consistently in the news in the late 1960s, the focus of concerted efforts to improve air quality in the city.[4]

Tasse's letter confirms the obvious: students, like adults, learned about their environment from the news as well as their lives. Undoubtedly, discussions in school that week, which at Westlake occurred in both biology and English classes, affirmed this list of problematic places; Edgewater Park, Muny Light, and Republic Steel were well-established targets of environmental activism. But even the letters that include no specific target of concern confirm that for most students—for most Cleveland-area residents—the most pressing environmental issue was pollution, which they tied directly to industry. They also expressed a growing urgency concerning political action. Shannon Havranek, a junior in Maple Heights, a working-class suburb south of the city, wrote, "Sitting around and talking about pollution doesn't help a dying lake and atmosphere. Act now. Make the industries improve their sewage disposal. Spend more money on pollution control. Impose heavier fines on littering." In the minds of children, the path forward seemed so clear.[5]

The letters capture the sense of environmental crisis in 1970 and, somewhat less clearly, an understanding of the ongoing urban crisis. Pollution emanated mostly from the city's core, especially the riverside mills and the lakeside power plants, but the children wrote mostly from surrounding suburbs—Westlake, Maple Heights, Cleveland Heights—a reminder of how much suburbanization had already reshaped the metropolitan area. Although the letters said little on the subjects of concentrated poverty, inadequate housing, crime, and racial inequality—all topics that probably seemed inappropriate for Earth Day letters—many students wrote with an understanding that Cleveland's problems could not be solved through the haze of pollution. The city was engaged in major urban renewal projects, putting special emphasis on reviving the central business district, part of the effort to speed the transition to a service city. But as Havranek put it succinctly, "The new improvements in downtown Cleveland will not be seen through the pollution." The letters raise serious questions: would the city survive the seemingly impossible confluence of crises described in the letters? What would become of a city suffering simultaneously under the weight of industry's wastes and the wrenching displacement caused by industrial decline?

Cleveland's first Earth Day is of special interest because in addition to suffering from problems common around the nation—pollution, litter, and even the proliferation of rats—the city had garnered an international reputation for its especially acute environmental crisis. In the years leading up to Earth Day, Cleveland appeared in the national press for a variety of reasons. Some of the attention was positive, especially in 1967, when it became the first large city to elect an African American mayor. But as the nation's urban and environmental crises deepened, Cleveland attracted mostly negative attention. The city was struggling to clean up Lake Erie, its greatest natural asset and the most imperiled Great Lake. In 1965, the national press detailed racism's consequences when the U.S. Civil Rights Commission held hearings on housing, schools, and employment discrimination in Cleveland so that it might understand the plight of African Americans in a typical northern city. Over the next three years, Cleveland experienced two intense riots, one before and one after Stokes entered office, both of which drew attention to the physical realities of the decaying ghetto. And the events of the summer before Earth Day, including the passage of a new air pollution ordinance, the creation of a water pollution control plan, and the Cuyahoga fire, had kept urban environmental issues in the news. In sum, by the time April 1970 rolled around, Cleveland had become emblematic of the intertwined urban and environmental crises. As Tasse put it in his letter to Stokes, "not every city can say they have a river that catches on fire." Or, to put it another way, Cleveland had become the city "where the river burns," just as the *Plain Dealer* had predicted.

Earth Day came at a critical moment in American urban history. White flight had remade cities in the previous decades. From Tampa to Milwaukee, from Boston to Los Angeles, metropolitan regions sprawled outward. In many American cities, underinvestment resulted in decaying housing, deteriorating infrastructure, and inadequate services in the urban core. Frustration among African Americans trapped in failed and failing neighborhoods fueled a series of Long Hot Summers, when riots and arson simultaneously protested and sped the destruction in ghettos around the nation. The Earth Day letters reveal the consequences of the increasing divide between the middle-class life of suburbia and the entrenched poverty of the inner city. Both suburban and inner-city children were living through environmental crises, but these crises were surprisingly dissimilar in nature. Children knew environmental problems were real and pressing, but how they experienced the environment determined how they articulated the problems.

As diverse as the writers were, they shared a trait that comes through in the letters: an attachment to place. This is especially true of Rady, who lived fifteen miles from downtown in a comfortable ranch home with a patch of woods beyond her backyard but who selected a distant power plant to represent her environmental concern. She thought herself connected to the industrial city to her east, perhaps connected by even more than pollution. It was "our city," she wrote, that was being strangled by pollution. Indeed, Rady's short letter was most poignant when she contemplated the future of her city. "In many years to come, space visitors to this planet may find the remains of a once great, but ignorant society," she predicted. "What will become of Cleveland?" she asked, and then, to Stokes more directly, "What do you plan to do?"[6]

CARL STOKES IS NOT SUPERMAN

On November 13, 1967, Carl Stokes stood in City Hall's Council Chambers and delivered his inaugural address. "In my first official statement as Mayor of Cleveland, I want to make it crystal clear that I intend to serve the best interests of all the people without fear or favoritism," he said, understanding that racial anxiety still governed the thoughts of many white Clevelanders, despite the long, mostly positive campaign that led to his election just six days earlier. "Yes, Cleveland is a city in crisis—a crisis shared with all the other great metropolitan areas of our country and of the world," he said, affirming that he knew just how difficult his task would be. "Our cities are the battleground in which American civilization is now engaged in a struggle for survival." Military metaphors were commonplace in the late 1960s, given the War on Poverty, the Cold War, and the actual war in Vietnam, but when most Americans' thoughts turned to urban battlegrounds they undoubtedly thought of the rioting that had wracked so many cities—or at least their ghettoes—during the previous three summers, each summer more violent than the last. And now, for the first time in history, a black man stood before a predominantly white city that he pledged to lead. "The enemy is not an organized military force, or even an ideology," he continued. "The enemy is a combination of tangible and intangible big and little problems—human problems and physical problems—problems that press thorns of misery on huge segments of our population—problems that make our environment irritable and unpleasant—problems that range from tangled traffic and downtown decay to race relations and the crying need for job making industrial development, from the needs of the neighborhoods to the need for port and jet age air development."

Carl Stokes could make a hell of a speech, no doubt about that. "Struggle for survival," "thorns of misery," "tangled traffic and downtown decay." He expressed so powerfully what many Clevelanders thought about their city. And Stokes was just as dramatic when speaking about his hope for the future. "This is a city renowned throughout the world for its industrial genius, its cultural achievements, and its accomplishments in many fields," he said. "We have what it takes to cure the blemishes of disease spots which now pock our community." And then, in nearly a shout, he repeated his campaign slogan, "I BELIEVE IN CLEVELAND." Stokes ended his inaugural address with the exhortation, "Let's roll up our sleeves and get to work!"[7]

And there was a lot of work to do. As he well knew, Stokes had stepped into the mayor's office at an inauspicious time. "After World War II, when the deterioration of our cities became apparent," he wrote several years later, "there was a complete failure to respond." Inaction had led to deepening problems in housing, employment, and public health. Recreational facilities were insufficient, public properties were ill-kept. Even as the city began to lose population, some schools became terribly overcrowded as the district struggled to maintain de facto segregation in the face of shifting neighborhood demographics. The city had even failed to make sufficient investments in basic infrastructure; roads, streetlights, and sewers needed considerable attention. As Stokes wrote in his autobiography, "Cleveland wandered into the late 1960s surrounded by its failures and fearful of its future." In essence, Stokes took charge of a faltering urban machine.[8]

The mayoral campaign had taken place in the shadow of the Hough riots, which had severely damaged the predominantly black East Side neighborhood in the summer of 1966. Many Clevelanders assumed that the presence of Stokes in the mayor's office would improve the lot of the black community and decrease racial tensions throughout the city. To put it bluntly, as some people did, Mayor Stokes was an insurance policy against further racial violence. If most whites had modest expectations about his ability to turn the city around, they at least thought he could bring an end to the mayhem. Stokes received 50.5 percent of the vote, winning by fewer than two thousand ballots. He gained the support of nearly the entire black turnout, as he assumed he would, but also something like 20 percent of the white vote. These were the people his campaign had sought to win over—open-minded folks who appreciated Stokes's energy and supported his policy ideas, as well as loyal Democrats who couldn't bring themselves to vote for Seth Taft, the Republican

𝓕𝒾𝑔𝓊𝓇ℯ 2. The Stokes campaign tried to avoid the issue of race in 1967, but it also recognized the historic nature of the election. Here Stokes drops off his petitions for his mayoral run in the summer of 1967 at the Cuyahoga County Board of Elections, with his wife, Shirley, at his side. Photo by Clayton Knipper. Cleveland Press Collection, Cleveland State University.

candidate. Other than being the right color, Taft had little intrinsic appeal to white ethnic voters. In addition to being Republican in a heavily Democratic city, he was an extremely wealthy man who until he threw his hat into the ring lived in Pepper Pike, a distant, exclusive East Side suburb. As the campaign progressed, the weakness of Taft's candidacy—he was neither a gifted speaker nor a natural politician—made it clear that if Stokes lost, it would be solely because he was black. Although the Stokes campaign tried to mute the issue of race, one of its slogans played up the historic nature of the city's choice: "Let's Do Cleveland Proud."[9]

Stokes campaigned on the themes of openness, inclusiveness, and community engagement. Each of these phrases signaled to long-neglected African American residents that their voices would be heard. The phrases were also designed to reassure whites, many of whom feared the consequences of a racial transition in City Hall just as they feared the transition in their neighborhoods. Stokes also ran on an extensive "Program for Progress," described as "Plans to Make Cleveland's Future Brighter." The program included thirteen major policy areas, including recreation (he would sell Shaker Lakes Park to Shaker Heights and invest in city parks), health centers (he would expand the

Health Department and emphasize the prevention of disease), and air and water pollution (he would make Lake Erie "the valuable recreation asset it should be"). His campaign convinced the *Plain Dealer*, which endorsed him over incumbent Ralph Locher in the Democratic primary, praising his "vigor and imagination," and then endorsed him again over Taft. Even the *West Side News*, which served an essentially all-white constituency, endorsed Stokes over Taft, praising his "sincerity, intelligence, enthusiasm, and courage." All this speaks to the predominant theme of his campaign: hope. Indeed, the anticipation of change became so great that Stokes, who liked to refer to himself in the third person, tried to keep expectations realistic, even reminding an audience a month before the election, "Carl Stokes is not Superman."[10]

CLEVELAND IS UNBEARABLE

Sixteen-year-old Debbie Mohorcic's Earth Day letter to Stokes opened with two assertive questions: "People or profit? Do you want to conquer pollution, or do you want pollution to conquer us?" It was a formal letter, neatly typed, and despite the aggressive tone, she signed it "Respectfully yours." She lived in a neighborhood of tidy homes—Cape Cods, bungalows, ranches—in the working-class suburb of Maple Heights, southeast of the Cuyahoga Valley's steel mills, just the type of place that had benefited most from the nation's long postwar boom, where white families with rising incomes secured better schools, cleaner air, and spacious lawns. But the only hint of the idyllic origins of Mohorcic's letter was the home address in the upper left-hand corner. "I wonder how much longer we will be able to exist under these conditions, which are becoming worse every day," she wrote. The "conditions" that concerned her were regional. She noted, as many students did, that Cleveland had made the federal government's list of the five most polluted cities in the United States, and the Cuyahoga was ranked among the ten most polluted rivers. "What contest are we trying to win?" she wanted to know. And then she made clear just how serious the situation had become: "By polluting the water the way we are, we are killing the wildlife (especially the fish), and by polluting the air we are going to kill ourselves."[11]

Maple Heights residents had physically escaped the city, but many of them continued to work in Cleveland's mills and factories, so the community was only partially removed from the city's industrial economy. Mohorcic seemed to understand this. She wanted to know why "big industries" were allowed to pollute so much, but she provided the answer herself. "Of course, these industries are bringing money to the city; but what is more important—the people

or the profit?" she wrote, repeating her opening question. Mohorcic had articulated the central proposition of the environmental movement. Appearing in
a variety of forms, this was the question environmental activists demanded
that politicians answer: are corporate profits more important than public
health or recreational opportunities? This was also a question that industry
could rephrase to meet its own needs: is a pristine environment more important than good jobs?

Many students from Maple Heights wrote to Stokes, the letters sharing
form and, at least partly, theme. Sixteen-year-old Pat Pivonka wrote most
passionately. "Our city is almost dead," she declared. "The lake is ugly and
polluted and you cannot eat the fish that are caught there. The air is always
dark, dreary, and smelly." Pivonka defined "our city" expansively, but she was
very familiar with a particular place exposed to industrial pollution. She had
relatives who lived near the Republic Steel Plant, at the southern end of the
industrial flats. "There is always red dust covering the houses—even though
the people wash down and paint the houses frequently," she wrote. Then she
pronounced, "The smell and the looks of Cleveland is unbearable."[12] How
could Stokes respond to that?

Some students, like Pivonka, wrote about specific sources of pollution, but
just as often students simply railed against "pollution" as a generic problem.
Air pollution garnered more attention than water, but dozens of students expressed concern about Lake Erie, especially its beaches, many of which were
regularly closed to swimming because they were fouled by sewage. Others
expressed concern about fishing, which had declined precipitously in the preceding years, helping fuel the "Save the Lake" movement in Cleveland in the
late 1960s. Maple Heights student Barb Gray wrote one paragraph on air
pollution and another on Lake Erie, ending the latter with, "What is the good
of having a lake when you can't fish or swim in it?" Jill Jaffe, writing from
Monticello Junior High in Cleveland Heights, an upper-middle-class suburb
on the eastern border of the city, offered to help clean the beaches so that she
could swim and water-ski. "But it takes a lot more than just the help of one
eighth grade girl," she added. "I'm sure that there are other people willing to
help." Jaffe, who had also attended an Earth Day assembly and helped her
classmates pick up litter around the school, wasn't alone in expressing an interest in helping. This, too, was a common theme.[13]

Surprisingly few students mentioned the Cuyahoga River in their letters,
and not all who did mentioned the fact that the river had caught fire just ten
months before Earth Day. The paucity of Cuyahoga references suggests that
the river played only a small role in children's conceptions of their city.

Unlike Lake Erie, the Cuyahoga held little recreational value, and most children rarely saw the river. It was largely hidden, invisible behind the mills in the wide southern flats and spanned by high bridges that afforded no view of the narrower northern stretches of the waterway. Although it was terribly polluted, the foul Cuyahoga was less intrusive than the streams of black smoke that issued from the great stacks of the mills and power plants. Its infrequent appearances in the letters remind us that children learned about their city mostly through their own experiences, and their experiences rarely included the Cuyahoga. Just as important, the paucity of references to the Cuyahoga reminds us that Clevelanders didn't need their river to catch fire to tell them that their city was polluted.

Those who did mention the Cuyahoga understood its unique ability to represent environmental degradation. For instance, the river figured prominently in the letter from Westlake student Craig Miller, who asked, "Would you please tell me how any river could become a fire hazard because of the oil on it?" He followed the rhetorical question with an understated, "That is really weird." The bulk of the letter from Maple Heights eleventh-grader Claudia Mendat reminisced about "a nauseating ride" on the *Goodtime II*, a small pleasure craft that gave her fifth-grade class a tour of the Cuyahoga and Lake Erie. "When I took the trip," Mendat remembered, "my fellow classmates and I spent the day watching the Cuyahoga River change colors, and smelling how bad the stench could become." To drive home her point, Mendat asked, "May I suggest that they change the name of this boat to the Pollution II?"[14]

In addition to relaying the Cuyahoga anecdote, Mendat's letter revealed that she had internalized the imagery and language of the environmental crisis as received through the media. "It is plain to see that our area is deteriorating at a rapid rate," Mendat wrote. "By 1980 we may be all walking around wearing gas masks in order to breathe," she predicted, using a common visual representation of air pollution. Earlier in the year, *Plain Dealer* political cartoonist Ray Osrin had used a gas mask in a play on Auguste Rodin's *The Thinker*, one of which sat on a pedestal in front of the Cleveland Art Museum. In the cartoon, the muscular statue is perched on a rock overlooking the badly polluted river, with smoking factories in the background and a gas mask secured around his face. Osrin's cartoon may have inspired some of the students who referred to masks in their letters, including thirteen-year-old Bob Adelberger, who asked, "How would the Cleveland Browns and the Cleveland Indians look playing ball wearing gas masks?" For Adelberger and Mendat, gas mask imagery connected their troubled world to an imagined, horrifying future.[15]

Children clearly learned about the environment from both personal experience and media exposure, and they expressed their concern using a variety of methods, from brief, polite requests for more information concerning what the mayor was doing about the problem to urgent demands for action. Despite the diversity, one approach appears frequently: narrating a personal experience with a troubled place. This was the case with Westlake's Robert Tasse, who described a "recent school field trip to the Cleveland Health Museum," during which he observed the city from the window of a bus. As they traveled toward downtown, Tasse struggled to see the skyline through the thick air. "It was so full of waste products, I could hardly see the top of Terminal Tower," he wrote to Stokes. "I thought that was pretty disgusting."[16] Like Tasse, many children learned this type of environmental lesson from a trip to the city. Take eighth-grade Cleveland Heights student Nancy Danker, who objected to the air pollution she saw while riding on the Shoreway, the East Side highway that hugged the lakeshore, "looking out the car window." Loren Clark of Westlake reported the same thing in greater detail. Writing the day after Earth Day, Clark complained about the Municipal Light plant, which according to her "emits black smoke all day," although she lived more than fifteen miles from the plant. "Upon passing the plant on the shoreway," she wrote, "I have to hold my breath or else choke." She continued, "I can imagine what the residents of Cleveland have to put up with when there is an offshore wind." This last sentiment is telling, of course, because as a resident of Westlake who apparently knew the pollution primarily through the windows of the car, she really could only imagine what residents of the city had to put up with. In letters like this, pollution appears as a real but distant problem, an occasional nuisance experienced mostly in short, memorable bursts, often while the children were on the move through the city, away from their cleaner suburban homes.[17]

Suburban children such as Mendat, Tasse, Danker, and Clark had special reason to emphasize urban pollution, of course: they were writing the mayor of Cleveland. Still, the letters make clear that children really did associate pollution with cities, even when it made its way into less urban settings, like out in Lake Erie. Several writers also complained about air pollution as it wafted out of the city and into their otherwise clean environments. Two months before Earth Day, for example, sixth-graders in Strongsville collected snow, brought it inside, and let it melt through a cloth filter. As the water dripped through, it left behind a layer of soot on the cloth. The children learned that Cleveland was to blame. Strongsville is twenty miles south of the city center, and from that distance Cleveland was unseen but certainly not unfelt. One of the Strongsville students, Ralph Simpson, wrote a terse but clear letter to Stokes: "You should get stronger laws in Cleveland. When I rode through it started to smell so bad that I wanted to leave right away," it read in its entirety. Richard Dusky, also from Strongsville, agreed, and he told Stokes that four years earlier, when Dusky was five or six, he was "coming home from a baseball game" and the "pollution was very bad."[18] Like so many of the suburban children who wrote to Stokes, the Strongsville students described pollution as an urban trait, something they both blamed on Cleveland and remembered mostly from visits to the city.

In a few instances, children indicated that they thought the environmental problems of the city derived not just from the presence of factories and power plants or from the poor policies and priorities of politicians, but from the people who lived there. Writing from Westlake, fifteen-year-old Shelley Stelmach told the mayor, "I chose to write to you because it seems to me you haven't done too much to clean up Cleveland." She went well beyond blaming Stokes, however. "Maybe I don't live in Cleveland but I can still see that this is a serious problem," she wrote. "I don't see how anyone could live in a house with a garbage filled yard; you'd think people had some pride in ownership." Stelmach had probably heard something about the garbage problem in Cleveland's ghetto, a constant concern in the late 1960s, but she didn't realize that homeownership patterns were different in Hough and Central than they were in Westlake. "I think you should encourage people to clean up their own property," she continued, "because, as I see it, pollution begins at home."[19]

AMERICA HAS BOUGHT A LITTLE TIME

In early 1968, *Trans-Action*, a social science journal based at Washington University in St. Louis, published a study of the previous fall's elections. "The Making of the Negro Mayors 1967" addressed the simultaneous elections of Stokes and Richard Hatcher in Gary, Indiana. Since the three authors, Jeffrey K. Hadden, Louis H. Masotti, and Victor Thiessen, were social scientists at Case Western Reserve University, the bulk of the piece concerned Cleveland. Despite the good press that followed the victories, the authors did not "find much cause for optimism in those elections" and concluded that "it would seem that the elections have only accelerated the pace of ever-rising expectations among Negroes." This conclusion followed the common assertion that frustration had grown among ghetto residents because their expectation of equal opportunity outstripped society's willingness to provide it. The authors feared that the threat of violence had actually increased because expectations shot up after the elections, and they feared that Stokes and Hatcher could not deliver results. They concluded, "The Negro community's frustration with the American political system will almost certainly heighten." While some American liberals proclaimed the elections of black mayors a great step forward on the long road to justice and equality, Hadden, Masotti and Thiessen concluded, "America has, at best, bought a little time."[20]

In victory Stokes had bought himself *very* little time. Taking office just six days after the election, Stokes entered City Hall unprepared to name a new cabinet and without faith or trust in many of the administrators who surrounded him. Exhausted by the campaign, Stokes was also unprepared to leap into the tasks at hand. So instead he took a family vacation after just two months in office, spending nearly two weeks in the Virgin Islands while people back home struggled through a heavy winter storm—a coincidence that had many Clevelanders saying "told you so." Scandals involving two close aides, both forced out before February, distracted the mayor and the press and gave even more Clevelanders the sense that Stokes and the people around him were not up to the city's challenges. The administration had gotten off to a slow start, as became evident to a national audience when the *New York Times* published an article by James M. Naughton, a *Plain Dealer* political reporter, under the headline "Mayor Stokes: The First Hundred Days." The piece described the early missteps at length, and its appearance in the *Times* confirmed one of Naughton's central points: Stokes was "under more intense scrutiny than any of his predecessors."[21]

Since the end of World War II, Cleveland had been nearly a one-party town, Taft's narrow defeat notwithstanding. Democrats had a lock on City Hall for twenty-five years, and party leaders greased the machine by providing plum jobs to supporters. Over the years, this led to the appointment and retention of ineffective employees, many of them in leadership positions. Add to this a lack of energy and vision at the top—a series of caretaker mayors—and it was no wonder Cleveland had a reputation as a poorly run and corrupt city. If one-party government failed Cleveland through ineptitude and inertia, after the 1967 election the situation changed abruptly. Cleveland suddenly looked more like a two-party town, with most Democrats backing Stokes, but with conservative Democrats lining up behind James Stanton, the City Council president, who quickly became a bulwark against the Stokes agenda. Stanton's resistance was no surprise to Stokes, who well understood that ethnic whites would be troubled by their sudden loss of power in City Hall.

Given the difficult politics inherent in the arrival of the new administration, Stokes needed to take care in his appointments, making certain that he found capable administrators who would remain loyal. Understanding that part of

Cleveland's inability to handle its myriad problems stemmed from poor leadership of the city's departments, Stokes pledged to "hire the best available individual for every policy making job at City Hall," using "capability" as the only criterion.[22] Given the typically low salaries in government service, however, he soon found himself struggling to attract more qualified managers without increasing budgets for personnel, which he was reluctant to do. At the same time, Stokes wasn't above making appointments for purely political reasons. For instance, in an effort to reach out to the ethnic communities of North and South Broadway, Stokes hired Ben Stefanski II, the twenty-nine-year-old son of a Slavic Village savings and loan president, to lead the Public Utilities Department. Stefanski had no background in Public Utilities, a large department that had charge of Municipal Light, the water supply, and the sewer system, all areas in need of renewed attention. Stefanski didn't know Stokes before the election, and he was as surprised by this call to service as everyone else in the city. Stefanski quickly became a trusted adviser to Stokes and a close, loyal friend—just the type of administrator the mayor needed. Still, Stefanski's inexperience and the obviousness of the political motivations behind his selection made him a lightning rod for criticism. His appointment signaled to many Clevelanders that the Stokes administration would be business as usual.

In one important regard, however, the new administration was revolutionary. As the mayor's brother and former congressman, Louis Stokes, put it in a recent interview, "black people had never been able to walk into City Hall and see people who look like them running the city."[23] That changed. Mayor Stokes appointed African Americans to high posts and made certain that hiring at all levels in city government would increase diversity. It is difficult to overestimate what this meant to the black community and, of course, to the individuals who now had the ability to find good jobs in municipal service. Some of these appointees became vital members of the administration, including Buddy James, a Legal Aid lawyer tapped by Stokes to head the Law Department. Perhaps the most visible African American leader in the administration, save Stokes himself, was Dr. Frank Ellis, who took over the Health Department in October 1968. Stokes had great expectations for a revamped Health Department. "The health of our people is at the top of our priority list," he said while introducing Ellis, adding that the Health Department would no longer be "buried in the City Hall basement and swept from our minds." Over the next three years, Ellis worked to improve service and public engagement, adding neighborhood health centers and making strides in disease prevention. Although he became an important public face of the administration, as he was introduced to the community he said, "This is not a time for speech making. It's a time for doing."[24]

In the summer of 1968, a civic advisory committee headed by Robert Morse, president of Case Western Reserve University, had identified Ellis as the leading candidate for the Health Department post, although the Glenville riots in late July delayed the announcement of his appointment. Ellis came to Cleveland with a strong reputation. He had earned his M.D. from Meharry Medical College in Nashville, had a stellar career, including years in the Army Medical Corps at the Kansas City Hospital and Medical Center, and when hired he was just completing a master's degree in Public Health from the University of Michigan. But it may have been Stokes's reputation that mattered more to Ellis's arrival in Cleveland. As the Stokes administration was winding down, Ellis reflected, "When I first thought about coming here, I said it had this same real significance, and that I wanted to be a part of that. There can never be another health director who served under Carl Stokes, you see." Other talented African Americans joined the Stokes administration with a similar sense of being part of history, including Bailus Walker, who was recruited by Ellis to the Health Department to head up a new rat control program. The Stokes administration got off to a slow start, no doubt, but as these and other appointees got to work, the pieces were in place for progress.[25]

Stokes may have been hindered by conservatives at home, but his administration benefited greatly from the liberal policies of the Johnson administration. His personal relationship with Vice President Hubert Humphrey and his star status as the first black mayor of a large city served Stokes well in Washington. Democrats controlled both houses of Congress and continued to support Johnson's War on Poverty by funding a series of programs designed to improve the plight of both urban and rural poor. New programs in housing, education, public health, and environmental protection worked their way through the chambers, and in hearing after hearing congressional leaders called on Stokes to testify in favor of increased federal involvement in urban affairs. In return, federal dollars flowed into the city. Cleveland applied for federal grants both large and small, from the expansive Model Cities program to the modest rat control program that Walker headed up. Although Stokes worked well with all the representatives from northern Ohio, beginning in 1969 he had a special relationship with the congressman serving the East Side, his older brother Louis, who shared an understanding of Cleveland's needs and a similar philosophy of activist government.

Federal dollars were essential to the cash-strapped administration, but Stokes knew he needed more. He had promised not to raise taxes during the campaign and so instead envisioned an expansive private-public program called Cleveland: Now! Stokes hoped to raise corporate funds to help jump-start programs that in turn could apply for federal dollars. He announced the program to great fanfare on May 1, 1968, using a half-hour television and radio program broadcast on all major Cleveland channels. The next day's *Plain Dealer* featured a double front page, the first dedicated entirely to Cleveland: Now! It featured a description of the program, designed to eventually raise $1.5 billion to spend on housing, jobs, and health initiatives, most of them focused on the inner city. Cleveland: Now! promised new health centers, job training programs, housing rehabilitation, and neighborhood cleanup efforts. As was common when Cleveland's daily papers covered Stokes, the news was accompanied by a photograph of the smiling mayor; this image caught him holding a basketball on a school playground surrounded by adoring kids, both white and black. At the bottom of the page, another article described the drive for eleven thousand new jobs, concentrated in the inner city, where unemployment was over 15 percent, remarkably high in a metropolitan region where only 2.4 percent of the workforce was out of work. The *Plain Dealer*'s first page also included an editorial offering unqualified support for the "imaginative and bold plan." Stokes's slow start was officially over.[26]

In the months after the announcement, the administration had success raising money. Despite a serious hiccough in the program caused by press attention to the fact that Ahmed Evans, the Black Nationalist at the center of the Glenville Shootout, had received Cleveland: Now! funds, Stokes continued to tout the initiative, speaking of it regularly. The assertiveness of the Cleveland: Now! program worked its way into the language of the city. The program didn't have the lasting impact Stokes would have liked, but he had changed the way people talked about their city. He had raised expectations about what even Westlake High School student Robert Tasse called "the NOW CITY." The fierce urgency of NOW, first articulated by Martin Luther King Jr. in 1963 and then reprised by Stokes in his renewal campaign, clearly resonated with many children, several of whom demanded action NOW! in their Earth Day letters.

TERRIBLE TO BE NEAR

When read together, the Earth Day letters sent to Mayor Stokes reveal a bit of sameness. The vast majority came from suburban kids who were overwhelmingly respectful and earnest. Writing in the formal setting of school, under the supervision of teachers, students followed the rules of polite society, from proper salutations to traditional, sometimes affectionate closings. They expressed concern about a fairly narrow range of problems. But a handful of letters stand out, serving as instructive exceptions. Among them are the letters from St. Wendelin's, a Catholic elementary school on the city's near West Side, just a few hundred yards from the Cuyahoga River on Columbus Road. The slender Willey Avenue arcs behind the school, down a steep grade, and into a gulch that carries the tracks of what used to be called the Big Four Railroad and a creek that used to be called Walworth Run. In truth, it is the creek that used to be, rather than its name, which persists. Walworth Run disappeared altogether in 1903, when the city finished burying the creek, turning it into a huge combined sewer that empties into the Cuyahoga at one of its many bends. Despite its location so close to the center of the city (it was just three blocks from the busy West Side Market), St. Wendelin's wasn't a prominent school, perhaps in part because it sat perched between the Nickel Plate and Big Four tracks, both of which carried heavy freight along the city's east-west industrial corridor. And the nearby streets, including the aptly named Train Avenue running along the bottom of the gulch, carried little traffic other than the trucks serving industry and the cars of neighborhood residents. There had been a time when Walworth Run served Cleveland's industrial growth admirably. It had been home to several oil refineries, some of which John D. Rockefeller consolidated into Standard Oil beginning in 1870. And just below St. Wendelin's the Standard Paint and Lead Works and the Walworth Run Foundry took advantage of the good rail connections.

By the time St. Wendelin's students took up the task of writing Mayor Stokes, their neighborhood had been terribly polluted for a hundred years. Lead and chemical wastes had spilled onto the ground and drained into the creek at first, and then the sewer. Factory stacks and locomotives had belched smoke over the valley—a century of sootfall. The city had buried the creek because for two decades it had served as an open sewer draining wastes from the city's union stockyards, less than two miles upstream from St. Wendelin's. The creek had disappeared, but so had the wastes—into the Cuyahoga. By 1970, some of the evidence of all this industrial development had disappeared. The refineries were gone, the trains were less frequent, and now the environment was both polluted *and* neglected.

The letters from St. Wendelin's say nothing about the industrial residues. The railroad tracks and the factory stacks just a few hundred yards from where the children wrote warrant no mention. Instead, the children focused on a lot closer to the school that served as a casual dump. "Have you ever seen Willey Hill?" ten-year-old Louis Rodriguez asked Stokes about the street that headed down to the tracks below his school. "Well, I have. I live five houses away and when I play I can smell it," he reported. "It really is a bad place, with broken glass, rats and garbage and even snakes." Eight-year-old Mark Hudak wrote much the same thing of the lot near the bottom of the hill, complaining of "filth, garbage, broken glass, waste and smell." This place was near his school, which worried him because "young children play there and live near there." To make his point clear, Hudak stated bluntly: "It is terrible to be near."[27]

St. Wendelin's student Melissa Stevens wrote perhaps the most heartbreaking letter sent to Stokes on the first Earth Day. "I am writing to you because I and others have a problem which I think you can help us solve," she opened hopefully. Like her classmates, she focused on the dump on Willey Avenue. "It has garbage and filth all around it," she noted. Then she added, "It involves danger." She thought that if Mayor Stokes knew of this place and the danger, he would "have someone to come and clean the mess." She wrote "please." Like all the children at St. Wendelin's, Melissa wrote about a place she knew well, a place she knew was dangerous, an environment that needed to be cleaned, a place that was terrible to be near, a place that *was* near. And yet she was willing to do her part. "If you have it cleaned," she wrote Stokes, "I promise I will do what I can to keep it that way. It should look like God wanted it to be. Thank you."[28]

Few inner-city schools like St. Wendelin's wrote to Stokes on Earth Day, but he did get a letter from a sixth-grade science class at Daniel E. Morgan School, in Hough, the neighborhood wracked by riots four years earlier, where decay and disorder were even more evident than on the near West Side. Mrs. Le Grande, who wrote a cover letter to the mayor, had led her science class in a brainstorming exercise on "how littering contributes to pollution." Le Grande explained that the students had "concluded that littering can be controlled," and she attached a list titled "Recommendations for Controlling Littering," which well described the environmental problems that so immediately affected these children. The list begins simply, reasonably: "All trash should be disposed of in suitable containers." Second, "the city should provide trash cans at every busy corner of the city." The children also hoped that garbage collectors could be "more careful when collecting garbage." The fourth recommendation remained practical: "Every car owner should be required to have a litter bag in his vehicle, available to occupants." Fifth, another policy recommendation, "Garbage should be collected twice weekly in heavily populated areas." This suggestion seems as if it might have been added by the teacher, and yet like the previous recommendations it was directly on task, as the students were, thinking of practical structural and policy changes that might lead to a cleaner Hough.[29]

Then the list begins to take on a different character, as if the brainstorming children began to connect their thoughts about litter to other aspects of the neighborhood they wanted improved. Street clubs could "concentrate more on the problems of pollution," they proposed. "Dog owners should be required to walk their dogs instead of allowing them to run free in the neighborhood," a solution whose wording suggests that the unleashed dogs, not what they left behind on the ground, posed the actual problem. "Breaking bottles and glass on the street and sidewalks should be out-lawed," the children wrote, conjuring images of a neighborhood strewn with broken glass. And then, moving completely away from litter, the class recommended that "the city should do more to rid the neighborhoods of rats and other pests." And the city should "provide supervisors for The Morgan Playfield," next to their school. Finally: "All laws, (present and new) must be enforced."[30]

Mrs. LeGrande's classroom nearly comes alive again in this list, the children moving from the concrete, the most practical, most on-task solutions to littering, to other, related problems: the dogs that run loose in the neighborhood, the rats, the unsupervised playground. This was a neighborhood out of control. It needed order; it needed law enforcement. All this in an Earth Day letter. We surely get a sense of crisis here, as we do from the letters of suburban students, but it is a different crisis altogether. Suburban children expressed concern for the environment of places to which they felt some connection but which were generally at some distance from home. For the children of Hough, like the children at St. Wendelin's, the environmental crisis wasn't experienced through a car window; they didn't see it on a field trip or an outing to a ballgame. They don't reference gas masks or Municipal Light. They didn't gather their sense of crisis from the news. They didn't point to distant smoky factories or polluted waterways. Their environmental crisis was near at hand and underfoot. It was behind the school yard where they played, in the streets where they lived.

Mayor Stokes understood that these children were living through a crisis from which they could make no retreat. This was an existence he knew well, through his experience growing up poor in Cleveland. He wrote about his childhood, "We had almost no notion of anyone's living beyond the horizons of our narrow patch of neighborhood." This was the only environment these city kids knew: the environment of the urban crisis.[31]

WHY CAN'T WE HELP THESE PEOPLE?

In the summer of 1968, Cleveland police were keeping an eye on Ahmed Evans, a Black Nationalist who had gathered a number of supporters and a cache of guns in his Auburndale Avenue apartment. On July 23, that surveillance went terribly awry. Rising tensions led to gunfire, though no one knows who fired first. The shootout in Glenville lasted hours and left seven people dead—three of them policemen. The shootout evolved into Cleveland's second major race riot in two years, as African Americans took to the streets of the city's East Side. Arson, looting, and the threat of spreading violence convinced Stokes he should call for the National Guard. On the night the conflict began, forty-year-old Dorothy Cassidy sat in her Maple Heights home and watched the news reports from Glenville. "It scares me," she wrote to Stokes. "I never felt this kind of fear before. Why should I & I'm sure others, have to be afraid in this great country of ours." Surely Cassidy's fear was real, fueled by the reports of intense violence—men holed up in a residential neighborhood, firing rifles and shotguns at police officers in the street. Even though Cassidy was ten miles away, seemingly safe in her suburban home, her connection to Cleveland was so strong that she worked out her anxiety in a letter to the mayor. "Surely the heat of the day has caused the troubles tonight," she wrote, trying to find an explanation. "I'm uncomfortable & hot in my nice, clean, suburban home, and I think what must it be like for so many cramped into sticky, hot, overcrowded apartments." Unlike many in the region who watched the violence unfold on television, she was empathetic toward those stuck in the ghetto. "Why can't we help these people get away from that atmosphere at least one day a week when it's hot," she suggested.[32]

Cassidy's proposal seems naive at first glance. Weekly escapes when the weather turned oppressive were unequal to the challenges of the urban crisis. Her suggestion ignored the other, more consistently oppressive forces at work on the black community—the forces that ensured chronic unemployment, a deteriorating housing stock, and inadequate public services. Still, Cassidy's letter expressed the possibility that the environment played some role in sparking the violence—and not just the heat, but also the cramped, overcrowded apartments. Indeed, the letter hints at how troubled Cleveland really was, that this violence, as extreme and shocking as it was, had not come out of nowhere. It came out of the ghetto. This chain of events—shootout, riots, and the arrival of heavily armed troops—affirmed to many Cleveland-area residents that the city had entered a period not just of decline but of crisis, and in

Cassidy's letter we see how intimately the urban and environmental crises were intertwined.

That April, Stokes had helped prevent violence after the assassination of Martin Luther King Jr., spending hours in and around Hough trying to calm emotions and ease tensions. Perhaps because black Clevelanders saw the tears of their mayor on television and in the paper, or perhaps because he spent days out in the streets, asking angry crowds to "cool it," while other cities burned, there was peace in Cleveland. "We must use the death of Dr. King as a stone upon which to build a better Cleveland and a better America," Stokes said. "To do less would be to make a mockery of his life." This performance during the King crisis helped solidify Stokes's reputation around the nation as an effective African American politician. But just four months after King's assassination, the Glenville riots revealed the limits of Stokes's ability to calm black anger. As the violence spread, he took the extraordinary step of removing white police officers and guardsmen from the affected area in an attempt to reduce violence between police and the African American residents of the East Side. This action may have saved lives, but it deepened white suspicions of the black mayor, especially among police officers.[33]

On the one-year anniversary of King's assassination, *The Humanist* published an essay by Stokes titled "Rebuilding the Cities," opposite Eldridge Cleaver's radical "Tears for the Pigs." Using the headline "Militant vs. Moderate on the Black Revolution," the magazine cast Stokes as the voice of reason merely through the stark contrast with Cleaver. "The people of the cities are tired of having their problems analyzed," Stokes wrote. Everyone knew what the problems were; now it was about finding the political will to create solutions. "There must be a massive attack on poverty—one that will require a whole new order of national priorities," he proposed. In what might have sounded like a strident message had it not been so directly contrasted with a polemic from the voice of the Black Panther Party, Stokes described how recent migrants into the city—the growing African American population—had "not come into a land of primeval forests and sweet, clear waters." Instead, "their inheritance is the dregs—the filth and decay and the leavings of people who have long since moved into clean, spacious new surroundings." Sounding something like Cassidy contrasting her own Maple Heights home with the neighborhoods of the inner city, Stokes drove the point home by purposefully conflating the deterioration of the natural environment with that of the city as a whole. "The once-clear Cuyahoga River has long since turned brown with refuse, polluted almost beyond help, and the lake itself is a deadly sea in which little lives beside the organisms of disease. Some call it blight. I call it tragedy."[34]

Even though his first term had been rocked by violence, Stokes remained a popular mayor. He ran for reelection in 1969 and won a second term by a more comfortable margin. Not surprisingly, during his four years in office Stokes heard from many racists about his personal and policy shortcomings. (The most offensive and threatening letters wound up in a special file.) The most rabid tended to write from beyond Cleveland, indeed from outside Ohio, but white resentment inside the city was unmistakable. Some of the bitterness came from older Cleveland residents, perhaps those who felt least able to pick up and move away from the gathering crisis, those attached to their neighborhoods and their fading city. Some of the most pointed letters went unsigned, including one from early 1969 that asked the mayor to "make the streets of Cleveland safe for ALL people and let the black man stop all robberies and mugging." Further, the writer wondered, "Why do these black women have so many youngsters, paid for by the whites?"[35] This letter, like many others, conveyed an understanding of urban culture informed by racism, one that blamed African Americans not only for their own problems but for the problems of the entire city.

In a similar vein, an elderly white woman who had voted for Stokes wrote to express her disappointment about the trajectory of Cleveland. Fearing bodily harm or damage to her property, she signed the letter only "An old tax payer." She had raised her own children without any help from the city, and now she didn't want to "support illegitimate children and their mothers." She had been unmoved by media coverage of East Side slums and "the filth where children play." She wondered, "Why don't these people living there take a broom and shovel and clean up their yards instead of throwing garbage out their windows." To this old taxpayer, the physical disorder of the ghetto revealed the flawed character of those who lived there, a common and long-standing conception.[36]

The strength of this white resentment reveals how difficult Stokes's job would be. It also reminds us that racial politics charged every interaction between Mayor Stokes and his correspondents, many of whom may not have known the city well but knew enough to read race into the landscape. Some pitied blacks trapped in the ghetto; others simply blamed them for their plight. The racial divide complicated everything in Cleveland at this critical moment, not just during the periods of open violence but as the city attempted to negotiate the long urban crisis. And race was a constant consideration for a black man attempting to manage a predominantly white city.

THE MORE INCLUSIVE URBAN CRISIS

The Earth Day letters are filled with urgency and fear, but it is difficult to determine how much stress children in the Cleveland area really experienced. Surely some students exaggerated their concerns for rhetorical effect, but expressions of anxiety about the future are frequent and vivid. Many of the children expressed concern not just for the future of their city but for themselves and even humanity altogether. A surprising number of students worried about dying young. Eighth-grader Nancy Danker, of Cleveland Heights, was made to "wonder whether or not pollution will kill me by the time I am twenty five years old." Glenn Gray, of West Technical High School, was even more dramatic. "I hope within a few years that the people of the United States do something before the world itself is *destroyed*," he wrote. Underlining "destroyed" six times was not enough. Gray added a postscript: "Do something *now* before we are destroyed!!!" And repeating Stokes's own urgent demand for action, Gray added across the bottom of the page in bold block letters: "CLEVELAND NOW!"[37]

The mayor's office responded politely to the letters, emphasizing the city's actions to date and promising continued vigilance in the fight to clean up Cleveland. Undoubtedly, students complaining about air pollution heard something about how the city had passed a tougher ordinance in 1969; students concerned with water pollution were probably reminded that city residents had passed a $100 million bond issue in 1968 that would help reduce water pollution through investment in sewers and sewage treatment. As would be expected, the mayor's office's replies surely affirmed the need to act but not the students' most dire predictions for the future.

In at least one instance, however, Stokes's office sent a particularly aggressive reply to a letter from a concerned student. In June 1970, two months after Earth Day, seventeen-year-old Bernard Sroka of Independence, a thinly populated white suburb extending along the Cuyahoga south of the city's mills, wrote Stokes to complain about "the layer of pollution hovering over the Cleveland area." Noting that it "stinks downtown," Sroka was concerned about the "blue gray haze" that had developed "even down here in Independence," more than ten miles from inner-city Cleveland. Sroka asked Stokes, "Why don't you try halting the pollution of our air, even it if means forcing the factories to close down and regulating auto use? Why don't you help make Cleveland clean and beautiful so that it could live up to its motto of 'The Best Location in the Nation'?"[38]

Stokes's reply suggests a growing impatience with the drumbeat of complaints about the environment. "The problems related to the crisis in the environment are serious components of the larger, more inclusive urban crisis," the letter said. "As mayor of the city of Cleveland, I must view them as such and act accordingly." The response touted the administration's many accomplishments related to the environment, claiming, "My administration has devoted more time, money and manpower to the fight against pollution than any previous administration in Cleveland's history." But the letter also pushed back against the very idea that the administration should dedicate more energy to solving environmental problems. "I face many more serious crises which affect the lives of my constituents to a greater degree than air and water pollution," Stokes wrote. These were the "problems of the poor," which "must receive highest priority. These include housing, jobs, food, clothing, and the ability to live in a society free of racial hatred." Sroka, a young man writing at a safe distance from the concentrated poverty of the inner city, can surely be forgiven for demanding different priorities for Cleveland's mayor, but Stokes understood that solving the environmental crisis would mean little if the urban crisis were allowed to persist.[39]

2 Hough and the Urban Crisis

On June 2, 1969, Carl Stokes joined Frank Ellis, director of the Health Department, and his recently hired deputy commissioner for environmental health, Bailus Walker, on a residential street in Hough, the densely populated and long-deteriorating East Side neighborhood. At the north end of Holyrood Road, part of a tangle of odd-angle streets of clapboard houses, town homes, and low-rise apartment buildings, Stokes, Ellis, and Walker announced a new program to control rats, funded by the federal government. Stokes knew that the $381,000 from the Department of Health, Education and Welfare wouldn't accomplish much without neighborhood involvement—hence the public kickoff. Stokes thrived in these kinds of situations; he was at his best as a politician out on the streets, shaking hands, smiling, and selling himself and his policies.

Holyrood Road may have been at the center of Cleveland's East Side slum, but it wasn't terribly dissimilar from lots of streets in the area. In fact, Stokes had grown up on such a street, just two miles away in Central. Stokes was raised by his mother, a domestic worker, in what he remembered as a "rickety old two-family house." His father had died when Stokes was just two, and his knowledge about the struggles of the poor came from watching his mother raise her two boys alone; his understanding of the problems of living in substandard housing came from that rickety house at 2234 East 69th Street. "We covered the rat holes with the tops of tin cans," he remembered in his autobiography. "The front steps always needed fixing, one of them always seemed to be missing." The family—Carl, his mother, and his older brother Louis—shared one bed in their one cold and drafty bedroom. Moving out of that home at age eleven and into the "dependable warmth" of Cleveland's first public housing complex—Outhwaite Homes, also in Central—"was pure wonder" for Carl. In their new home they found "a sink with hot and cold running water, a place where you could wash clothes with a washing machine, an actual refrigerator." Stokes felt, and never forgot, the real physical differences that came with his new, modern home.[1]

From that critical transition in his life, Stokes learned that government can make a very positive impact on the lives of citizens, a lesson that helped guide his political career. Standing on Holyrood Road that morning, Stokes could not make grand claims about the transformative potential of the new rat control program, but the federal money could make a difference through little steps: by helping train city workers, paying for rodenticide ("that's a fancy word for rat poison," Stokes told the gathering), and funding a community education effort to encourage residents to improve their homes and their behavior so as to make Hough and other rat-infested parts of the city less accommodating to the pests. For this reason, the city "will need the cooperation

Figure 3. At the "Rat Control Kick-off," Mayor Stokes stood with Director of Health Frank Ellis and his new deputy Bailus Walker, surrounded by a small crowd of press and Hough residents. Ellis and Walker wore coveralls, contributing to the imagery of taking some visible action—a central theme in the Stokes administration. Carl Stokes Photographs, 1968–1971, container 2, folder 101, Western Reserve Historical Society. Used with permission.

and the involvement of citizens if the program is to achieve its potential," Stokes announced to the small crowd.[2]

The main event of the kickoff wasn't a lecture on proper garbage storage or "environmental hygiene." Rather, it was a demonstration with the poison, which city workers placed in rat burrows around nearby homes. This, too, fit with a fundamental Stokes administration strategy: do something visible. Rats and the burrows they made around buildings and in vacant lots were obvious signs of a neighborhood's failure and of government's failures, too. Rats scared children and sometimes bit them. They spread disease, and they gave neighborhoods an unhealthful, even chaotic feel. Still, everyone knew—Stokes, Ellis, and Walker included—that rats didn't produce Cleveland's problems, not even the problems in Hough. The rats were symptoms rather than root causes. Stokes, like other politicians before him, understood that treating symptoms was easier than identifying and removing the causes. Symptoms were visible, tangible, and perhaps even manageable. Root causes were just the opposite. Perhaps the pressing question that morning should not have been could the city control the rats, but rather when would the city stop fighting symptoms rather than trying to cure the disease?[3]

In his four years as Cleveland's mayor, Stokes pressed liberal solutions to inner-city problems, re-created local government so that it might better respond to the urban crisis, and participated fully in federal programs designed to improve conditions in troubled neighborhoods. And through it all, the programs and the reports, the activism and press conferences, Hough took on special meaning. Observers could begin to believe that Hough *was* the urban crisis. The obvious problems of racism and segregation, unemployment and the concentration of poverty in the ghetto, helped Hough, and neighborhoods like it around the country, define the urban problem. Containing and curing the crisis in the ghetto became the primary strategies for reformers, both in and out of government. Public and private activism made a difference in individual lives and particular places, but the trajectory of Hough—and Cleveland as a whole—remained unchanged. Liberal policies simply could not stop the deterioration of Hough's residential environment.

90 PERCENT OF CLEVELAND'S POPULATION DO NOT KNOW

Just about the time Stokes and Walker announced the rat control program, city employee Gary Bound began reading meters in Hough. A resident of Old Brooklyn, a white working-class neighborhood on the southwest side of Cleveland, Bound might as well have been traveling to a different world as he crossed the Cuyahoga River and entered the basements of the rapidly deteriorating ghetto homes and unkempt apartment buildings. Bound was so moved that he typed up a lengthy letter to the mayor, eloquently expressing his shock at what he saw in those basements. "They're so rotten and foul that it's like being swept into an abyss of rotting grime, germs and garbage. The dampness, the decay—and I am *not* over-emphasizing—the stench is beyond proper description. You simply 'must' see it to actually believe it, and still it all strikes as like a horrid nightmare, an unreal horror story." After describing this situation, "the horrible basements and wretched backyards," Bound proposed that the city use some of its Cleveland: Now! money to buy some "outside help" to aid these residents, giving them instructions and encouragement "to teach them how to clean-up, how to improve their lawns, how to reconstruct and save their homes and basements." Bound's visits to Hough had convinced him that the neighborhood's direst problems were physical. He described an environmental crisis that city residents faced every day.[4]

Bound was clearly a sympathetic observer, but his proposed solutions suggest how little he could actually see, even as he toured the darkest corners of what psychologist Kenneth Clark had called the *Dark Ghetto* in an influential book published four years earlier. Such deterioration could not be explained merely by the lack of interest or ability of the current Hough residents to improve their environment. Bound saw Hough's physical problems, but he could not clearly discern their causes, a nearly universal failure, especially for those who lived outside the ghetto. Bound could not appreciate the powerlessness of residents who for the most part did not own the buildings in which they lived, who could not gain the type of employment that could help them purchase better housing, and who found it difficult to escape a deteriorating neighborhood because of racism among landlords, real estate agents, bankers, and many residents of white communities that resisted integration.

By the mid-1960s, neighborhoods like Hough—increasingly referred to simply as "the ghetto," regardless of the city in which they appeared—had become a primary domestic concern in the United States. The riots of the Long Hot Summers, which began in earnest in 1964 in Harlem, North Philadelphia, and several other inner-city neighborhoods, spread alarm among Americans as they watched their cities burn on the nightly news. Increasing media attention was matched by increasing scholarly attention. Kenneth Clark's 1965 book bridged those worlds because he was a scholar *and* an insider, and he wrote in the sharp prose of a journalist. Clark's emphasis on the distinctiveness of ghetto life, its "all-encompassing" nature and the pathology that affects all its residents, even those who escaped, influenced contemporary discussion about failed urban neighborhoods. A forty-year resident of Harlem, Clark described ghetto residents as prisoners, trapped physically and, more problematically, psychologically. According to Clark, all the ghetto's problems—indeed all of urban America's problems—stemmed from this reality. High rates of delinquency, homicide, drug abuse, and school dropouts all derived from the central fact of forced segregation. The poverty and powerlessness of the ghetto was self-perpetuating so long as the damaging forces of segregation buffeted African Americans. Clark described for a newly attentive audience the "normal chaos of ghetto communities" and the colonial relationship ghettos and their residents had with the city beyond the "invisible wall."[5] Despite the wide readership of *Dark Ghetto* and the power of its descriptions and explanations, most Americans, even those who had seen failing urban neighborhoods firsthand, never fully integrated the consequences of systemic racism into their understanding of the ghetto. Even Gary Bound, who deeply felt the plight of the poor, failed to appreciate the power of that invisible wall.

Bound may not have fully recognized the causes of decay, but at least he had been in the bowels of the ghetto, and he used this experience to help him understand the troubles of the people stuck there. "I, in my many hours of silent meditation," he wrote to the mayor, "have often wondered why these negroes were really bitter and angry, why they rioted and revolted. NOW I KNOW!!!" Bound knew these people needed help, were demanding help, but still were not getting it. Like the residents of Hough, he wondered why help was not forthcoming. Bound believed that if everyone could see what he had seen, things would change. "I think I can safely estimate that 'at least' 90% of Cleveland's population do not know, do not realize even, what this tragic situation is over in this negro area," he wrote, adding, "It certainly does make my heart weep to realize this myself." Really seeing Hough, as Bound had, might be a step in the right direction, but merely witnessing was not enough.[6]

Stokes wrote a brief and polite response to Bound's three-page letter. He praised Bound for his "concern about the future of Cleveland" and said he had referred Bound's "interesting thoughts" to several staff members "for review." As the Stokes administration knew well, however, the city had been struggling to solve the problems of Hough for more than a decade—Bound's "interesting thoughts" had been thought before by many in government and in the church organizations, nonprofit agencies, and charitable foundations that had been at work in the neighborhood. That spring Stokes himself had stood on East 81st Street just south of Hough Avenue, with representatives of Inner City Housing Inc., a joint effort by the large local banks, including Central

National Bank, to announce the rehabilitation of forty-two apartments in three buildings. Neither that small endeavor, nor the investments of time, energy, and capital of all the other involved organizations, could stop the rot.[7]

THE CRISIS GHETTO

Bound discovered Hough's problems in 1969, but other Clevelanders had begun investigating the growing troubles in the 1950s, as the neighborhood entered a rapid demographic transition. In 1950, Hough had nearly 66,000 residents, 95 percent of whom were white. Just five years later, the population had grown to over 82,000 and it was over 50 percent black. By the end of the decade, the neighborhood had already begun its population decline, and three quarters of its 71,000 residents were black. This demographic change reflected Cleveland's attempt to accommodate more than 165,000 additional African Americans in the two decades after 1940. Many of the blacks moving to Hough came from the South, but others came from the adjoining Central neighborhood, which had become home to Cleveland's black population during the first Great Migration of the 1910s. As white ethnics, including Jews and Italians, moved out of Central, the physical condition of the neighborhood deteriorated. This decay helped make it the focus of public housing efforts in the 1930s, as the city demolished hundreds of buildings to make way for the Outhwaite Homes and Cedar Apartments projects, both of which replaced old clapboard homes with midrise brick apartment buildings. By the 1950s, demolition well outpaced rehabilitation, and Central began a dramatic population decline, losing 7,000 residents in that decade and another 25,000 during the 1960s, most of them moving farther east, especially into Hough, Glenville, and Mt. Pleasant.[8]

Hough's white residents read the racial transition and physical deterioration of Central as foreshadowing. The same changes would reach their streets—it was just a matter of time. In a pattern that played out across the urban North, whites fled as blacks arrived; more than half the people who lived in Hough in 1950 had left by 1960. In addition, the whites who left Hough in the early years of transition were disproportionately white-collar, meaning that the neighborhood's income composition was changing as rapidly as its racial demographics. The transition was so rapid and obvious that the Cleveland Foundation, a venerable organization dedicated to the region's success, initiated and funded a study by social scientists at Western Reserve University, an eminent institution that sat just east of Hough. That work, published in 1959 by Marvin Sussman, a sociologist, and R. Clyde White, a professor of social work, described a neighborhood under considerable stress. Sussman and White hoped to provide an "exact description of the facts about Hough, its people, their hopes, wishes, needs, and living conditions as these were in October–December 1957." To do this, they combined a demographic analysis with interviews of residents in the two-square-mile neighborhood. Their data quantified the racial turnover and revealed other trends, including a rise in the number of children and a gradual increase in crime. But the most significant problems were physical and subjective. Recreational facilities, including parks, were increasingly overcrowded and worn out, according to residents. More important, the growing population was packed into existing structures. Only sixty-five housing units had been built in Hough in the 1940s, when the population was overwhelmingly white and fairly stable. As the population grew in the 1950s, construction added essentially no new residential space. Instead, according to Sussman and White, the division of single-family homes into apartments had led to "dilapidation."[9]

Excluded from most areas in metropolitan Cleveland and forced to compete for units in constricted space, blacks paid premiums on real estate, and the extreme population pressure and high rents discouraged many types of investments. Upgrades to kitchens and bathrooms, new windows, doors, porches, and even new roofs became unnecessary to attract tenants. Apartments in dirty and unkempt buildings rented anyway. Worse, property owners with large mortgages, many of them absentee landlords, subdivided single-family homes and made extant apartments even smaller. Some began renting out previously unused spaces in basements and attics. Much of this conversion work was shoddy, and even newly created spaces deteriorated quickly. Real improvements rarely came because property owners could charge high rents for even degraded units. Tenants held little sway over landlords, who sometimes remained unknown to them or shifted frequently as investment properties changed hands.[10]

Despite the stress from population growth, Sussman and White didn't describe a neighborhood in crisis, and for good reason. While the arrival of blacks signaled the arrival of blight for some Clevelanders—including the white families who quickly moved out—Hough remained a lively community in the late 1950s. Although 90 percent of blacks in Hough had lived in their homes less than five years, the high mobility had not prevented the creation of strong social ties. Most black residents had family connections in the neighborhood, and even more told Sussman and White that they had made good friends with neighbors since their arrival. Hough gained a reputation for extreme poverty, but most families earned paychecks, and they built—or brought with them—the types of institutions that strengthened communities, especially churches. For instance, in 1956 Liberty Hill Baptist Church moved out of its handsome brick building on Kinsman Road in Central and into a much grander structure on Euclid Avenue in Hough, where a beautiful sanctuary welcomed worshipers under a great dome, illuminated in part by large Tiffany stained-glass windows facing the side streets—four in each direction. The Star of David adorned nearly every surface in the church, and Hebrew phrases were scattered about, including on the windows.

The Liberty Hill congregation had moved into what had been the Euclid Avenue Temple, completed in 1912, when Hough was a much wealthier neighborhood with homes that nearly matched the grandeur of the temple. The Baptist congregation retained the Jewish symbols, accepting both the building's history and the Jewish history played out in the stained glass that adorned the room. Those unfamiliar with Jewish symbols and Hebrew might miss the references to Abraham or Jehovah and wouldn't be able to translate "Hallelujah," but to those who knew the Bible the two stone tablets were unmistakably the Ten Commandments. Here and in other temples that became churches, the continuities of the two faith traditions lived on in the sanctuaries they shared.

The Liberty Hill building well represented the demographic transition, but casual observers might miss the broader continuities. Just fifty years earlier, immigrant Jews had occupied a neighborhood in distress—Central—where the city had initiated efforts to improve housing conditions. A 1914 report by Cleveland's Department of Public Welfare called the Jewish and Italian neighborhood "some of the worst conceivable housing conditions" with "extreme and hodge-podge overcrowding." Indeed, population density along Scovill and Central Avenues, 208 people per acre, was well above the "overcrowded" densities that would plague Hough in the 1950s. The study also found a majority of the buildings, most of them wood frame, in a "poor or only fair state of repair." The author, Mildred Chadsey, chief inspector of the city's Bureau of Sanitation, expressed concern about the cleanliness of yards and the homes themselves. All this would sound familiar to observers of Hough as it transitioned into an African American neighborhood. There was something very recognizable about the arrival in poverty, the struggle to move out of squalid housing, and the movement to better neighborhoods. This wasn't a black story; it was an urban American story. It was a story well known to the Jews who moved their temple from Scovill Avenue in Central, to Euclid Avenue in Hough, and finally to an even larger facility in suburban Beachwood.[11]

In the 1950s, Hough grew in population but not in prosperity. Money flowed in, but too much money flowed out. All the necessities of life were expensive, especially rent. Worse, rent and mortgage money mostly left the neighborhood, as landlords tended not to live in Hough, and banks essentially ceased making new loans in the area, assuming that the racial transition made investment there a poor risk. In addition, residents found themselves paying too much for groceries, as too few stores catered to a largely captive population. Storekeepers, like landlords, didn't reinvest in the area—stores didn't expand, didn't gain new refrigeration units or new displays, just as homes didn't gain new plumbing and appliances. In short order, this crowded community looked sick, as building owners neglected painting, failed to replace the rotting piers under listing porches, failed to pick up garbage that accumulated along fences and in overgrown lawns. Capital flowed from Hough, and the neighborhood deteriorated under the weight of population pressure and Cleveland's harsh weather.[12]

If Hough looked sick by 1960, by 1965 it *was* sick. A special mid-decade census found just 59,000 people, meaning the neighborhood had lost more than 20,000 residents in a decade. The population decline reflected a deterioration of conditions, including the abandonment of housing units no longer habitable or worthy of repair. It also represented a continued desire of many residents to find better housing elsewhere. Despite the population loss, Hough still had almost 46 people per acre, or more than four times the density of some white working-class neighborhoods, such as Tremont on the near West Side. And Hough was now nearly 90 percent black, an indication of the completeness of the racial transition and the uniqueness of the black experience in postwar urban America.[13]

Using the 1965 special census data, Walter Williams, a researcher for the Johnson administration's Office of Economic Opportunity, determined that Hough was part of a new kind of place: a "Crisis Ghetto." Data showed that over the previous five years poverty had declined nearly everywhere in the city, even among blacks—not surprising, given the strong economic growth at the time. Still, the census found that real income had actually declined in Hough, Central, and Kinsman, down 2 percent in male-headed families and a remarkable 15 percent in female-headed households. Unemployment rates also rose, but only among blacks living in the Crisis Ghetto, where poverty rates had increased more than 10 percent. What's more, the deleterious effects of the ghetto had "spread beyond the economy to the total environment—to schools, to street associations, to the preservation of life itself." In sum, Williams concluded, "in 1965 the average Crisis Ghetto inhabitant was worse off than he had been in 1960, both absolutely and relative to others in the city."[14]

Williams used data to describe growing despair in the Crisis Ghetto, but the national media were just as likely to use physical descriptions to convey the depths of social decay. This was not mere shorthand or symbolism. The physical deterioration was real. John Skow, writing in the *Saturday Evening Post* in 1967, described Cleveland as "worn out and feeble." Problems were most evident in Hough, where large wooden homes with "front-porch columns that upheld the Sunday-pot-roast respectability of the McKinley Administration" were now "split and peeling."[15] A month earlier, in an article under the headline "Cleveland's Ghetto," *New York Times* reporter Paul Hofmann described Hough as "one of the sickest and most sinister neighborhoods in the nation." Hofmann quoted disaffected residents and described recent troubling events, but the article's most powerful paragraph described the scene.

> Hough lives in a mood of suspended rage. Shattered windows, garbage heaps, loitering men and mousy prostitutes outside the few saloons still in business, youth gangs ensconced in vacant homes, older people too afraid to go out and dejectedly staring out of windows, groceries sold at marked-up prices behind half-closed grilles in a handful of stores just a few hours a day, burglaries, muggings and arson as a way of life, shots in the night, and rats—this is Hough today.[16]

"And rats"—the crescendo that drove home the chaos. Of the many physical markers of the urban crisis, rat infestations became perhaps the most sensational.

The danger posed by rats to human health was nothing new in the 1960s, of course. In 1909, the U.S. Department of Agriculture referred to the brown rat as "the worst mammalian pest known to man." Once primarily a rural nuisance responsible for substantial crop damage, rats also spread deadly diseases for centuries before scientists uncovered their role. Especially as the carriers of the fleas that spread bubonic plague and the lice that spread typhus, rats have been complicit in the deaths of hundreds of millions of human beings across the globe. What was new in the 1960s, however, was the connection of rats to a specific kind of place, as symbolic of urban decay. Just fifty years earlier, when rats lived in a wide variety of places in dense American cities—along wharves, in public markets, warehouses, and stables—no urban neighborhood could banish the pests. As the century progressed and the middle class moved out of the crowded central city and into modern homes, built with concrete basements and without privy vaults or stables, broad swaths of suburban, auto-dependent America made for poor rat habitat. At the same time, the densest urban neighborhoods, with overflowing garbage cans, poorly constructed and maintained plumbing, and porous outbuildings and basements, still supported large rodent populations, allowing rats to evolve into the quintessential marker of urban despair, of the failure of certain places to progress.[17]

Politicians responded to the growing connection between slums and rats, and perhaps thinking it easier to eradicate the pests than diminish their habitat, they created programs to control rats. Even the lackadaisical Locher administration, which controlled Cleveland's city hall from 1962 to 1967, felt obligated to engage in rat control, initiating a pilot eradication project in Hough in the fall of 1966. Later the city expanded the program to include all the city's infested neighborhoods. In 1967, the city surveyed 20,000 residential properties, and its Bureau of Neighborhood Conservation, which had been created just two years earlier, "baited and gassed infestations on over 7,000" of them. That year more than half the complaints to Division of Health sanitarians involved rats; one in every four Cleveland families lived in a rat-infested dwelling, and forty-eight Clevelanders were bitten by rats.[18]

Cleveland wasn't the only city to recognize the seriousness of rat infestations, and national politicians began to envision a federal role. In the spring of 1967, Lyndon Johnson delivered a special message to Congress concerning his priorities in the ongoing War on Poverty, which began with the passage of the Economic Opportunity Act of 1964. Although the War on Poverty addressed both urban and rural problems, such as through job training programs and Head Start education support, many of the new federal programs focused on the problems of the slums. Johnson's 1967 legislative agenda was typically far-reaching, with the expansion and creation of programs such as "Operation Green Thumb" and the Jobs Corps. Among the new programs was federal rat control, introduced with the goal of "Protecting the Slum Child." Johnson noted, "The knowledge that many children in the world's most affluent nation are attacked, maimed and even killed by rats should fill every American with shame. Yet, this is an everyday occurrence in the slums of our cities." Congress at first balked at further expanding federal involvement in municipal affairs, but in the fall it passed a bill allotting $40 million over two years to the Department of Health, Education and Welfare's "partnership for health" grant program, which would allow cities to apply for matching funds to support rat control efforts.[19]

TOTAL RESTORATION OF THE LOCAL ENVIRONMENT

By the time Stokes, Ellis, and Walker stood on Holyrood Road in 1969, the city had been engaged in a long battle with rats, one that predated Mayor Locher's tentative efforts. Eight years before Stokes announced his new control program, Cleveland asked the U.S. Public Health Service to study the rat problem in preparation, theoretically, for a coordinated attack. The 1961 City Council resolution asking for federal help described a health and safety hazard caused by increasingly poor sanitation and growing rat populations, and it noted that the city did not have the proper administrative structure or expertise to tackle the problem. The council resolution explained the problem's spread by claiming that "the continuous movement of people from one neighborhood to another and from other cities to Cleveland results in a lowering of sanitation standards of everyday life due to a lack of knowledge and the habits of the people resulting in the continued deterioration of some neighborhoods in the city." In other words, through ignorance of the customs of urban living or simply low standards of cleanliness, migrants arriving in Cleveland's crowded inner-city neighborhoods caused a spike in the rat population. The resolution left unstated that these new arrivals, and those moving from one neighborhood to another, were black.[20]

The resolution reflected a revolution in thinking about the relationship between slums and the people who lived in them. Some fifty years earlier, Progressive Era reformers had expressed an environmentalist understanding of poverty and impoverished places, arguing that degraded places created degraded people. Progressives feared that the children of the slums would be demoralized by their surroundings, learning poor work and hygiene habits. By the 1960s, the causal arrows had shifted for many observers, who, like the City Council, were now more likely to blame the bad behavior of residents for the quality of the environment. This understanding informed Mayor Locher's approach to Hough and other degraded neighborhoods. In describing the role of his recently created Neighborhood Bureau of Conservation, Locher claimed, "It will help to educate and guide the new migrant in adapting to the cultural patterns of big city living." The bureau also dispensed expert advice on home maintenance, by sponsoring workshops and distributing pamphlets, mirroring the efforts of natural resource management, which relied on the wisdom of experts to help people make better choices. Locher, a Democrat with support among Cleveland's still powerful white ethnic communities, wasn't unsympathetic to ghetto residents, but he understood why so many

Clevelanders blamed slum residents for slum conditions. "Life in a shack, harsh surroundings, and an inferior education often make it difficult for the newcomer to conform to the rules and the customs of city living," Locher said in 1966. "The non-conformity stirs prejudice against him. There is great need for a program that acculturizes the newcomer to his new surroundings."[21]

This way of thinking wasn't entirely new, of course. Urban residents had expressed concern about immigrant behavior since the mid-nineteenth century, and teaching newcomers how to live in the city had been a core mission of the Settlement House movement in the Progressive Era. As the Great Migration dramatically increased the African American population of northern cities, especially Cleveland, Detroit, and Chicago, the famed University of Chicago sociologist Robert Park linked deteriorating social conditions with the unpreparedness of southern arrivals. "The enormous amount of delinquency, juvenile and adult, that exists today in the Negro communities in northern cities is due in part, though not entirely, to the fact that migrants are not able to accommodate themselves at once to a new and relatively strange environment," Park wrote in 1925.[22] Through the twentieth century, policy makers' assumptions about the inability of blacks to accommodate to urban living, through lack of experience or knowledge, or simply cultural inclination, prevented officials from seeing the more complex relationship between poverty, race, and urban decay.

Not everyone was so certain about how the arrows of causation lined up. Morris Thorington, who lived in the southeast neighborhood of Lee-Harvard and commuted into Hough, where he owned a beverage store and delicatessen, had drawn his own conclusions about the people he served every day, some of whom he clearly admired. "The moral character of the family don't change as much as you might think by the home they are living in," he said in 1966. "It is not that Hough is a morally decayed neighborhood. It is rather because Hough is decayed that it is drawing these morally-decayed people into it because people come from all over the city to do their dirt down there at Hough." In this way, Thorington's conception of the inner city thoroughly mixed people and place. Indeed, although the lines of causation varied, Americans continued to link degraded places to degraded people. The ghetto bound people and place—and rats—together in decay.[23]

After the city's 1961 request, the federal government conducted a study of the rat problem, surveying 10 percent of Cleveland's blocks and giving policy makers excellent data. The study, led by Clyde Fehn, a sanitary engineer with the Communicable Disease Center, determined that 28 percent of the city's properties showed signs of rat infestation, with the problem most severe in the areas surrounding downtown, especially African American neighborhoods. Forty percent of Hough's properties showed signs of rats, but other East Side neighborhoods were even worse, including Central. Fehn's report, completed by the summer of 1962, made clear what any interested party already knew: "Rat infestations, rat bites, and transmission of rat-borne diseases have long been associated with substandard housing areas. This association is evident in Cleveland." The immediate causes of rat infestations were also well known. As Fehn summarized, "Inadequate storage of refuse, extensive use of illegal refuse containers, and excessive amounts of stored refuse are the principal causative factors in the rat problem." Fehn placed a high value on educating residents and adjusting their behavior, but he had a broader vision. His report cast a wide net in assigning blame, and he suggested several avenues for improvement. Citizens would have to be educated on how to prevent infestations, by storing garbage correctly and not leaving pet food out in yards, for instance, but the city had responsibilities, too, including increasing garbage pickups to twice weekly and creating a new Bureau of Environmental Health, "devoted to all phases of environmental sanitation." Many city services would have to improve, including building inspections, street cleaning, and the use of rodenticides in the most troublesome locations. The city also had responsibilities to make physical changes in infested neighborhoods, including removing vacant buildings and adding garbage cans to street corners in crowded neighborhoods.[24]

In 1966, four years after the initial report, Fehn produced a follow-up, in which he described no progress. The city had taken some relatively easy steps, such as distributing educational pamphlets and passing an anti-littering ordinance, but other, more costly recommendations led to nothing, not even the addition of garbage cans to street corners. Most striking, however, Fehn expressed an obvious disappointment in the behavior of slum residents, noting that "deficiencies in refuse storage" reflected "primarily the failure of citizens to place refuse in available containers and the failure to keep covers on the containers." Indeed, Fehn blamed a "deterioration of citizen behavior," including littering and stealing garbage cans, for the ongoing rat infestation. He was more forgiving of the city's behavior.[25]

Not all observers were so forgiving of the city. Kenneth Clark, writing about ghettos generally, saw the gathering trash as evidence of the city government's failure to provide equal services to all residents. "To lecture the miserable inhabitants of the ghetto to sweep their own streets," Clark wrote in *Dark Ghetto*, "is to urge them to accept the fact that the government is not expected to serve them."[26] Like Clark, Stokes was unlikely to blame the poor for the trash and rats in their neighborhoods. He took a comprehensive approach, one that reflected Fehn's long list of recommendations in 1962 and not the follow-up report's focus on resident behavior. In January 1968, just two months after he entered office, Stokes thanked Dr. Joanne E. Finley, the acting health commissioner, for taking the initiative in applying for a Department of Health, Education and Welfare grant to take on the rat problem. The proposed program was just the kind of visible action Stokes desired. Significantly, Findley's extensive grant request, titled "Establishment of an Environmental Improvement and Rat Control Program," placed the onus on government—not the residents.[27]

Finley, who held a master's degree in public health from Yale and an M.D. from Western Reserve University, described a grand expectation for the program: the overall improvement of environmental health. She hoped the program would "restore the total environment to a more desirable condition," while eliminating the rats, which were "symptomatic of the present state of environmental deterioration." Finley's application revealed a broad understanding of Cleveland's predicament. She knew that the city had been built "by individuals who regard the resources of their environment to be boundless in quantity and justifiably exploitable." Because of this, she asserted that the municipal government had a moral obligation to save the city's environment from "debasement by its citizens"—by which she meant the exploiters, not the exploited. Finley's application reflected a new tone coming from Cleveland's City Hall. It was time to stop blaming the poor for the physical conditions of the ghetto.

According to Finley, although the city had a legal and moral obligation to act, it didn't have an effective bureaucratic structure or the resources needed to succeed. The city's bureaucracy fragmented responsibility for the environment. Eight different city departments had a stake. Health and Welfare handled air pollution and public health; Public Utilities handled water pollution and garbage collection. Public Properties managed recreational spaces; Public Service managed the streets. Community Development contained the housing and building divisions; Public Safety was responsible for the dog pound. All this meant that the urban environment could not be regulated holistically. And environmental health, Finley noted, suffered. Finley called the rat control program "a logical and feasible first step toward total restoration of the local environment." It would feature community education and involvement, a revised sanitary code, better laboratory facilities, and a new home improvement and rat-proofing program. Much of the outreach would operate through Neighborhood Opportunity Centers, created and funded by the

Office of Economic Opportunity to help wage the Johnson administration's War on Poverty. The opportunity centers were staffed by local residents, who would help teach their neighbors how to take simple steps to make their community less attractive to rats. The outreach staff would also report infestations, helping city employees identify where eradication should take place.[28]

The federal grant allowed the city to hire Bailus Walker, who joined the Department of Health in part to manage the rat program. Thirty-six years old at the time, Walker held a master's in public health from the University of Michigan and was working toward his Ph.D. at the University of Minnesota. He arrived from Dayton, where he had briefly worked on that city's rat control program. He came with a good understanding of Cleveland's problems, having spent a summer in Central working at his uncle's grocery store on Scovill Avenue, where many of the customers came from Outhwaite Homes. More than family ties and a personal connection drew him to Cleveland, however. Like many African Americans around the country, Walker was emotionally invested in the Stokes administration. In a recent interview, Walker described "an air of excitement among many of us and across the country about Carl being the first black mayor of Cleveland." Stokes "brought a lot of energy to the city; a lot of enthusiasm." That enthusiasm, and a wave of new hires in the city administration, Walker included, led to late hours, brainstorming, and innovation.[29]

After working in Cleveland for a year, Walker understood the special environmental pressures on inner-city residents. He noted in a journal article that "the health needs of inner-city residents are acute." Using language that would come to be associated with the environmental justice movement, he described the connection between an "impoverished neighborhood" and "the pall of smoke and odors emanating from a nearby industrial operation, dump, sanitary landfill or incinerator." The environmental hazards were myriad. "Vacant lots, vacant and vandalized structures, abandoned automobiles and discarded appliances add a new dimension to health and safety hazards in inner city neighborhoods." The inner-city environment, with its rat bites and high carbon monoxide exposure, required health professionals to develop new strategies to protect children, who had a significantly lower life expectancy than other Americans. "The overriding need for this strategy is brought into full view when we recognize that the environment of the urban ghetto child does more than depress him, injure him or otherwise overwhelm him; it kills him as well." Echoing Kenneth Clark, Walker concluded that he could not believe that in the ghetto "the mind and the emotions or the physical health go unscathed." Here all the failings of the city came together. The total environment failed. And still, Walker had faith in government and faith in Stokes to make a difference—to do something visible and meaningful.[30]

A SENSE OF PLACE AND PURPOSE

In March 1968, Carl Stokes sat in the U.S. Capitol before the Senate Subcommittee on Housing and Urban Affairs, surrounded by fourteen other Clevelanders—city officials, leaders of the business community, and prominent citizens engaged in the housing issue. Stokes hoped this extraordinary turnout would help convince senators that Cleveland was serious about solving its housing problems and that the city needed federal support. Among those in attendance were George Grabner, chairman of the Greater Cleveland Growth Association, which had replaced the Chamber of Commerce; Paul Unger, chairman of the mayor's Urban Renewal Task Force; and Jim Huston, president of PATH (Plan of Action for Tomorrow's Housing). Despite the broad showing, the presence of Stokes clearly mattered most. A transformative figure, Stokes sat before the panel considering public housing legislation and testified through experience—not just as the chief executive of the nation's tenth-largest city but as a former resident of public housing. Stokes spoke eloquently from a position of power for a constituency that rarely found a voice in Congress.

Stokes was blunt, as he always was, about having lived in one of Cleveland's projects, but what impressed the senators most was his command of the bill then under consideration and his point-by-point explanation of how Cleveland would benefit by its passage. "We can do things on our own in our city," Stokes said. "But the fact is that we are going to need additional technical and financial assistance from the Federal Government." Here in a nutshell was the issue. Like all big-city mayors, Stokes wanted control over reforms within his city, but he also wanted the additional resources that could come only through federal programs. Specifically, Stokes supported the doubling of money for the Model Cities program, a dramatic increase in the funding for homeowner rehabilitation in renewal areas, and the establishment of a reinsurance program that would help property owners in riot-prone neighborhoods acquire fire insurance—the disappearance of which in places like Hough had caused further capital flight as business owners closed up shops for which they could not secure insurance.[31]

Just a month before, President Johnson had described "the crisis of the cities" and the moral imperative for national action in a special message to Congress. Johnson had asked for full funding of the War on Poverty and for expanding federal involvement in public housing and neighborhood redevelopment with a new appropriation of $2.34 billion. Johnson also revisited his Model Cities program, initiated in 1966, which he hoped would "encourage the city to develop and carry out a total strategy to meet the human and physical problems left in the rubble of a neighborhood's decay." Outlining the provisions of the housing legislation before the subcommittee, Stokes repeated Johnson's phrase concerning the human need for a "sense of place and purpose," which reminded the mayor of one area of conspicuous failure in housing policy—"what to do about people's lives within the inner city."[32]

Both Stokes's appearance in Congress and Johnson's message the month before spoke to the great entanglement of federal policy in urban issues. The federal government's involvement in housing dated to the early 1930s, when the Public Works Administration funded the building of several large projects, including Outhwaite Homes. This involvement expanded significantly with the Housing Act of 1937 and then again after World War II, when the public housing program that once aimed to merely provide adequate housing morphed into slum clearance and urban renewal. Federal intervention in the housing market provided some clean and suitable homes, but altogether it did little to improve housing quality in central cities or reduce the great number of Americans who lived in substandard housing.

Depression-era policy responded to the growing problem of dilapidated housing in urban cores, where older tenements had been built without electric wiring and little or no indoor plumbing, and for the first time federal initiatives addressed the working poor's inability to afford suitable housing. But federal policy was informed by more than the need to bring housing up to modern standards. Sociological theory, first articulated at the University of Chicago in the late 1910s, compared urban growth and decay to ecological processes. By the 1920s, planners and policy makers commonly thought of the city in biological terms. Neighborhoods had life cycles—they got old and diseased. The concept of "urban blight" gained broad currency in the 1930s, just as governments began to root out slums through demolition. "Dry rot," *Business Week* called it in 1940; the *Saturday Evening Post* called it "an anemia" four years later.[33]

Theorists might disagree about the causes of blight, but they agreed it was contagious, just as the strengthening analogy would suggest. Because urban blight spread like a disease, the concept reinforced the idea that the problems of slums were containable, and therefore localized. This way of thinking—nearly universal in the early postwar era—hid a significant assumption: that the causes of slum conditions actually lay in the neighborhoods themselves, in their poorly kept and outdated buildings or their uneducated and unemployable residents. Theorists, planners, and policy makers essentially ignored the larger metropolis in which the slum grew. In other words, pathologizing slums hid the fundamental flaws of metropolitan growth, flaws that ensured inequalities of investment across space and inequalities of power and wealth across populations. Structural issues that encouraged the outward movement of people, employment, and capital went unaddressed.

Johnson's approach to the urban crisis improved on these older theories of blight, emphasizing involvement of residents in articulating and solving neighborhood problems, taking a comprehensive approach—addressing both physical and social issues simultaneously—and, of course, spending a considerable amount of money in the process. The Cleveland representatives testifying before the Senate Subcommittee on Housing and Urban Affairs in the spring of 1968 praised this approach, especially the increased spending. Among them was James Huston, a lawyer by trade and the president of PATH, who commended federal involvement in housing, even quoting the goals of the 1949 Housing Act: "A decent home and a suitable living environment for every American family." Huston also described the work of PATH, created in 1966 by the Greater Cleveland Associated Foundation. In early 1967, it issued a report on housing conditions in the region and made a series of recommendations to the city, the state, and the business community. PATH found sixty thousand substandard dwellings in metropolitan Cleveland, nearly 90 percent of which were in the city itself, and noted that a quarter of Cleveland residents lived in "rat-infested" dwellings. No solution was in sight. The vast majority of new housing was being built outside the city, and promises by government to supply public housing had gone unfulfilled. Although the report described a crisis in housing that seemed to affect the city much more than its suburbs, PATH declared, again echoing the 1949 legislation: "We have one housing problem in Greater Cleveland—how to provide decent homes for all our citizens in a suitable environment."[34]

The PATH plan of action made forty-five recommendations to improve housing and the residential environment. Noting that federal policies had heretofore encouraged suburban development, largely through tax incentives and mortgage insurance, PATH recommended that Cleveland apply for a Model Cities grant, which would help fund comprehensive community planning and implementation in the city's worst neighborhoods. Now, a year after noting the many failures in Cleveland and describing the dire housing situation, Huston testified before Congress that a "new spirit" had developed and "forward movement" had begun—this due to Stokes, who undoubtedly flashed his famous smile as he listened. Neither of them would have anticipated the tone of PATH's follow-up document, published in March 1969, which found that despite some progress, "the housing crisis is even more critical." Thus far, the PATH study, like so many that came before, had not become the watershed document that reformers hoped it would.

EVERYTHING OF ANY VALUE WAS STRIPPED OFF AND TAKEN AWAY

As residents of ghettos around the nation gathered in protests and riots in the mid-1960s, the national press stepped up coverage of the nation's inner-city troubles. The struggle to understand what was happening, to discern root causes of the physical deterioration and the social disaffection, led to even more studies conducted by all types of analysts inside and outside government. Among the organizations that turned its gaze to the city was the Civil Rights Commission (CRC), created by Congress in 1957 "to provide means of further securing and protecting the civil rights" of citizens. The CRC's primary means of action was to conduct and publicize investigations into critical issues, including voting rights and the desegregation of schools and housing.[35] By the spring of 1966, Cleveland's inner city had garnered enough attention that the CRC began planning a week of hearings there in April. CRC staff made contacts in Cleveland, arranged for the appearance of prominent officials, including Governor Jim Rhodes and Mayor Locher, and gathered a list of other speakers who might provide insight into housing, welfare and education, employment, and police-community relations—four topics each afforded a full day of attention. The CRC selected two sites for its Cleveland hearings: the federal building downtown and the Liberty Hill Baptist Church in Hough. At the latter site, the hearings would take place in the auditorium, at the rear of the building. As the six commission members took the broad stage and the witnesses appeared one by one, no doubt this felt like civic space rather than a religious venue. Most important, given the location, the witness list, and the testimony about housing, Liberty Hill's auditorium felt like Hough.

Reverend Paul Younger sat in the large, plain hall, notebook in hand. Younger was a white minister whose calling brought him to inner-city Cleveland from his childhood home in Mt. Kisko, New York. Younger and his wife, Betty, also an activist for the poor, had moved to Hough in the late 1950s, while they were in their twenties, and they lived on 86th Street, just a few blocks from Liberty Hill. By 1964, Younger was working for Protestant Ministry to Poverty, focusing his efforts on Cleveland's East Side ghetto. In the summer of 1965, he had marched with members of the Congress of Racial Equality (CORE) and Students for a Democratic Society, along with residents of Hough, to protest the lack of citizen involvement in the Council for Economic Opportunity, the War on Poverty program that promised "maximum feasible participation." The protest culminated in the parading of a rat-infested couch through the city, carried by children at first and then by activists. When the protesters reached City Hall, several of the marchers took dead rats from the couch and laid them on the steps. Among them was Grady Robinson, chairman of the Cleveland branch of CORE, a national civil rights organization that had been especially active in the movement to integrate Cleveland's schools, and Hattie Mae Dugan, a young mother who had recently moved back to Cleveland to be near family. Robinson, Dugan, and two others who carried the rats were cited for breaking public health codes. Younger, who apparently didn't touch the rats, was spared a citation, as were about twenty-five other protesters there to argue that "only the poverty-stricken could understand the problems of the poor," as the *Plain Dealer* summarized.[36]

By the time he arrived at Liberty Hill for the CRC hearings, Younger had become an important member of Cleveland's large civil rights community, and he saw in the crowd many familiar faces. Indeed, Younger may have been disappointed that he didn't see more *unfamiliar* faces, for only one hundred people assembled in the spacious auditorium—clearly a gathering of the faithful. One of the largest headlines related to the week-long event summarized the Saturday afternoon gathering accordingly: "Crowd Is Thin at Rights Public Housing Hearings." Despite the headline, newspaper coverage of the hearings was respectful. It was also thin; little of the testimony made its way into the papers. Perhaps the *Plain Dealer* and the *Cleveland Press* assumed the public had heard it all before, especially since many of those who spoke had long been in the press.[37]

After statements by Governor Rhodes, Mayor Locher, and state and local officials from the CRC, the first witness was Hattie Mae Dugan. Expanded by dozens of questions from the panel, Dugan's testimony was wide-ranging, addressing inadequate police protection and segregated schools. She also re-told the story of her arrest for placing rats on the City Hall steps. But the soft-spoken Dugan was most effective when describing her apartment, in a poorly kept building on East 93rd Street. Photographs illustrated her points—a slow-draining tub that was impossible to clean, light fixtures hanging by their wires, and a garbage-strewn hallway. There were no photos of rats, but Dugan declared, "The kids they play with rats like a child would play with a dog or something. They chase them around the house and things like this."[38]

Reporters were so touched that many of them featured Dugan's testimony in their stories, including one in the *New York Times*. Some of the commissioners, among them Notre Dame president Theodore Hesburgh, had already been moved by Dugan's story, having visited her building earlier in the day and given witness to the conditions in the heart of Hough.

Although housing was the general topic of the first two full days of testimony, the commissioners asked several witnesses about rats in particular. Among those who took the stage was fifty-two-year-old Velma Jean Woods, who had come to Cleveland at about the same time as Rev. Younger, moving with her husband, who was transferred by Chrysler from Detroit. They had moved to an apartment building on East 93rd Street which, according to Woods, "they just began to zone" for African Americans. Her use of the term "zone" suggests how systematic the transition process could appear, even though racial segregation had no legal sanction. Her building, the Clevelander, had seventy-two apartments, and hers was just the second black family to move in. Woods noted that only some of the whites moved out right away, while others were content to live in the building, which was still in good shape. Two custodians worked full time, and, Woods noted, "they really kept it up." What drove the remaining white occupants away were significant increases in the rent. According to Woods, landlords could expect blacks to pay nearly twice the rent. Despite the higher income, landlords let the building deteriorate as the black population increased. Woods described some efforts to organize the tenants, who knew they overpaid for their apartments and could see the worsening conditions around them. Woods talked matter-of-factly about rats and roaches, but powerlessness clearly fed her anger.[39]

Clyde Fehn also testified, introducing his rat reports into the record, summarizing his findings for the panel, and narrating a slide show that mostly revealed poorly stored and scattered garbage. A few images of dead rats illustrated Fehn's objective conclusion: "There are lots of rats." Although brought in to introduce scientific evidence of the rat problem, which Fehn agreed was a serious health concern, he was more interested in augmenting his reports with observations about behavior on Cleveland's East Side. Fehn had recanvassed the city in February and was disappointed with what he saw. "I would say that there has been a very serious deterioration in human behavioral patterns and attitudes," he said. Further, "I noticed from 1962 to 1966, that there has been a very serious deterioration in the attitudes and behavior of people in Cleveland, especially with regard to empty houses." He showed a home that had been abandoned just a month or two earlier but had already been stripped of its toilets, tubs, and aluminum siding. "Everything of any value at all that could be stripped off was stripped off and taken away."[40]

The last person to offer testimony regarding Cleveland's housing situation was Dr. Joanne Finley, who was then working for the Cleveland Welfare Federation on a U.S. Public Health Service grant designed to improve public health planning. Finley had also recently agreed to join the city's Department of Health and Welfare and would in a month become its acting commissioner. At first, Finley answered questions about the relationship between prenatal care and poor birth outcomes in the ghetto, and the high incidence of tuberculosis in poor, crowded neighborhoods. Perhaps inevitably, the questions eventually turned to rats. Finley listed some diseases linked to rats, but she quickly drew the conversation back toward broader health concerns, mentioning for the first time the high incidence of hypertensive heart disease among blacks. After she described her goal of creating a proactive health department dedicated to improving residents' health, especially through disease prevention, and made clear her emphasis on sound science and health planning, the last question came from Commissioner Erwin Griswold, an East Cleveland native and the long-time dean of Harvard Law School: "Do you hope to be able to make some progress on rats after July 1?" when Findley would become Cleveland's acting Health Commissioner.[41]

On its last day in Cleveland, the CRC heard testimony from a variety of community figures, including Ruth Turner, of CORE, and Reverend Donald Jacobs, president of the local NAACP. Carl Stokes, who was then a member of the Ohio legislature and had unsuccessfully run for mayor the year before, also took the stage. Stokes spoke briefly but passionately on a wide range of issues, including the discriminatory practices of labor unions and the Locher administration's many failures. He was blunt and aggressive and concluded with a jab at the broader community.

> Metropolitan Cleveland's citizens must be awake to the facts that unchecked and uncontrolled disease does not stop at the city boundary; nor do the rats that often carry the diseases know they are to stop there; water and air pollution affects all of the county; all Cuyahogans bear the cost of welfare; and an unemployed person who takes recourse in crime will go wherever he thinks his efforts will be most fruitful.

Here Stokes deftly combined old conceptions of creeping blight with white fears of the failure of race containment. Urban problems will leak to the suburbs, Stokes promised—pollution and crime and even the rats. As Stokes reminded his audience, all boundaries, even municipal lines, are porous.

Participating largely as an intent observer for most of the CRC hearings, Younger also joined the last group of witnesses, taking the stage to a round of applause. Younger emphasized the need for jobs—good jobs—and the need for employers to train inner-city workers. He also made clear the powerlessness felt by Cleveland's poor. In public housing they were subject to managers entering their apartments with passkeys; those on welfare could expect midnight inspections from caseworkers in search of violations. Altogether this "managed life" disempowered the poor, who were already so obviously constrained by their economic plight. Younger ended with a plea for maximum feasible participation, noting that he and other Hough residents had seen "federal program after federal program come into Cleveland with high promises, but come in with a plan that is administered to us, done for us and which over and over again ends in nothing because the money is taken, but the work is not done." Resident participation would end this, Younger said. "Neighborhood people are committed to their neighborhood."[42]

Younger's work for the commission didn't end that afternoon. Along with several prominent Clevelanders, Younger was a member of the subcommittee formed to continue investigating civil rights in the city. Over the subsequent months, he headed a group addressing "municipal services." The preliminary report he crafted just three weeks after the hearings focused primarily on rodent control. Noting that Cleveland ranked with Chicago and Boston as one of the "most heavily rodent infested large urban communities in the nation," Younger argued that the city needed more frequent garbage pickups—the same recommendation Clyde Fehn had made four years earlier. He also noted that "inadequate street cleaning, repair and lighting contribute to the decline of crowded neighborhoods' self image and desirability for residence." He recommended better litter ordinance enforcement, the placement of litter baskets on street corners in crowded parts of the city, and the development of "tot lots" to improve recreation opportunities, especially in neighborhoods where demolished buildings provided unused space.[43]

In early 1967, Younger helped the subcommittee write a follow-up report in which he noted some improvements, including movement toward better containers for garbage, especially for large apartment buildings. The Rotary Club had given $4,300 for a four-block demonstration rat-kill program, which encouraged the city to expand rat control. But the city had not yet placed garbage cans on street corners, nor had it converted demolition sites into tot lots or vest-pocket parks. Here was yet another report that said essentially the same thing as many that had come before and many more that would follow. Even the little things that might have signaled a slowing of Hough's decline had not been achieved or attempted. Younger, an optimist, may have had great hope for the future, but unfortunately he died in a car accident in 1969.[44]

TO SAVE HOUGH

The Civil Rights Commission came to Hough because press attention already had. Part of the barrage of coverage came from *Press* reporter Paul Lilley, who had written a series of articles in February 1965, the last appearing under the headline "Crisis in Hough." After his extended reporting in the neighborhood, Lilley recommended a number of immediate steps, many of them directed toward improving the environment. "City health officials should start an immediate sanitation campaign against rats, vermin, filth, garbage and rubbish that plague and overflow congested backyards," he declared. Further, "street sweepers and flushers of the service department should visit the area regularly. Retail store owners should be made to sweep sidewalks in front of their establishments."[45] After a year with no improvement, another Lilley article ran under the headline, "Coming Year Will Tell Whether Hough Dies." Now Lilley called Hough "a powder keg as explosive as that which touched off the Watts disaster last summer in Los Angeles."[46] The presence of the CRC that spring didn't reduce tensions, nor did it pressure the city to act. The powder keg sat as the summer heated up.

On the evening of July 18, 1966, the owner of a bar at 79th and Hough Avenue denied a black man a drink of water. After some shouting and flared tempers, the owner posted a sign on the door, "No water for Niggers," which greatly inflamed the situation. A slow police response allowed a large crowd to gather, and overly aggressive police tactics in subsequent hours fueled the rage, as officers broke down doors and rampaged through apartments seeking snipers who had apparently fired from buildings along Hough Avenue. That night police and firemen dodged all varieties of missiles thrown by the crowds, including gasoline fire bombs. Arson and looting damaged or destroyed many of the neighborhood's largest stores, especially along Hough Avenue's commercial strip between East 71st and East 93rd. Three Sav-Mor Supermarkets were hit, as was Al's Cut-Rate Drugstore and King Kole Clothing Company. The second day of rioting saw sixty-seven more fires, mostly in abandoned houses and commercial buildings. The *Press* later reported that after twelve years on Hough Avenue, Starlite Delicatessen owner Joe Berman would have to call it quits. "There's nothing for me here anymore," he said. The arrival of the National Guard didn't immediately stem the violence, but once it subsided, the neighborhood tallied the damage from the worst rioting in Cleveland's history. Four people had been killed, most dramatically Joyce Arnett, shot once in the head through a window. She was twenty-six years old, a mother of three young girls, including seven-year-old twins Lynette and Jynette.[47]

On the evening of July 21, a number of Hough residents gathered to discuss the disorder. Among them were Daisy Craggett, DeForest Brown, and Fannie Lewis, leading figures in Community Action for Youth (CAY), a demonstration project funded largely by the federal government to combat juvenile delinquency in the neighborhood. They drew up a lengthy statement and submitted it to Mayor Locher the next day. "Our neighborhood—Hough—is in trouble," it began. "Our real troubles go far beyond the troubles of the last few days." They categorized the roots of the riots: unemployment among the neighborhood's men; the physical deterioration of the community, which has made it "a symbol of despair and degradation"; and the failure of welfare to allow the poor to live "decent dignified" lives. "As citizens of Cleveland, we ask other Clevelanders to acknowledge that to save Hough is truly to save our entire city." Surely more Clevelanders would now agree that Hough required attention. The CAY statement was straightforward and clear, perhaps even indisputable.[48] Four days later, as peace was returning to Hough, the *Press* editorialized about the talk that was sure to follow the riots. "Absolutely nothing new will be said," the *Press* assured its readers. "It has all been said a thousand times." This seems clear enough. The neighborhood needed better housing, better recreational facilities; the people needed jobs. "Everybody knows the recipe for lifting up the area," the *Press* continued. The real problem was that nobody was willing to cook.[49]

A month after the Hough riots, Mayor Locher found himself in Washington sitting before a Senate subcommittee concerned with the federal role in solving the urban crisis. Chaired by Abraham Ribicoff, a Connecticut Democrat, the subcommittee was a largely sympathetic group. Locher was a Democrat, too, after all, even if he was an ineffective one. His task wasn't easy, however, as he defended the policies of a city just a few weeks removed from serious civil disobedience. Locher might have been a well-meaning man, but he found it hard to accept blame for Cleveland's problems, placing it first on the people of Hough. "We must not forget—nor sweep under the rug—the problems of the individual unaccustomed to urban life," he said, " 'air mail garbage' [trash thrown out apartment windows], discrimination, breakdown of the family structure, three generations on welfare, and a growing disrespect for law and order. And poverty—at the root of it all—poverty." Locher repeated the arguments he had made just months earlier before the Civil Rights

𝓕𝒾𝑔𝓊𝓇𝑒 4. Riots in 1966 caused extensive damage, especially in the deteriorating business district along Hough Avenue, but even before the violence and arson that July, Hough had become a "Crisis Ghetto." Photo by Jerry Horton. Cleveland Press Collection, Cleveland State University.

Commission: many of the residents of Hough, accustomed to rural poverty, had yet to learn how to live in urban poverty.[50]

Locher couldn't hide his disappointment in the people of Hough, but he appreciated the depths of the problems facing urban America as a whole. "We have other problems in our cities," he said, "which have an indirect but none-theless real bearing on our least advantaged citizens: air and water pollution, economic development, the need for better transportation facilities—both highway and transit—and the continuing erosion of our tax base with an accompanying lack of access to adequate supplemental financial resources to provide the municipal facilities and services which our citizens need, expect and demand." In the face of "the extensive catalog of urban ailments," the details surrounding the Hough disturbances might seem rather insignificant, or at least Locher might have hoped.[51]

Locher wanted to draw attention to the broader urban crisis in part because he had been called to Washington to explain what happened *after* the riots as much as what had caused them. A Cuyahoga County grand jury investigating the disturbance had just released an alarmingly unrealistic report on the rioting. Senator Ribicoff opened the questioning by reading from the report, dated August 9: "This jury finds that the outbreak of lawlessness and disorder was both organized, precipitated, and exploited by a relatively small group of trained and disciplined professionals of this business. They were aided and abetted wittingly or otherwise by misguided people of all ages and colors, many of whom are avowed believers in violence and extremism, and some of whom also are either members of, or officers in the Communist Party."[52] Extrapolating from the vague testimony of two undercover cops who had infiltrated the Communist Party in Cleveland, the jury had allowed Cold War concerns about communism—undoubtedly mixed with racist assumptions about the gullibility and immorality of ghetto dwellers—to blind them to the very real concerns of Hough residents. Part of the jury's thinking came from the fact that the violence had not been random. Some buildings escaped harm, most likely those owned or operated by people who treated residents fairly, such as those who didn't overcharge for poor-quality merchandise. According to the jury, this meant that "the targets were plainly agreed upon," and therefore planning must have taken place. But the jury may have had broader concerns in mind. "What this country and this community need," the report concluded, "is not so much a blood bath but a good cleansing spiritual bath."[53]

Even beyond its preposterous conclusions, the grand jury report seemed to have been written to heighten tensions purposefully. For instance, the report asked that "all decent law-abiding citizens proclaim their support of law and order and their support of policemen and firemen in carrying out their duties toward that end." The report at least recognized that poverty "served as the uneasy backdrop for the Cleveland riots," allowing that population density, exorbitant food prices, poor housing, high rents, and unenforced building codes all combined to make Hough "a feeding ground for disorder." But the report noted of Hough residents: "Frequently they find themselves bewildered and unable quickly to adjust themselves to the demands of their new surroundings and thus find themselves frequently at cross purposes with the authorities and the older residents of the area in which they find themselves currently."[54] In other words, the poor surroundings didn't demand too much of residents; rather, the residents failed to adjust to the environment.[55]

Incredulous at the tone and conclusions of the report, Ribicoff let Locher have it, adding a moving description of the real crisis at hand: "In city after city across this great land of ours, people are aware. The problem is there for people to see if they will only look. They would see seething masses living in poverty and unhappiness and frustration—living in conditions that you would not even house cattle in." Locher attempted to defend himself by listing the many meetings he'd had in Hough concerning ghetto conditions, to which an unswayed Ribicoff noted that there is nothing more frustrating than having to go to meeting after meeting and getting no results. After Ribicoff made clear that he thought Locher had failed Hough and Cleveland, Senator Robert Kennedy attempted to move the conversation forward, asking Locher how much federal funding he would need to fix the problems of Cleveland. Locher, who had been asking for block grants throughout the questioning, knew that there had been a substantial underinvestment in the city in recent decades. Instead of describing the costs of repairing the ghetto, however, he took up the issue of water pollution, and the specific problem of separating the city's combined sewers and treating phosphates at sewage treatment plants to save Lake Erie. "It would come in the neighborhood of 1 billion dollars if we are to do the job right." And, he concluded, "that is just one thing."[56]

Even as Locher traveled to Washington to explain Cleveland's failings, citizens of Hough gathered to create their own narrative of the disturbances. Five noted lawyers, including Louis Stokes, Jean Capers (the first African American woman on the City Council), Stanley Tolliver (a prominent civil rights lawyer), and Carl Rachlin (a CORE lawyer from New York City), conducted open hearings on three evenings at Liberty Hill Baptist Church. The public was invited to testify, and twenty-six people did. The first was Earl Rowe, an Office of Economic Opportunity social worker who had a law degree and lived at 3439 E. 145th Street in Mount Pleasant, a working-class neighborhood southeast of Hough. He described the conditions that led to the riots, emphasizing overcrowding:

> You find, well, I know of one family which always comes out in my mind, a husband, wife, four children sleeping in one bed with rats and mice regularly crossing the children's faces at night. This is overcrowded conditions. Other conditions with housing seem to be the lethargy or the missing garbage collectors in the Hough area, consequently many of the homes are covered with filth and debris and it is a very great sore spot to try to get regular collection. The debris is not only in exterior apartment dwellings, but in the interior also. There are abandoned dwellings which have become accident traps, broken windows and the dwellings have been standing for years and the city of course has promised that once the protocol is completed and once the tear-down orders given, these buildings will come down. So the overcrowded conditions of blight and filth and deterioration and the abandoned dwellings seem to be the main core of housing complaints.

The people of Hough, Rowe made clear, had not caused the problems of Hough.[57]

Most of the testimony that followed Rowe's rich description of the physical environment concerned police misconduct, especially during the disturbances themselves. Some witnesses told stories of police officers bursting into homes, forcing families out into the rain, and ransacking their apartments. Few of the witnesses made connections between the injustices during the disturbances and the broader injustices described by Rowe, but Dennis Hilliary, who had lived in Cleveland all of his twenty-two years and had been at the 79er's Club the first night of the riot, expressed his thoughts rather succinctly: "People are not dumb to the fact that these people are living off us niggers." He left somewhat vague who "these people" were, but everyone in the room surely understood.[58]

The Cleveland Citizens Committee on Hough Disturbances wrote a lengthy statement after the testimony concluded. Not surprisingly, the committee attacked the official explanation of the riots as determined by the grand jury, finding fault with both its details and its conclusions. Hough's citizens, and those who came to represent them, were especially concerned about certain passages in the report. For instance: "The Grand Jury's statement concerning the welfare department's 'paying mothers to have babies' conveys a gross ignorance about the facts of public welfare. Anyone knowledgeable about public assistance payments to welfare clients would know that seventy-three cents a day could hardly be the motivation for bringing a child into the world." But the broader concern had to do with the grand jury's failure to identify the real causes of the disturbances. "Despite the numerous studies, reports, and investigations of overcrowding and code violation in Hough, no meaningful remedial action has resulted," the statement read. "The residents of inner-city areas such as Hough have become cynical and angry over the repeated failure of city officials to keep their promises. They are asked to live in dilapidated housing with rats and roaches while the city expends all its resources on high rise apartments and innerbelt highways." The last comment connected policy failure in Hough to real changes taking place just three miles away—downtown.[59]

PRAY FOR CLEVELAND

In the spring of 1967, as the nation girded for another round of inner-city violence, *Jet* magazine ran a short piece under the hopeful title "How Cities Can Avoid Another Long Hot Summer." An accompanying map identified fifteen trouble spots around the nation, including Detroit, Baltimore, and Los Angeles. Despite the release of energy in the riots of 1966, Cleveland made the map. *Jet* called for better police-community relations and jobs programs for young black men. Unfortunately, the picture looked bleak in Cleveland, "which is expected to be one of the first cities to explode," largely because "the summer job outlook is depressing." Several small incidents of "window breaking and looting" seemed like foreshadowing, and more ominously, "reports have circulated that this year's disturbances will not be confined to the Negro areas." Suggesting that racial conflict might evolve into street warfare, *Jet* reported, "White motorcycle gangs are armed and ready to shoot it out with black nationalists, who also have a supply of weapons and ammunition. No one is sure what will happen there this summer. Bumper stickers read 'Pray for Cleveland.' "[60]

Several of the nation's inner cities indeed exploded that July—most destructively in Newark, where twenty-three people died in six days of violence, and Detroit, where forty people died over five days. A major incident never developed in Cleveland, but tensions remained high. Reporting from "rat-gnawed Hough" that summer, journalist John Skow described a community on the edge, where nothing had been resolved as a result of the violence the year before. "Hough, a 50-block-by-10-block infection of crumbling three-story apartment buildings and huge, rotted frame houses dating from a time when summer meant sweet corn and Citronella, is still owned by rats that can't be frightened and landlords who can't be found," Skow wrote. "Its backyards are still splattered with rain-soaked garbage and burst mattresses. Derelict buildings stand empty and gutted as before."[61]

Hough escaped a major disturbance in 1967, but Cleveland's fortunes changed the following year, when Stokes was in office. In mid-July, a group of

Black Nationalists living in Glenville, by then a predominantly black neighborhood well on its way toward the decay that had laid low Central and Hough before it, engaged in a shootout with police officers. Four hours of firing from inside and around what Skow called the "shabbily respectable" clapboard homes and small brick apartment buildings of Glenville left seven men dead. The gunfire and swarming police touched off looting and arson in the neighborhood. Hardly just another urban disturbance in a long string of them, the Glenville Shootout suggested a deepening conflict. Reporting from the mayor's side as he patrolled Hough and Glenville, Skow concluded, "The illness had reached a new phase." For his part, Stokes couldn't hide his disgust and disappointment. Elected just six months earlier, in part with the expectation that the mere presence of a black man in City Hall would end rioting, Stokes had in fact helped prevent disorder earlier that year after the assassination of Martin Luther King Jr. As cities around the nation burned, Cleveland remained calm. Stokes and other black leaders walked the streets and helped talk through the anger. Now Stokes was on the streets again, approaching young black men out after curfew and giving them rides home.[62]

As the Glenville crisis deepened, Stokes made a bold and unprecedented decision. On the second day, he removed white police officers from the affected neighborhoods and set up a perimeter with the help of the National Guard. Inside the cordoned area, a volunteer patrol of citizens and the few black Cleveland police officers tried to keep the peace. White police took their exclusion as a professional affront, and white business owners accused Stokes of abandoning them and putting their property at greater risk. More broadly, the removal of white officers and guardsmen from Hough and Glenville served as an object lesson in the creation of two Americas, "one black, one white—separate and unequal," in the words of the Kerner Commission, which had been created by President Johnson to investigate the causes of the 1967 riots and had issued its report that February. The violence, including arson, lasted for five days, and the damage to businesses was extensive, but the cordoning off of Hough and Glenville may have saved lives, although it did nothing to salvage a sense of progress in race relations in Cleveland. A year later, Ahmed Evans was convicted by an all-white jury of murdering the police officers and sentenced to die in the electric chair. (He died of cancer while in prison in 1978.) Views on the verdict ran along the city's racial divide. Of all the boundaries that ran through metropolitan Cleveland in 1968, the race line may have been the most impenetrable.

On June 3, 1969, the day after Stokes and Walker stood in Hough introducing the rat control program and less than three weeks before the Cuyahoga caught fire, the mayor held a news conference at City Hall on the problem of "law and order." A room full of reporters and cameramen listened to an unusually dour Stokes talk about "crime on the streets." Stokes had good reason to be frustrated. Cleveland was experiencing a spate of violence—an average of one murder a day in May—during which a Cuyahoga County prosecutor's investigation of the Civil Service Commission had prevented Stokes from hiring new police officers. Stokes felt hamstrung by petty politics, and the violence showed no signs of letting up. Although the crime wave reached a variety of neighborhoods, Hough was at the center of the city's social disorder.[63]

Not surprisingly, the press conference didn't slow the violence. Racial conflict plagued the far East Side, where a long series of incidents kept Collinwood High School in the news. On June 6, vandalism, menacing, and fighting led to arrests—mostly among young whites marching to protest attempts to integrate the student body. So much violence racked other parts of the city that the *Press* reported the latest three homicides in a single article on June 9. All three deaths occurred on the East Side, including one at the Diamond Market on St. Clair Avenue, where Murray Diamond killed a Black Nationalist, Daniel Carter, after he had broken into and looted the store. Later that day, a clash between whites and blacks in Woodland, south of Hough, led to the stabbing death of Donald Waight, a young white man. That murder brought people out onto the streets, where the next day Stokes was joined by his rival, Anthony Garofoli, a councilman who represented the Little Italy neighborhood, notorious for defending its borders and schools from the intrusion of blacks. The two walked together and begged for calm. That afternoon the *Press* reported another four homicides—the 124th, 125th, 126th, and 127th in the city that year. The police, already stretched thin and unable to keep a lid on all the simmering conflicts, were able to prevent a march of a hundred whites up Woodland Avenue to the mayor's home, just over a mile away. Unsatisfied, a large group of angry white "youth" broke windows and battered cars "with concrete chunks," the hard bits of a city rapidly falling apart. Several blacks accidentally strayed into harm's way and were harassed, beaten, and repelled.[64]

A month later, Stokes sat in Washington, testifying before Congress yet again, this time before the House Select Committee on Crime. Stokes spoke about the need for gun control and the political impossibility of getting a bill passed at the state or local level, given the strength of the gun lobby. At the same time, Stokes made it clear that while he supported "law and order," that very phrase had become politicized and some Americans took it to suggest suppression of dissent, if not the suppression of those who were struggling for equality. Stokes then broadened the conversation because, he said, "crime is part of the urban crisis, along with deteriorated housing, unemployment, inadequate health care, air and water pollution, inadequate public transportation and education." Stokes understood that solving the crime problem would require tackling the crisis of the urban environment.[65]

A COMPARATIVELY LIVABLE NEIGHBORHOOD

Cleveland's rat control program was subject to annual reviews. The 1970 report, written in part by Clyde Fehn, walked that fine line between praising progress and reporting a continuing problem that was worthy of continued funding. The report commended Walker's leadership and noted the reduction of reported rat bites and signs of infestation. Indeed, confirmed and reported rat bites had dropped from an average of seventy per year in the early 1960s to thirty in 1969. The authors seemed especially optimistic about the city's housing stock, even in the target areas, the most degraded of the city's neighborhoods: Near West, Central East, Hough, and Glenville. Relative to other large cities, the evaluators found, these neighborhoods were "comparatively livable," a phrase that may suggest more about how dire the urban crisis had become across the nation than about the quality of life in Cleveland's ghetto. Still, the review determined that "prospects are good for the future betterment of residential environment and living conditions," and it recommended an acceleration of conservation efforts rather than the slum clearance approach of an earlier generation—an indicator of the evolving nature of urban policy.[66]

Despite the generally positive tone of the report, for Hough there was bad news. Altogether, rat infestation rates for the city's target neighborhoods had fallen from 41 percent of properties in 1969 to just 19 percent in 1970, a good sign that the nearly $400,000 federal investment had paid off. But in Hough, unlike the other three neighborhoods, active rat infestation increased from 20 percent of the properties to 30 percent. Several other environmental factors also failed to improve—there was no budge in the number of abandoned vehicles, the number of abandoned appliances grew significantly, and refuse storage remained problematic. Notwithstanding the two areas of improvement, in numbers of abandoned homes and incidents of high weeds on empty lots, the data showed that Hough's physical decline continued unabated. Despite demands for help, the riots, the public scrutiny—even national scrutiny—the years of federal involvement, the extensive community organization, and the appearance of Stokes, Ellis, and Walker on Holyrood Road in June 1969, the neighborhood had not improved. Hough was still a crisis ghetto.

The decline persisted well past the end of the Stokes administration in 1971. Hough's population fell to just over 45,000 in 1970, and a decade later it dropped to 25,000, meaning the neighborhood lost 65 percent of its population in just twenty years. Cleveland as a whole, dragged down by the collapse of East Side neighborhoods, continued suburban development, and industrial decline, lost 35 percent of its population over the same period. In his 1975 dissertation, Bailus Walker maintained his faith in the ability of municipal governments to adjust to the urban crisis and provide basic environmental health services. But the numbers for Hough, where a Cleveland Department of Public Health study located 75 percent of the city's substandard housing in 1971, suggested that not all places would survive.[67]

In May 1972, just as Carl Stokes was beginning his career as a television news anchorman at NBC in New York City (part of what was marketed as a "news team that cuts through the garbage"), the Cleveland City Planning Commission began a study called "Housing Abandonment in Cleveland," a sign that the city's problem had shifted. No longer did Cleveland struggle to build housing for the poor—it worked to demolish unoccupied units. Arson raged on the East Side in the 1970s, as owners used insurance policies to wring all the capital they could from otherwise unprofitable properties. In Hough, following the trajectory of Central, blight increasingly gave way to empty lots.[68]

Local and federal policy failed Hough, just as it did ghettos around the nation. Crime persisted, the "normal chaos of the ghetto" continued, but fears of rioting and broader racial tensions eased as populations declined and blacks made their way into housing markets through much of the East Side, including the middle-class suburbs of Cleveland Heights and Shaker Heights. Open space increased in Hough, some of it created purposefully to provide recreational opportunities, but most of it created unintentionally as vacant lots accumulated. The federal rat control program persisted through the Nixon administration and beyond, outlasting many of Hough's homes and residents. And as the neighborhood lost its people, and the press stopped reporting on the rats, the landscape gradually lost its meaning. The urban crisis had spread.

3 Downtown and the Limits of Urban Renewal

On Friday, June 13, 1969, at the end of a long week of conflict and violence, Carl Stokes stood at a prominent corner in downtown Cleveland shoulder to shoulder with some of the city's economic elite. Wearing a hard hat and his famous smile, Stokes joined Edward Carpenter, Central National Bank's chairman of the board, and John Gelbach, its president, in a cornerstone ceremony at the bank's nearly completed twenty-three-story tower. The small crowd included reporters and photographers from the *Plain Dealer* and the *Cleveland Press*, crews from local television news programs, and representatives from the Tishman Corporation, which was overseeing the construction. They stood along East 9th Street and watched as officials placed several items into a time capsule—including that morning's *Plain Dealer* and the previous afternoon's *Press*. Carpenter, Gelbach, and Stokes all made remarks destined for inclusion in the time capsule, with the mayor's words captured on tape.

A keen politician, Stokes never missed a chance to celebrate the building of a new Cleveland, and his comments for the time capsule spoke not just to a future generation but to those who were listening that June. He began with a brief salutation to whoever might be mayor—in the same "hot seat," as he put it—in 1990, when the time capsule would be opened, but then he leapt immediately to issues of substance. "In this year of 1969, Cleveland, like the other major cities of America, is confronted by a crisis of immense proportions—a crisis in the urban environment." A curious opening for a message to the future, this passage suggests that Stokes understood that this crisis would matter not just in 1969 but in 1990 as well. And the phrasing indicates that he had found a new way to talk about what was happening to his city. Cleveland wasn't just in the midst of an urban crisis. This was "a crisis in the urban environment."[1]

Stokes then launched into a list of Cleveland's problems. "The city which is a monument to man's ingenuity and enterprise, the rich repository of great commercial, cultural and educational achievements, is also a monument to man's neglect and failures in the areas of deteriorated housing, air and water pollution, race relations, inadequate health care, high unemployment rates, inadequate mass transportation, high crime rates and insufficient attention to the problems of our senior citizens." He purposely mingled a variety of issues in this compendium, as he made clear when he turned his attention to his Cleveland: Now! program, which he touted as "a massive 10 to 12-year rebuilding and rehabilitation effort." Cleveland: Now! would address the total environment, social and physical. In case the program had not been successful in creating "a much better Cleveland" by 1990, Stokes pleaded to posterity: "Let me say this: we were trying. We were trying hard to make Cleveland a great city, not only for ourselves but for all of you."

Stokes's letter to the future said nothing about Central National Bank, or about banking generally, but he *was* speaking to those who had assembled that morning. The mayor's program to reinvest in a long-neglected landscape, Cleveland: Now!, had gained the support of the city's economic elite since its creation in May 1968. Corporate officers from prominent Cleveland companies, including Republic Steel and Union Bank, led the fundraising, with the help of the Cleveland Development Foundation. Instantly successful, donations totaled over $5 million, not entirely from corporations, and Cleveland: Now! became a model private-public collaboration. The enthusiastic support for Cleveland: Now! reflected the commercial elite's recognition that it needed the city and its mayor to help protect its investments, most of them clustered downtown in the several dozen blocks surrounding the new bank tower they were celebrating. And Stokes wanted them to know he was trying.

If Stokes's remarks set the day's events in the larger context of Cleveland's problematic trajectory, bank president John Gelbach took a narrower view, placing Central's new tower in the context of downtown, where a number of significant changes encouraged more optimistic visions of Cleveland's future. Much of the change sprang from the adjacent Erieview urban renewal development, which encompassed 163 acres on the east side of the central business district. Based on a 1960 plan by I. M. Pei, Erieview would remove dozens of buildings, adjust the street grid, and create a modern neighborhood of office towers, apartment buildings, parking garages, and open plazas. Approved during the administration of Mayor Anthony Celebrezze and pressed by Mayor Ralph Locher, the plan was now bearing fruit, with Stokes more than happy to wear hard hats and turn ceremonial shovels. "Urban renewal is taking place rapidly all around us," noted Gelbach. After nearly thirty years with little significant development, Cleveland's skyline was now growing, most notably with the recent completion of the forty-story Erieview Tower and the ongoing construction of a thirty-two-story federal building, also on East 9th Street, two blocks north. Gelbach noted that development of Cleveland State University had also begun a few blocks to the east, where a cluster of modern buildings expanded the small campus of Fenn College, acquired by the state in 1964 to serve as the germ for the new university. "All Cleveland can be proud of such progress," Gelbach concluded. "At Central, we have faith that these changes will meet the needs of a growing Cleveland for many years to come."[2]

Who could fail to notice the contrasting visions of Stokes and Gelbach, one speaking of crisis and the other of progress? Even while standing on East 9th and Superior, Stokes could see the city's ongoing deterioration out in the neighborhoods. Gelbach saw the booming service economy and downtown development, the creation of a new landscape with ample parking and easy highway access, office towers and inviting plazas. Although observers at the time might not have recognized it, both were talking about the crisis in the urban environment; it was working its way through downtown as surely as it was through Hough. Both places had entered a prolonged phase of radical physical change, one through decay and arson, the other through eminent domain and demolition. These places were linked by policy, too: urban renewal, designed to speed the process by which the physical city would be remade to meet the demands of the service city. That morning, Stokes and Gelbach stood in a landscape filled with meanings, some carried over from much earlier eras and some recently created. What was happening downtown—the bank tower before them and Erieview behind—was as much an attempt to control the meaning of the central business district as it was an attempt to shape physical space. But what was happening downtown could do little to stem deterioration in the neighborhoods beyond. In 1969, few observers believed that employment trends foretold permanent change, but prosperous industrial Cleveland was collapsing, to be replaced by a city that would serve far fewer people.

ON THE GROW WITH CLEVELAND

Four years before the cornerstone ceremony, Central National Bank marked the seventy-fifth anniversary of its founding with the publication of *On the Grow with Cleveland*, a richly illustrated history that linked the evolution of the city with that of the bank. Along with headshots of prominent businessmen, the book contained street scenes and aerial photos that revealed the transformation of downtown. Pictures of smoking industry along the Cuyahoga in the early pages gave way in the later chapters to the gleaming visions of "space age" Cleveland, the white concrete embrace of the Innerbelt Freeway and the clean lines of Pei's Erieview plan. The accessible prose coupled Central's growth with that of the city. In 1890, flourishing shipbuilding and steel industries helped Cleveland become the nation's tenth-largest city. Burgeoning Great Lakes trade and rail commerce fed the growth of the banking sector, too, and that year the new Central joined eleven other national banks headquartered in Cleveland. The bank's founder, Jeremiah Sullivan, rented space in the recently completed nine-story Perry-Payne Building on Superior Avenue, strategically located between the Cuyahoga's industrial flats and the Public Square at the center of downtown. One of the earliest Cleveland skyscrapers built with an iron superstructure, Perry-Payne was clad in decorative stone and had oversized windows. It was the most impressive edifice in the warehouse district, and it attracted the offices of iron ore and coal dealers as well as Central National Bank.

Despite the difficult economy of the 1890s, Central persisted and Cleveland grew. In 1905, both marked their good fortune with the completion of the massive Rockefeller Building at West 6th and Superior, just a block east of the Perry-Payne, which it dwarfed. A real estate venture of John D. Rockefeller, who had retired from Standard Oil a decade earlier, the seventeen-story Rockefeller Building became Central's new home. Designed by a local firm but inspired by the style of Louis Sullivan, the Rockefeller Building featured an ornate stone and iron facade that emphasized the steel superstructure. For many years, the skyscraper held aloft two large CENTRAL NAT'L BANK signs, one pointing east, the other west. Inside, a stunning Italian marble lobby greeted bank customers. In 1927, after a corporate merger greatly expanded Central's capital holdings, the bank purchased a narrow seventeen-story building at 308 Euclid Avenue, built in 1916, and moved its headquarters into this neoclassical tower in the heart of Cleveland's commercial district. After riding out the Great Depression, Central moved its headquarters yet again, this time to the colossal Midland Building, part of the Terminal Tower group south of Public Square. There Central conducted business in a cavernous banking room, its rich oak columns and walls contrasting with bright travertine floors. The epitome of urban grandeur, the room had been built for Midland Bank, which did not survive the financial crisis that set off the depression. After Central's move was complete, the headquarters on Euclid were demolished.

All this moving about reflected the growth of both the Central National Bank and the central business district, but it also reveals how important it was for the bank to occupy just the right building in just the right spot. Central had moved four times in sixty years, never traveling more than five hundred yards with each move, and now it was less than half a mile from its initial location. The architecture and the interior design of the buildings it occupied spoke to the prominence of the locations—the iron and carved stone facades, the rich wood and marble interiors. Each building suggested strength and stability; each move reflected the constant need to adjust to the shifting real estate market and the changes in foot traffic downtown. Central needed to be where the action was, and the action kept moving—from the warehouses tied close to the river, toward Public Square and the growing business core, then to Euclid Avenue and the thriving retail corridor, then to Terminal Tower, where Central hoped tens of thousands of commuters would find its grand banking floor both impressive and convenient. The expanding and shifting economy drove continuous physical change to which Central and the rest of Cleveland continuously adjusted. Industrial growth altered the landscape throughout the region, but changes were most intense downtown, where real estate prices rose the fastest and where small distances had the greatest financial significance.

In June 1969, Stokes came to East 9th and Superior to celebrate what turned out to be Central's fifth and final move. The bank had grown rapidly in the 1950s and 1960s, adding branch offices throughout the metropolitan area. New buildings in suburban communities featured drive-up windows—twenty-five of the thirty-nine branches had them by 1964. Central tried to keep up with the movement of its customers farther and farther from the urban core. The bank's 1969 annual report highlighted the movement of the bank into downtown's evolving financial district and expressed great pride in the new tower, but a map at the back of the report illustrated the other movement—to the periphery. The dark map, with Cleveland's municipal boundary clearly marked, showed the constellation of branches across the metropolis. The central business district remained critical to the bank: six of the locations, including the new headquarters, were downtown. But twenty-six of the forty-eight branches were outside the city. Central was on the grow with the suburbs.

Central staged the cornerstone ceremony to provide what bank officer F. J. Blake described in an internal memo as "some good publicity at minimal cost," and the newspapers and television stations obliged with stories and images of progress. Indeed, the building of the Central National Bank tower was big news in Cleveland. When Central first announced the coming tower, the *Plain Dealer* ran a front-page banner headline: "Bank to Build Skyscraper."

Four years later, with the building completed, Stokes returned to the tower for a dedication ceremony, held in the lobby due to poor weather. The event was photogenic enough to earn space in the next day's papers, and to be certain that Cleveland noted the occasion, Central took out a full-page ad in the *Plain Dealer* declaring, "Central National Bank looks ahead with Greater Cleveland and Ohio."[3]

A VIGOROUS, VIBRANT, PULSATING HEART

Two years before Stokes helped fill the time capsule, a similar group gathered on the site for a carefully orchestrated groundbreaking ceremony. After a hovering helicopter signaled the height of the tower to come by unfurling a Central National Bank sign, Mayor Locher joined Edward Carpenter and John Tishman in turning shovels while wearing personalized Tishman hard hats. The key figures said a few words of praise for the first major bank construction in Cleveland since the onset of the Great Depression thirty-five years earlier. Just five blocks from its previous headquarters, the new tower would put Central at the heart of what the bank called "the new financial district in downtown Cleveland." Cleveland Trust, Union Commerce, National City, and the Federal Reserve all clustered along or around East 9th. At the groundbreaking, Carpenter emphasized location, noting, "This carefully selected site joins the well-established business hub of the city to the area of new commercial development in Erieview."[4] Central's tower joined the city's past with its future.

Erieview was one of the most ambitious downtown urban renewal plans in the nation. Created by I. M. Pei & Associates in 1960, the plan featured clusters of midrise buildings surrounding plazas and punctuated by several new towers. It called for a new federal building, just across the street from City Hall, and a hotel or motel on the lakefront, but most of the construction would create modern residential buildings and office space. All the new buildings would have access to parking facilities, either underground or in nearby garages. The plan removed some small streets and alleys so the buildings could gather around open pedestrian spaces. The plan also removed all surface parking, which had slowly crept into the area as owners demolished unprofitable buildings and secured income by charging commuters for spots near the business core. In addition, light industry, which occupied many of the existing buildings, had no place in Pei's Erieview. Altogether, the plan envisioned the demolition of 224 of the existing 237 buildings and the displacement of more than five hundred businesses, including restaurants, taverns, retail stores,

repair shops, and custom manufacturers. Federal renewal policy had emphasized the rehabilitation and conservation of existing buildings since 1954, but
Erieview included no program for rehabilitation. Among the few buildings to
survive were St. John's Cathedral and the Cleveland Press building, although
the latter did not long outlive the newspaper, which folded in the early 1980s.

The year after the city planning commission adopted the Erieview Plan,
I. M. Pei & Associates printed a beautiful, oversized, twenty-six-page pamphlet with illustrations and explanations. Bright watercolor paintings of the
buildings to come were augmented by a series of sharp maps contrasting the
old cluttered city with the clean lines of modern Cleveland. Mayor Celebrezze
provided an introduction in the form of a letter to the people of Cleveland.
"Under this program," Celebrezze wrote, "a large downtown area will be reclaimed and redeveloped to give the core of our city a vigorous, vibrant, pulsating heart." Celebrezze praised the plan's "bold vision" but also noted the
"practical and realistic means" by which it would uplift the economy. "By
redeveloping the central city," he continued, "we revitalize all of Greater
Cleveland." Such was the assumption that a prosperous metropolitan region
needed a prosperous downtown.[5]

With Erieview, Cleveland took a significant step toward a re-envisioned,
service-centered city. Pei's plan banished manufacturing from downtown's
eastern edge, largely replacing it with a residential community that, in Pei's
words, would provide "dwellings for families who wish to return to the advantages of city life." Elegant apartments would be convenient to downtown's
services, retail, and jobs. Pei dedicated more than half the site to "open lawns,
tree-lined malls and parks" that would "provide an orderly and attractive setting for the buildings and a pleasant environment for the people who occupy
them." An elementary school, also proposed in the plan, would make the new
neighborhood even more attractive to families. Part of Erieview would be
built on stilts over the lakefront railroad tracks. This terrace would hold a new
public park, while beneath it two levels of parking would house an additional
two thousand cars. Arising from and near the terrace would be four thirty-story
residential towers with stunning views of the lake to the north and downtown
to the south and west. Altogether it was a beautiful vision of a postindustrial
city based on the predicted growth of service jobs downtown and the ability
of an improved urban environment to lure middle-class residents back to
the core.

The problem with the vision was that it contained the ideas of too few people. The top-down planning process encouraged little buy-in, and the emphasis on demolition and the creation of a completely new aesthetic for the area

failed to elicit excitement within the city's middle class. Indeed, real estate research suggesting latent demand for downtown living was badly off. Few of the residences envisioned by Pei were built, although the four-hundred-unit Chesterfield apartment building, planned before Pei's involvement, overcame a decade of delays and filled one of the vacant lots in Erieview in 1967. Apparently "the advantages of city life" had yet to outweigh the many disadvantages, and most Clevelanders watched the slow progress of Erieview from their car windows or on their television sets, not from the windows of their "luxurious apartments."

Pei's conception of the future may have been mostly right, but the architecture was all wrong. Modernism's rejection of the past, its purposeful removal of old meanings from urban spaces, left Clevelanders unmoved by Pei's clean but sterile vision. As *New York Times* architecture critic Ada Louise Huxtable wrote of downtown Cleveland in 1973, "at night the area is empty: it is a surreal wasteland of deserted towers and echoing spaces from Public Square and the Beaux Arts mall overlooking Lake Erie to Erieview Plaza. It is as if catastrophe struck at sundown." Huxtable cast some blame on Pei, whose plan was "long on desolate, overscaled spaces, destructive of cohesive urbanism and defiantly antihuman," although she saw signs of hope in the continued construction of Cleveland State University's campus, just a couple of blocks away, and at the adjacent Playhouse Square, where the city hoped to revive a more traditional urban landscape around beautiful but underused theaters.[6]

The Erieview plan was not responsible for the eerie quiet of downtown Cleveland, of course. It was merely a general guide for development. Implementation required that the city receive federal capital to buy properties and demolish existing buildings. The city would then sell development rights to companies through a bidding process. In essence, renewal funding allowed cities to purchase, assemble, and clear urban land for redevelopment at below-market prices. In theory, almost certain profits would attract developers and spark competitive bidding on the right to build in Erieview. That didn't happen. The low demand allowed those who did bring their capital to the table to move away from the plan's original design. This occurred right away, when the federal building morphed into a tower rather than the low-rise structure enclosing a plaza envisioned by Pei.

Central National Bank had been courted to build in Erieview, where developers would have altered the plan to allow a bank tower near Lakeside Avenue. But Central thought the site, just three blocks from where it actually built, too far from the banking hub, a reminder of the importance of even short distances in the central business district. Central's lack of interest in Erieview might also have given pause to the developers, who needed to attract large tenants to the site. As Tishman put the finishing touches on the Central tower just outside the redevelopment area, Erieview was still mostly surface parking, with only two major buildings completed: the Erieview Tower in 1964 and the federal building in 1967.

As the years passed with so little construction, the entire urban renewal enterprise became suspect. And as the tenth anniversary of Erieview's passage approached, Clevelanders expressed doubts about the plan's ability to remake downtown as Pei had promised. To be certain, the old neighborhood was swept away, but mostly what Erieview provided was an object lesson in the failure of government to predict market desires and accelerate land-use transitions through the infusion of capital. Perhaps more important, Erieview, especially its first two towers, came to symbolize for many Clevelanders the failure of government to understand where renewal was truly needed—in the neighborhoods. While the towers rose, the expansive East Side renewal plan, University-Euclid, languished. The announcement of that plan, which City Council had approved in 1961, far predated actual renewal efforts, and the specter of eventual takings and demolition greatly impeded capital investment in Hough. Private investment essentially ceased in neighborhoods marked off for renewal. While meeting in Cleveland in April 1966, the Civil Rights Commission examined the city's stalled urban renewal projects. Data gathered for the hearings revealed that over the preceding five years more housing had been destroyed than constructed, and the University-Euclid project had not built or remodeled a single dwelling unit. Data like these became fodder for Stokes's mayoral campaign in 1967 and a source of frustration and embarrassment after he won that November.

In this context, building in downtown was dispiriting in Hough and other deteriorating residential areas. As the city prioritized its work, progress in one area meant delay—and decay—in another. In July 1966, as the Hough riots began to subside, the trustees of Community Action for Youth gathered to craft a message for Mayor Locher, which they titled "Statement and Recommendations by Hough Citizens." Primarily concerned with the most obvious causes of the violence—unemployment and poverty—the statement also made clear the added frustration imparted by the contrast with downtown's redevelopment. "The progressive physical deterioration of Hough has made the community a symbol of despair and degradation," the statement read, "while new office towers rise around it and plans for greater structures are

Figure 5. The Erieview project swept away more than two hundred buildings in the hope that a modern neighborhood of office towers and apartment buildings would revive downtown, but for years Erieview Tower, seen here in front of the newer federal building, stood in a sea of parking. The city's focus on downtown renewal raised concern in the neighborhoods, especially since it didn't seem to be working. Photo by Bill Nehez. Cleveland Press Collection, Cleveland State University.

proclaimed. Hough sees progressive dilapidation and derelict buildings as reminders that only others count. Hough must have the opportunity to share in the amenities of the other America. The promise of urban renewal must be fulfilled for Hough."[7] Cleveland had created many urban renewal zones, covering six thousand acres—more than 10 percent of the city's area and more than any other city in the nation—but the Locher administration had failed to keep its projects moving forward. Since all of them had fallen behind schedule, the office towers in Erieview, symbols of progress and transition for some, became symbols of continuing neglect for others.

The residents of Hough had good reason to suspect that urban renewal worked in the best interests of people other than the city's poor, for whom the program had ostensibly been created. From the start—1949, when the federal Housing Act initiated the program—Cleveland had been an eager participant in urban renewal. It had the backing of the city's establishment, not just the politicians who expected to parlay federal dollars into visible local action but also the economic elite, both the old industrial corporations and the newer financial giants. In 1954, the economic powers came together to create the Cleveland Development Foundation to promote renewal projects, especially by facilitating the relationship between public action (such as planning, property acquisition, and demolition) and private developers, who were to build new housing, modern industrial plants, and eventually office towers. John C. Virden, chairman of the board of the Cleveland Federal Reserve Bank, became the first president of the new foundation. Among the other participants were officers from the city's largest and most visible corporations: Republic Steel, Cleveland Electric Illuminating, Standard Oil, Cleveland Trust, Central National Bank, National City Bank, Union Bank of Commerce, the May Company, and the Higbee Company. In all, eighty-three companies joined the Cleveland Development Foundation, and their subscriptions helped create a $2 million revolving fund used to expedite renewal planning.

It wasn't just that the city's most powerful economic and political forces backed renewal that made Hough residents suspicious. It was the way they talked about it. At the center of renewal was the concept of blight—disease that spreads and threatens the well-being of the entire city. Battling blight required serious intervention—some supporters called it surgery. The Cleveland Advertising Club published a brief, widely distributed report on the city's urban renewal program in 1955. "Twenty-six square miles of cleared land," the introduction began, "stripped of its unwanted burden of slums and squalor . . . are emerging in the central areas of Cleveland."[8] Before a congressional panel investigating urban renewal in 1963, Mayor Locher testified, "Erieview will rescue and beautify what has been a derelict neighborhood in the middle of the city." "Unwanted," "derelict," "squalor"—powerful words used to justify the most severe government intervention in the landscape possible: purchase through eminent domain and subsequent demolition.[9]

Hough residents also knew that Erieview would not serve their interests. The new housing would be market rate and out of reach for the working poor. Indeed, as the city defended its decision to undertake such a large renewal project downtown, it became clear that Erieview's primary purpose was to encourage corporate investment in the central business district and, just as important, to protect the investments that had already been made. At the 1963 congressional hearing, Locher argued that Erieview needed to be large so that new construction could secure Federal Housing Administration mortgage insurance, claiming that developers hoping to build apartment towers in the area could not win FHA backing because of the poor physical environment. Locher claimed that by clearing away the old, Erieview would "assure environmental protection of a large enough area" to obtain FHA financing. In other words, Erieview established what Locher called "investment security." Edward W. Sloan Jr., president of a large Great Lakes shipping firm and chairman of the Cleveland Development Foundation, was even more blunt before the same panel: "the clearance of blighted and nonconforming buildings," he said, "will permit private development," and the size and attractiveness of Erieview would "assure the security of investment."[10] Originally a program designed to improve residential environments, in Cleveland urban renewal was now intended to create viable investment environments.

On June 18, 1969, five days after the ceremony at Central's tower, Stokes announced that plans for Plaza 9, a seven-story office building just to the north of Erieview Tower, had been finalized. Four days later, Stokes attended the groundbreaking for another Erieview project, a new home for the Public Utilities Department on Lakeside Avenue. The five-story building would house the city's engineering, water pollution control, light and power, and water divisions. In a very upbeat speech, Stokes listed all the construction then under way or recently completed in the area, including the Union Commerce Garage and the Central National Bank tower. Suddenly the long-stalled renewal program was moving again, and Stokes linked the good feelings of Erieview's progress with the American moon landing, which had taken place just two days before, when Ohio native Neil Armstrong took his historic giant leap for mankind. "Anyone who cares to should feel free to collect rock samples, moon walk fashion, and take them back to City Hall for analysis by our department of community development to determine why life did not exist here to this extent under previous administrations." Following Stokes's lead, the press began asserting a new theme: Erieview, the urban renewal project that got off to a sluggish start, would soon be out of space.

A LOOK OF STRENGTH AND BEAUTY

In August 1967, Stokes kicked off the formal phase of his mayoral campaign at an open-air meeting on Woodland Avenue and East 75th Street, where an urban renewal site had been cleared for industrial development that had yet to materialize. Stokes had a well-crafted stump speech, which varied somewhat depending on the setting. It contained two key points. First, he would sell Municipal Light to an eager Cleveland Electric Illuminating Company, the private corporation that supplied power to most of metropolitan Cleveland. The sale would bring in $60 million, which the city could invest in physical improvements: better street lighting, more playgrounds, swimming pools, recreation centers, and resurfaced streets. The Muny Light sale was Stokes's positive message. He had a negative point, too: Locher had been an ineffective leader, most evident in his poor handling of urban renewal. "Only in Cleveland," Stokes said, "would a city administration spend one and a half million dollars to buy a brand new Addressograph-Multigraph building on Lakeside Avenue because it would not conform to someone's notion that the site on which it was located should be a green mall for a new hotel which has not been built and apparently will never be built."[11] The small modern building had been purchased as part of the Erieview project, and now it sat empty, paying no property taxes, as Stokes pointed out, all because the city was following Pei's notion of what downtown should be.

A week later, Stokes gave another campaign speech on the thirty-eighth floor of Erieview Tower, near the emptied Addressograph building. The Top of the Town Restaurant gave members of the Cleveland Club who attended spectacular views of the lake and downtown. Stokes looked out and saw, he said, "a sleeping giant."[12] Approaching the tower that evening, he also saw a giant building standing in a sea of parking. The city was pocked by renewal's scars, the vast empty lots that were evidence of the Locher administration's flaws and perhaps of the failure of the entire urban renewal enterprise. But unlike the East Woodland urban renewal site where Stokes kicked off his campaign, the thirty-eighth floor of Erieview Tower was not an especially suitable location for making an argument about the failure of projects to move forward. The forty-story tower had reshaped the city's skyline, pulling it dramatically to the east. Looming over the new reflecting pool that ran toward East 9th Street, the tower suggested that Erieview might actually take its proposed shape. The skyscraper was more than just the starting point for redevelopment: it was the linchpin of the plan. "No office building in any other U.S. city will attract attention so immediately and so unequivocally," Pei claimed. "It stands at the hub of an entire downtown redevelopment project designed to complement it, service it and heighten its importance—a setting unequaled by any office building in the U.S. It will appeal particularly to tenants who require large areas of office space and a location of dominance and prestige in the heart of the city." In this preeminence of the Erieview Tower, Pei had misplaced his hopes for the entire plan.[13]

Following modernist principles then in vogue, Erieview removed essentially all connections to place and history. The new buildings connected Cleveland to modernity but removed the associations Clevelanders had with this part of town. In the planning, design, and construction of Erieview, locals had little input. The tower's design came from the New York office of architectural partners Wallace Harrison and Max Abramovitz, who specialized in the international style—sleek towers of glass and steel. Harrison and Abramovitz were in the midst of building similar towers around the United States, including the Marine National Exchange Bank in Milwaukee (1961), Bank One Tower in Columbus (1964), Erie Savings Bank in Buffalo (1969), and First National Tower in Louisville (1972). Although some of the towers, including the U.S. Steel building (1970) in Pittsburgh and the Fiberglas building (1969) in Toledo, held the headquarters of industrial firms, the partnership's success was due in large part to the era's explosion of bank skyscrapers. Harrison had also served as lead architect for the United Nations Headquarters and was engaged in the expansive Empire State Plaza, which remade downtown Albany with many of the same features as Erieview, including a rectangular reflecting pool. The proliferation of international-style towers, which varied in height and the tint of their glass but little else, made certain that Pei's pronouncement that Erieview would attract attention like "no office building in any other U.S. city" simply could not come true.

Modernism's intentional removal of connections to place and the past muted Erieview's ability to revive Cleveland's downtown. People would work in the offices and park their cars in the garages, but the thriving public spaces Pei envisioned did not develop. The tall, flat towers deflected and accelerated Lake Erie's winds, making the plazas especially uncomfortable, and the buildings themselves, impressive from a distance, sparked little attraction up close. Older downtown buildings featured Americanized European styles—Italianate, Romanesque, beaux arts, and the like—but regional stone, local brick, and touches of ironwork made each structure unique and of the place it occupied. The buildings carried local names—Perry-Payne, Rockefeller—that connected architecture to local families. The principles of modernism prevented local touches in Erieview. Standing on the plaza, staring up at the tower, Clevelanders might think themselves in Albany, Pittsburgh, Milwaukee, or, if the wind off the lake was especially sharp, Buffalo.

Erieview Tower was the tallest building constructed in Cleveland since Terminal Tower, which had dominated the skyline since its completion in 1927. The contrast between the two structures is stark. Built as the crowning feature of a union railroad terminal complex to the southwest of Public Square, Terminal Tower quickly became the pride of the city. Constructed by real estate developers Oris Paxton Van Sweringen and his brother Mantis James Van Sweringen, the new train station transformed downtown, and not just because the tower lorded over the skyline. All manner of rail lines came together at the site—passenger rail, commuter rail, and trollies all met there. Most important to the Van Sweringens was the rapid transit that linked their Shaker Heights development to downtown via the Kingsbury Run valley. Altogether the complex was an impressive, efficient machine where passengers and baggage transferred from one form of travel to another. Along the way, people could eat, shop, and get a haircut. Inspired by other city-within-a-city developments around the nation, including Grand Central Terminal in New York City, completed in 1913, the Cleveland complex contained all the major components of a modern downtown: a variety of retail shops, a department store, a massive bank building, and a luxury hotel. Grand Central and Terminal Tower were so successful that they encouraged the construction of other center-city, mixed-use developments, including Cincinnati's Carew Tower, completed in 1931, and New York's Rockefeller Center, constructed from 1930 to 1939.

At the center of the Cleveland complex, balancing the transit hub below and to the rear, was an office tower in the front that reached over seven hundred feet. It was the tallest American building outside New York City for more than three decades, and it served as a fitting symbol of Cleveland's industrial might. Like skyscrapers around the country, the tower helped reshape the meaning of downtown. The historian Oliver Zunz calls skyscrapers "vertical expressions of corporate power," a description that suits many early towers, including Woolworth and Singer in New York. But skyscrapers were much more than that: they were vertical expressions of downtown's preeminence in city life and the urban economy. Even in the early 1900s, Americans began to judge cities by their skylines and individual towers. Successful cities had successful downtowns; successful downtowns had skyscrapers. In this way, Terminal Tower signaled the success of the entire Cleveland metropolis. The power of that tower ensured that skyscrapers that came later—including Erieview—would instantly gain significance.[14]

That is why Central National Bank's 1969 tower held so much meaning for the city, why the newspapers gave it so much attention, why the news cameras came to capture the groundbreaking ceremony, returned for the enclosure of the time capsule, and then for the building's dedication, and why the mayor attended all three events. Central's tower was charged with meaning, even before Tishman broke ground, because all large skyscrapers had the potential to redefine the city, as Terminal Tower had forty years earlier. Given the importance of the building, Central hired the prominent architect Charles Luckman, the former president of Lever Brothers who had followed his passion into architecture and, among other things, designed the Prudential Tower in Boston, which when completed in 1964 became the first building outside New York taller than Terminal Tower.

Blending older forms and materials with the sleek style of modernism, the Central National Bank tower contrasted with the East Ohio building just across East 9th, which when it opened a decade earlier became the first of many large glass boxes to populate downtown Cleveland—a style that Central had no desire to replicate. Bank officials may have been drawn to Luckman because he had a reputation as a flexible designer, one less interested in making an artistic statement than serving the needs of the client. Luckman had also recently finished work on the Madison Square Garden complex, on which he had collaborated with the Tishman Corporation, the same developer leading the Central construction project. Following instructions, Luckman avoided steel and glass curtain walls in Cleveland, and instead the firm used Ohio bricks—lots of them—as the major exterior material. Rounded brick pilasters rose from the ground floor to the top of the building, lending a hint of tradition in an otherwise modern skyscraper and, as the bank's annual report boasted, "giving it a look of strength and beauty." Writing in the *New York Times*, Ada Louise Huxtable called it simply a "conventionally pleasant red brick" building.[15]

Inside, the open bank floor mixed contemporary styling with traditional materials, travertine marble and burled elm. Central's new tower spoke mostly to the future, however, at least to the future its leaders imagined. A modern pneumatic tube system facilitated communication among workers on the bank's twelve floors, easing the movement of the paperwork at the heart of the business. More important, although the building contained an expansive traditional banking floor, it also featured three "auto-tellers," drive-through lanes that allowed customers to pull up to television monitors, speak through intercoms, and pass materials into the building using that same pneumatic technology. Customers pulling off Superior Avenue could make a choice: climb a ramp up into the adjoining six-story, 350-spot parking annex or drive straight, under the garage, and conduct their business from the convenience of their cars.

A DEPRESSING EFFECT ON REAL ESTATE

The week before Stokes spoke at Central's cornerstone ceremony, he received a letter from George Salapa, executive vice president of the Cleveland Real Estate Board. Salapa described a recent meeting of the board, at which members "discussed the acts of hoodlumism that have occurred in the downtown area in the last few months." The board was concerned that the approaching summer season, when more people would make the trip downtown, would bring further increases in crime and "the resultant publicity may keep people away." Salapa noted that crime "had a depressing effect on real estate values and businesses, especially shopping, entertainment, restaurants, and the like." He recommended an increased police presence, including overtime for some officers and more strategically placed beat policemen.[16]

The Cleveland Real Estate Board had good reason for concern. Image had grown increasingly important to downtown's vitality. Metropolitan residents, many now living much farther from the core than before and most now moving about in automobiles, had choices about where they spent their time and money. Things that people had long tolerated about downtown—including dirt and disorder—had grown intolerable. People who worked downtown expressed concern, especially when they relied on the willingness of customers to make the trip. Sanford Frumker, a dentist with an office in the prominent Williamson Building, wrote Stokes after two of his patients had been accosted on the street at Public Square. "I love Cleveland," he wrote. "I love downtown Cleveland. I most anxiously want you to succeed. That is why I am urging you as a first priority to get adequate police protection to downtown so it will be safe."[17] Like the Real Estate Board, Frumker had a vested interest in the viability of the central business district, but he also linked Stokes's success to that of downtown, reflecting a common understanding of the singularity of this place. Downtown was critical to the property tax base and long a center of employment growth. As the urbanist Charles Abrams wrote in *The City Is the Frontier*, his 1965 plea for better planning and greater federal involvement in the urban landscape: "The cities with pulsating downtowns are the cities that thrive." Central business districts are "part of the fuel that makes cities flicker."[18] If downtown's flame went out, Cleveland would lose its way. As downtown goes, so goes the city. Or so the theory went.

All this intensifying concern was relatively new, and not just related to a spike in "hoodlumism." For more than a hundred years, Cleveland's downtown, like those in industrial cities around the nation, had grown because market forces identified this central place as especially valuable. Many sectors of the economy demanded central locations: businesses from manufacturing and warehousing to banking and insurance all jostled for their place in the core, near docks and railroad terminals. Retail followed. The largest department stores, the May Company and Higbee's, had located on Public Square by the end of the 1920s, and smaller shops put themselves in the paths of pedestrians who filled the city's sidewalks. Hotels and restaurants, theaters and taverns, so much of what makes a city a city, serving residents, commuters, conventioneers, and tourists, all clustered downtown, the closer to the center the better. Cleveland policy makers didn't have much to do with this growth, this demand for downtown real estate, but after World War II, cars and trucks helped destabilize real estate demand by allowing greater decentralization. The "fluid city" Mabel Walker had predicted in 1947 was emerging in the 1950s, and the central urban question became, how do we keep downtown vibrant? And then, in short order, the question morphed into, how can we revitalize the core?

In the attempt to answer these questions, in 1959 the City Planning Commission developed a plan for the central business district: *Downtown Cleveland 1975*—the short, fifteen-year horizon revealing how rapidly conditions were evolving and the need to continuously update plans to match changing realities. The plan asserted that "the heart of Cleveland is exceedingly important to the health and well-being of the City of Cleveland and to the entire Cleveland Metropolitan Area." One-sixth of those employed in the region—124,000 people—worked downtown, and thousands more came to shop, but increasing vacancies, especially in the retail corridor of Euclid Avenue, were a special cause for concern. At the same time, although office vacancies remained low, no large buildings had been constructed downtown between 1930 and 1957, an unprecedented hiatus in investment.[19]

The primary purpose of the City Planning Commission, which dated to 1915, was to prepare for and manage change, and although the 1959 plan was based on a clear-eyed understanding of the trends working against downtown, the authors recognized the limits of the changes the city could encourage. "Cleveland is a northern industrial giant—neither young nor old—fronting a great inland sea," the plan acknowledged. "It cannot and should not assume the personality of some other type of city, but rather should magnify and celebrate those qualities which are native to it and which indeed make it 'Cleveland.'" In other words, the planners would not attempt to change the character of the city—just modernize industrial Cleveland.[20]

The plan opened with a summary of "desirable measures," some of which involved direct government action, including the improvement of public spaces, such as the mall and Public Square. Other measures required the city to encourage private action, such as marketing downtown to corporate employers. The plan recommended improvement to transportation systems, including making downtown more accessible by car through the redevelopment of surface streets and the establishment of parking near freeway exits. The convention center would have to be expanded to keep pace with other cities that were investing in their facilities. And Cleveland desperately required a modern "convention-type" hotel. First on the list of "desirable measures," however, was "improving and maintaining the physical attractiveness of Downtown through the elimination of drab facades, inappropriate signs and other aspects which detract from the appearance of Downtown, in order to offset the competition offered in this respect by the newer suburban business and shopping centers." Cleveland, like the rest of America, was entering an era in which building owners covered older, ornate ground floors with modern facades—using plain, often artificial materials—in the hopes of attracting or retaining customers. In retrospect, it obviously wasn't the old-fashioned stone and brick facades of downtown that jeopardized retail; nevertheless, the effort to retrofit older buildings with bright new facades reveals an understanding that image mattered more than ever. To attract shoppers, conventioneers, and employers looking to build new office space, all of whom had choices, the city would have to be clean and attractive, with plenty of parking and safe streets and pedestrian areas.

The downtown plan envisioned extensive redevelopment along the lakefront. The city would expand port facilities so it could capture a greater share of the increasing lake traffic promised by the creation of the St. Lawrence Seaway, completed in 1959. The plan also envisioned improving the lakefront airport, which had opened just twelve years earlier, so that it could handle more and larger aircraft. The needs of commerce would be balanced with the recreational needs of residents through the addition of piers for excursion boats, a new aquarium, and a sports arena, all adjacent to the existing Municipal Stadium and linked to the mall by a "pedestrian way" that would soar over the Shoreway and the railroad tracks that separated the city from the lake. All this represented a gradual pushback against industrial dominance along the city's waterfront.

The city's general plan, published in 1950, stated the obvious: "both the lakefront and river valley were taken over by railroads and industry." The New York Central traveled along the lakeshore, joined by the Pennsylvania near downtown, and part of the lakefront had been given over to dumps, where spoils from harbor dredging and burning trash would eventually add new land, much of it to be used by the expanding airport. The 1950 plan noted that "a growing number of citizens have long felt that the economic side of Cleveland could share the lakefront more fairly with Cleveland's people as a whole." The city had been acquiring land for the expansion of parks, as well as filling in the lake to increase recreational opportunities (and space for parking).

"When the whole lakefront is given the development it deserves, we will prove to Clevelanders and visitors alike that our greatest natural asset can benefit everyone living here." The general plan made no attempt to reclaim the Cuyahoga River from industry, however, and the entire valley remained classified as "General Industrial" or, around the steel mills, "Unrestricted Industrial," where "blast furnaces, oil refineries, and stock yards" needed room and access to rail or water transport and "make noise, smoke, and odors, and frequently fire hazards." Clearly the general plan, and the more focused downtown plan that followed nine years later, envisioned an industrial city that better accommodated its own citizens, but an industrial city nonetheless. Only in one large area—along the river from Harvard Road in the south nearly to the terminal complex in the north—would industry be "unrestricted."[21]

The 1959 downtown plan contained typical modernist goals, the most important of which involved the "separation or removal of conflicting land uses" and "the strengthening of sound use areas." This meant land uses would be clustered by type in the attempt to increase efficiency and reduce the troubling diversity that gave downtowns their chaotic feel. To emphasize the segregation of land by use, a beautiful color-coded map categorized every inch of downtown, placing buildings and blocks into "sound use areas." Bold colors compartmentalized space: the Major Business Core in pink; Government Centers were dark green; public open spaces appeared light green. The plan included the creation of residential areas, indicated in yellow, one of which occupied a portion of what would become the Erieview urban renewal zone. But *Downtown Cleveland 1975* also designated substantial acreage for "conveniently located Downtown warehousing and industrial activities" and the "encouragement of modern industrial park type development." Indeed, much of the area that became Erieview fell into two land-use types, Industrial Research and Light Manufacturing, and nearly a third of the entire planned area was set aside for industry. That Pei would banish manufacturing from Erieview just a year later was an indication of his distinct vision for the Cleveland of the future and how rapidly expectations for downtown were evolving.[22]

In another sign of the modernist influence over the city's planners, *Downtown Cleveland 1975* reimagined Public Square as a transportation hub and performance space. The city's most historic spot would be dramatically altered, with Ontario Street closed and the northern half of the square regraded. New sitting areas and plantings would be added, but, shockingly, "the traditional monuments" of Moses Cleaveland, the city's founder, and Tom L. Johnson, its most famous mayor, would be "replaced in newly-designed spaces." Even the Soldiers and Sailors Monument, Cuyahoga County's impressive

Civil War memorial, would be taken from the square, where it had been a fixture since 1894. Removing these monuments would have detached much of the history and meaning from this place, and purposefully so. In the modernist vision, Cleveland would have to leave its past behind.

TOM L. JOHNSON ENDURES

A month after attending Central's cornerstone ceremony, Stokes went to Public Square to celebrate the birthday of Cleveland's favorite politician, Tom L. Johnson. Cleveland State University urban studies professor Tom Campbell and members of the venerable City Club, an organization dedicated to providing forums for political debate, gathered with Stokes around the bronze statue of Johnson, which remained steadfast on the square despite the plan to remove it. Johnson sat facing southeast, smiling and holding a copy of Henry George's famed treatise *Poverty and Progress*, which had inspired so many Progressive reformers, including Johnson. A four-term mayor in the first decade of the century, Johnson was a champion of municipal ownership and of the power of government generally. He battled to end the private operation of streetcars, initiated the creation of Municipal Light, the city-owned power company, and backed the development of Cleveland's Group Plan, which had transformed downtown Cleveland. Johnson died in 1911, and the statue took its place on Public Square just five years later. The back of the monument explained that it had been "erected by popular subscription in memory of the man who gave his fortune and his life to make Cleveland as he often expressed it 'A happier place to live in—a better place to die in' and located on the spot he dedicated to the freedom of speech."

Stokes linked himself with Johnson in both style and substance. Johnson was a great communicator who reached out to common Clevelanders. Stokes emulated this approach through his regular town hall meetings, held around the city. To show how similarly the two politicians envisioned the city and their mayoral roles, that afternoon on Public Square Stokes quoted Johnson at length: "Good sanitary conditions, public parks, pure water, playgrounds for children and well paved streets are the best kind of investments, while the absence of them entails not only heavy pecuniary loss, but operates to the moral and physical deterioration of the city's inhabitants." Clearly all those concerns remained alive. But Stokes also noted that much had changed in the city—and not all of it for the better. Despite decades of change, Stokes said, not everything had been swept away: "the Soldiers and Sailors Monument over there is the same and perhaps the pigeons, but styles and dress and

Figure 6. Stokes linked himself to the popular Progressive Era mayor Tom L. Johnson. At a celebration of Johnson's birthday anniversary on Public Square, Stokes pressed his own progressive agenda, including a plan to construct public housing in the Lee-Seville neighborhood. Carl Stokes Photographs, 1968–1971, container 1C, folder 66, Western Reserve Historical Society. Used with permission.

architecture are different. Yet Tom L. Johnson endures. His heritage to us endures."[23]

Ever the opportunist, Stokes engaged in some political grandstanding, even beyond connecting himself to Johnson's legacy of working for the people of Cleveland. "What peculiar tricks history plays," he said. "Not only are the streetcar tracks paved over so that Tom L. Johnson wouldn't recognize his town and not only are the diesel fumes of the people's busline contributing to the pollution of the people's environment, but the statue itself faces, not city hall or the lakefront which he sought to preserve for the people—no, indeed, the statue of Tom L. Johnson, you will notice, faces Lee-Seville." The year before, Stokes had proposed building 274 single-family homes on vacant land already owned by the city's housing authority in Lee-Seville, a middle-class black neighborhood nine miles south of downtown, and by the summer of

1969 the construction of public housing outside the city's impoverished central neighborhoods had become a major issue. Stokes mentioned it at every turn. Standing on Public Square, he reached for a symbolic connection with Tom Johnson, who was facing south, but not actually toward Lee-Seville. Had those present followed Johnson's gaze, they would have turned to see Terminal Tower. Stokes's talent, of course, was seeing beyond downtown's skyscrapers and into the city's neighborhoods.

The Lee-Seville battle took on extraordinary significance, drawing attention away from the long crime wave, the rotting ghetto, Erieview redevelopment, and the death throes of Lake Erie. Most public housing conflicts around the country focused on the issue of race. In Cleveland, that issue was muted by the shared race of Stokes, most Lee-Seville residents, and those who would probably occupy the public housing. Stokes described the Lee-Seville development as an attempt to redraw the municipal map, moving poor residents to the city's edge, a step toward ending the concentration of poverty at the city's core. "We have to give the poor people a chance to have their own garage, their own piece of property," the *Call and Post*, Cleveland's African American newspaper, quoted him as saying in the early stages of the campaign for the development. "We have to give these people a chance to be part of the affluent society." As many Lee-Seville residents saw it, however, the plan threatened to compromise their middle-class achievement by bringing the ghetto into their neighborhood. The conflict, expressed in these broad terms, moved into City Council, which was considering a series of bills that would fund the infrastructure—roads and sewers primarily—necessary to support the development. Much to Stokes's chagrin, opponents found broad support in the council, and the bills stalled.[24]

The evening before the cornerstone ceremony at Central National Bank, Stokes had wrangled with angry Lee-Seville residents opposed to the mayor's public housing plan. Held at the neighborhood's elementary school and attended by six hundred people, several hundred of whom stood outside listening to the proceedings over a public-address system, the meeting had turned confrontational, as the *Plain Dealer* reported at length. Three days earlier, Stokes had organized a "housing rally" on the mall, at which he claimed "the Lee-Seville issue has become a test of whether public housing for the elderly and the poor must be confined to the core of the city." Stokes condemned City Council, calling out individual members for their failure to move bills through the chamber. Much of the stalled legislation concerned environmental improvements, especially air and water pollution control efforts. Stokes blamed council president James Stanton, a fierce political rival, for forcing the delays in an effort to embarrass the mayor and prevent the construction of public housing in Lee-Seville.[25]

Stokes made his case for Lee-Seville wherever he went, but his use of Public Square and the mall reflected the importance of these spaces for political speech. Surrounded by public buildings, many of them grand and heavy beaux arts blocks, the rectangular mall had a remarkably serious quality. Conceived of in the late 1800s and backed by Tom Johnson in the early 1900s, the mall was at the center of the Group Plan created by Daniel Burnham, John Carrere, and Arnold Brunner in 1903. Burnham, the Chicago architect who had gained renown not just for his skyscrapers but also for his work on Chicago's World's Columbian Exposition in 1893, was an obvious choice to work on the plan, which would follow his principles concerning the appropriate grouping of buildings and the creation of vistas using open spaces. Carrere and Brunner were both well-known New York architects steeped in the beaux arts style popular for public buildings, including the New York Public Library, designed by Carrere's firm and then under construction.

Following the general principles of the City Beautiful Movement, the Group Plan placed civic institutions around an open, landscaped green that would enhance views of the facades. The plan emphasized symmetry and order, two qualities so evidently lacking in the jerry-built industrial city. Despite Mayor Johnson's enthusiastic support for the Group Plan and its new vision for downtown, the buildings around the mall gathered slowly. The federal building came first, in 1910, then the Cuyahoga County Courthouse a year later, followed by City Hall in 1915. The public auditorium joined the mall in 1922, and the public library, paired with the federal building at the south end, in 1925. Music Hall was added to the auditorium in 1929, and finally the Board of Education building took its place between the library and Music Hall in 1930. In addition to these expected buildings, the mall gained another stately public building in 1923, when the Federal Reserve Bank, created in 1914, moved into its own building, a substantial Italian Renaissance structure on Superior Avenue between East 6th and 9th Streets. The Federal Reserve's selection of Cleveland as one of the nation's twelve regional locations served as both recognition and affirmation of the city's status as a financial center. And the placement and architecture of the building made it seem like part of the plan.

Not all aspects of the Group Plan became reality. Burnham envisioned a new union passenger depot on the lake end of the mall, along the New York Central and Pennsylvania tracks. The depot's location would ensure that crowds of pedestrians would move through and enjoy the mall. Passengers would disembark, leave the station, and see before them a grand and orderly space. Failure to reach agreement with the various railroad companies prevented the creation of the new station, which was eventually superseded by the Van Sweringens' union terminal plan for Public Square, five blocks to the south. Still, Burnham's unbuilt depot made centralization the most evident theme of the plan. The drawing together of government buildings, the placement of the station, even the planning process itself, which Burnham preferred not to be too democratic lest he have to alter his vision to meet the desires of the people, all spoke to centralization. The Group Plan helped Cleveland make the claim that even in profit-centered industrial America beautiful urban landscapes might be built, and, of course, government could make it happen. It was just the first wave of the transformations that would come later in the century, as expanding power allowed government to reshape the physical city to serve visual and cultural ends rather than merely facilitate economic growth. All this seemed so progressive, in the language of the day, but ironically Burnham's modern city would be filled with neoclassical facades. The beaux arts public buildings, so common in American cities, affirm that this was a half-step in the remaking of cities. Burnham, Carrere, and Brunner were looking backward just as much as forward.

PERSPECTIVE CANNOT BE ATTAINED BY REMINISCENCES

At the close of 1966, Central National Bank finalized its purchase of the six-story Ellington Apartments, a stately building that had anchored the corner of East 9th and Superior since 1884. All the tenants would have to move by March 1967, and the building would have to come down to make way for the bank tower. In an editorial marking the beginning of the demolition that summer, the *Plain Dealer* praised the "Change for Better," calling the Ellington "another Cleveland landmark which simply fell victim to age and deterioration." This was an odd assertion, of course, since what it really fell victim to was Central's interest in having that prime corner downtown. Central offered enough money for the land to persuade the owners of a down-at-the-heels apartment building to let it go, and the bank transformed the corner from its mid-rise past to its high-rise future. This was market-led urban renewal.[26]

There was nothing new about this kind of transaction. Industrial cities worked this way. Older buildings gave way to new. On rare occasions entire neighborhoods disappeared. City residents sometimes marked demolitions with nostalgia for bygone eras, sometimes pined for meaningful buildings as they disappeared or mourned the passing of favorite businesses, but the very idea of demolition to make way for the new elicited little protest, since everyone knew that the construction of cities was predicated on destruction. A century of demolition had given rise to larger and larger buildings, to housing with better plumbing and wiring, to inspiring architecture, physical displays of the city's wealth. Demolition was most intense in and around downtown, where competition for valuable space drove the continuous recycling of real estate. Until the early 1930s, downtown—in Cleveland and in all large industrial cities—was in constant flux at its skyscraping core and its expanding edge, where commercial uses pressed into formerly residential neighborhoods and single-family homes fell by the dozens.

Market forces did not act alone. In the twentieth century, local governments combined new tools, such as planning and zoning, and old powers, especially eminent domain, to purposefully remake parts of the city. Driven by a new ideology that described some places as diseased or obsolete, Clevelanders began to see the value of government-led clearance. The city cleared more than one hundred acres—and dozens of buildings—to make room for Burnham's Group Plan. Many of those buildings were replaced by lawn. Building the mall required the removal of the tenderloin district, full of saloons, brothels, and gambling joints; it was just the type of place Progressives hoped to eliminate from the city. Then in the late 1920s, using the indispensable government power of eminent domain, the Van Sweringen brothers cleared a thousand buildings in the very heart of downtown to make way for the union terminal complex. Stretching from the southwest corner of Public Square nearly to the river's edge, the complex replaced hundreds of businesses—hotels, saloons, small factories, warehouses, and retail shops. The area had also been home to working-class residents of various ethnicities, some of them living in the temporary housing provided by hotels and almost all of them living in crowded, dirty conditions, hard up against the industry in the valley. This is the way slum clearance had worked for decades. The expanding downtown and expanding industrial plants forced the demolition of the city's oldest and often its most poorly kept housing.

What was gained from all this demolition allowed Clevelanders to forget what was lost. Few Clevelanders walked the mall and lamented the disappearance of the tenderloin, which reappeared elsewhere anyway, just to the east, farther from the core. And Terminal Tower already dominated the skyline before the finest building in the old neighborhood—the seven-story, red-brick Romanesque Telephone Building on West 3rd Street—met its inevitable demise. Over decades, the creative destruction of city building inspired much praise and little protest.

The Great Depression changed everything. The transformative capitalist engine idled, and older buildings decayed—noticeably. Reformers, planners, and politicians aggressively asserted the need for government action. In early July 1933, Cleveland hosted a conference on slum clearance. Attended by planners from around the country, the meeting featured a variety of lectures from leading urban theorists. It also featured a welcoming talk by Cleveland mayor Ray T. Miller. Giving his sense of the problem at hand, Miller emphasized that cities had grown too fast, without planning—surely a problem in Cleveland. Now, with the deepening economic crisis, the consequences of chaotic development were becoming clear. "We have cities in which acres of land lie idle with other acres covered with congested slums, productive of unhealthy living," Miller said. And municipalities' number-one planning tool—zoning—hadn't worked well in places where buildings already existed. "I speak of re-building our cities, because to me slum clearance is more than merely demolishing antiquated dwellings and replacing them with modern structures. We must consider this subject as one which involves, in the final analysis, a possible re-building of large sections of our cities." What Miller and others at the conference desired was federal support for this rebuilding. In this, and in many other ways, Miller's vision presaged the postwar urban renewal program, even down to the abandonment of building public housing as a primary goal. Indeed, Miller emphasized the need for more parks: "I believe the day is coming when cities generally will demolish large areas of unprofitable buildings and devote them to recreation and education," he said presciently. "I believe that every city will eventually have its central park." Miller's vision, like Pei's nearly thirty years later, featured a new kind of city, where order, beauty, and recreation joined economic growth as urban goals.[27]

With the struggles of urban renewal in the early 1960s, and the widespread demolition that came with the building of highways, the practice of clearing away the old to make way for the new began to raise questions, sometimes from powerful places. What changed wasn't just the pace of the destruction, which indeed quickened thanks to the infusion of federal dollars, but also what was built. In the 1960s, the demolition of the Ellington Apartments paled in comparison to the destruction just a block north. With little or no protest, building after building fell in the Erieview section. One of those who *did* protest was Teresa Grisanti, who lived on St. Clair Avenue near East 12th Street, on property that Pei had designated for the construction of Erieview

Tower. A long-time owner and resident of a mixed residential and commercial building, of the type that was so common of nineteenth-century cities, Grisanti had taken good care of her building, which inspectors determined was indeed structurally sound and not "detrimental to the public health, safety or welfare" of the city—the legal standard for the taking of blighted property. Still, Grisanti's building was in a blighted district, which, by law, allowed the city to take her property through eminent domain, demolish her sound building, and sell the property to a developer. With the help of her son Alfred, a former downtown councilman, Grisanti sued the city, but the courts upheld the urban renewal plan, never fully considering the actual condition of Grisanti's building or even those around it, which the building inspector had declared problematic. Grisanti appealed all the way to the United States Supreme Court, which dismissed the case in November 1962 for want of a federal issue. By then the city had garnered federal support for the project—$33 million in loans and a capital grant of nearly $10 million. And the city had already contracted with the Erieview Corporation to build the tower.

In upholding every aspect of the city's urban renewal powers, Cuyahoga County's Common Pleas Court placed Erieview in the broader sweep of the city's history. In the decision, Judge Donald Lybarger wrote, "The engineers of the past did a good job of planning for the little city then of small consequence. But is a large part of the downtown area of the great metropolis of Cleveland to lie moribund in the cocoon which was woven for it when a village more than a century ago?" Trusting in planning and the vision of Pei, Lybarger fully supported the government's right to remake the city, even when faced with unwilling property owners who found themselves in districts that municipal employees had deemed blighted. Further, the court determined that it should not substitute its own opinions about what property was blighted for the opinions of the experts. In other words, the Common Pleas Court found, and all higher courts affirmed, that under current law the city's building inspectors had the authority to set in motion a process by which any property might be removed from the hands of its owner.[28]

Courts around the country were affirming the authority of cities to conduct urban renewal, and the forceful assertion of government power raised eyebrows and ire. Despite the fact that Erieview had broad local support—it passed City Council with a unanimous vote in 1960, for instance—the size of the takings area and the high quality of many of the buildings slated for demolition made it a favorite target for opponents of the federal program. In June 1963, the Comptroller General of the United States issued a lengthy report on Cleveland's program titled "Premature Approval of Large-Scale Demolition for Erieview," which argued that inspection of the buildings had been per-functory and that, contrary to federal law, only 20 percent of the buildings in the area were actually substandard. Indeed, many of the buildings identified as problematic by the city had only minor defects, such as the absence of self-closing doors for fire safety, which could have been easily rectified. In-stead of notifying property owners of building code violations, the city had counted the buildings as substandard. One such building was only twelve years old at the time of inspection and was found in need of chimney pointing and "venting of toilets." This was enough to earn the substandard classifica-tion. What was worse, the federal inspectors apparently rubber-stamped the local determinations of blight. Outraged congressmen, led by William Wid-nall, a Republican from New Jersey, called on Mayor Locher to explain Cleveland's action. Locher surrounded himself with the city's business elite when he testified before Congress in the fall of 1963, and in a unified front Cleveland's most powerful men explained Erieview's demolition of blighted and nonconforming buildings as necessary to permit private development—an odd but ultimately successful argument in defense of growing government power.[29]

Despite the court challenge and the hubbub in Washington, Erieview pro-ceeded. By Christmas 1963, forty-five buildings had been demolished. As Erieview Tower rose over the next year, workers cleared the remaining acre-age of phase one. By the fall of 1966, demolition in Erieview II had begun, with cleared sites temporarily used for parking. Backed by federal grants and loans, the demolition greatly outpaced development, which required private-sector capital and the prospect of profitability. Soon Clevelanders began to wonder just what was going on, as surface parking occupied nearly the entire site. Even the Cleveland Development Foundation, created a decade earlier to speed urban renewal, began to challenge the Locher administra-tion's ability to oversee the process, going so far as to call the city's staff in-competent. A series of articles by *Plain Dealer* reporter Donald Sabath revealed just how problematic urban renewal had become, how little progress had been made in Erieview and elsewhere in the city. In June 1966, the U.S. Department of Housing and Urban Development, which then administered urban renewal, issued a "16 Point Immediate Action Program," listing spe-cific steps Cleveland needed to take in order to remain eligible for federal dollars. All these actions concerned the University-Euclid project—the focus of the Civil Rights Commission hearing that spring. Over the next six months, Locher's administration was unable to complete the construction of new rec-reation areas, improve building inspection, or increase the frequency of garbage collection—each of which had been enumerated in the HUD list. In fact, in January 1967, HUD secretary Robert Weaver wrote that "few, if any of the objectives can properly be considered to have been fulfilled." In light of this continued incompetence, Weaver took the extraordinary step of freezing federal urban renewal funds awarded to Cleveland. They were not released until after Stokes entered office later that year.[30]

The accumulating scars of urban renewal and highway construction helped spark a movement for historic preservation around the United States. In Cleveland, fittingly, protests became more vocal and organized as yet another downtown building—the Mechanics Block, a five-story Second Empire gem on the corner of Prospect and Ontario—was threatened with demolition in 1970. Among the most vocal citizens was Maxine Levin, who had taken up the preservation cause after the death of her husband, a prominent attorney and long-time supporter of downtown. Levin garnered the attention and support of the popular *Plain Dealer* columnist George Condon, who lamented that summer, "Before we begin planning again for the unpredictable future, perhaps we should salvage what we can from the past, such as the Mechanics Block, a valuable heritage representing the city that used to be."[31]

Not everyone agreed with Levin and Condon, of course. The Greater Cleveland Growth Association reacted against the fledgling preservation sentiment in its summer 1970 issue of *Clevelander* magazine, which contained a new "perspective" feature that opened with the questions, "Remember the all-night Leader drug store at 9th and Superior? PJ's? The Ellington Apts? The Hickory Grill?" The brief column was accompanied by two images, one a small sepia-toned horizontal photo of the Ellington, and the other a large vertical photo of Central National Bank's new tower, which had replaced the drugstore, the grill, and the apartments. If the images themselves failed to convey the intended message, the prose made it clear: "True perspective cannot be attained by reminiscences and nostalgia, at the expense of what today means." The purpose of this new "perspective" column would be to remind readers "that although yesterday may be interesting, it is only a base from which to move forward."[32]

After years of sporadic protest, Cleveland's preservation movement gained municipal support in 1971, when the city created a landmarks commission. The commission couldn't prevent the demolition of buildings but could at least begin the process of surveying and marking the city's historic assets. The movement gained an organizational center in 1972 with the creation of the Downtown Restoration Society. The very name of the organization spoke to the movement's primary area of concern, where so much architectural heritage had already disappeared and more was threatened. The protests concerned not just what was lost but also what was coming, which sometimes was merely a parking garage or a nondescript modern building, as was the case with the Mechanics Block. The Downtown Restoration Society's key figures included Maxine Levin and Tom Campbell, the Cleveland State historian who had stood with Stokes to remind Cleveland of its proud history and Tom L. Johnson, the embodiment of progressive government.

WE WERE TRYING

In May 1990, bank executives opened the time capsule at the corner of 9th and Superior. The date, set at the laying of the cornerstone just twenty-one years earlier, was intended to mark the one hundredth anniversary of Central National Bank's creation, but the executives who opened the capsule worked for Society National Bank, which had purchased Central in 1985. Ironically, the disappearance of Central National Bank said more about the changes in the city than anything the capsule held, the contents of which the *Plain Dealer* listed in its coverage of the "event," which itself was hardly a moment of celebration. Not only had Central National Bank disappeared through acquisition, but Cleveland too continued to disappear. Since the enclosing of the time capsule, the city had lost another 250,000 residents, shedding a third of its population. Although optimists could find reason for hope that the decline was slowing, clearly the growth promised by urban renewal had not materialized.

Among the items removed from the time capsule was the Greater Cleveland Growth Association's "Outlook for Greater Cleveland in 1990." As one might expect, the pro-growth business organization predicted great things for Cleveland, making no mention of the "crisis in the urban environment" at the core of Stokes's note to the future. Instead, the Growth Association predicted that the Cleveland region would have 4.7 million citizens by 1990, or about 1.8 million more than the metropolitan area actually had. "Steelmaking and metal manufacturing, spurred by new, exotic and still undiscovered applications of research in space travel and other new knowledge, will continue to be the base for the region's economy," the association predicted, missing altogether the collapse of the American steel industry, especially as a major employer. And the association predicted that a new airport out in Lake Erie, which Locher had proposed in 1966, would "provide citizens of Greater Cleveland and nearby areas with the best air service in the nation to all parts of the world." In sum, the outlook for 1990 asserted that Cleveland would be the focal point of a vast, thriving metropolis stretching from Toledo to

Pittsburgh. This wildly optimistic forecast suggested that Cleveland's business community assumed that the setbacks of the 1960s would be temporary, that they shouldn't prevent fantastic visions of future success.[33]

The brief *Plain Dealer* article describing the opening of the time capsule did not dwell on the broader trajectory of Cleveland or even its downtown, and instead highlighted the comments left by the then mayor Carl Stokes. After spending several years as a news broadcaster in New York, Stokes was now back in Cleveland serving as a municipal judge, although he apparently did not return to the bank for the time capsule's opening. The *Plain Dealer* offered no commentary on the capsule contents, no critique of the off-base predictions, and no assessment of the mayor's speech. But the article ended with a final quote from Stokes that suggested its own critique: "We were trying."[34]

4 Policy and the Polluted City

East 55th Street runs through some of Cleveland's most troubled neighborhoods. A five-mile thoroughfare extending due north from the industrial South Side, it stretches along Outhwaite Homes in Central, under the Pennsylvania Railroad bridge and past the western end of Hough Avenue, before ducking under the New York Central's tracks and rising over the Shoreway, just before ending at Lake Erie. Here, on June 17, 1969, Mayor Stokes joined Governor Rhodes for the dedication of the recently completed East 55th Street Marina. After the Coast Guard ceremoniously raised an American flag over the new facility, Kiely Cronin, the city's director of port control, introduced a few local and state officials, the governor made some remarks, and then Stokes stepped forward to speak. "The greatest significance of this ceremony today is the recognition we are giving to cooperation between the State of Ohio and the City of Cleveland," he said, only hinting at the increasingly important but strained relationship between the two. He continued, shifting to a happier theme: "The state and the city have combined to bring into being a facility which utilizes Lake Erie as the priceless recreational asset it can and must be, a source of delight, relaxation and fun—'recreation' in the true sense of the word—not only for Greater Clevelanders but for visitors from the whole northern part of the state."[1]

Stokes was a careful speech maker, writing out in advance even short talks, like this one, wanting to be certain that he hit the right notes and took advantage of the opportunity to deliver a message. Having pressed two important themes—state and local cooperation and the need to make the most of natural assets—the mayor went further, pressing another theme that had come to dominate his thinking. "While we have the governor here—and this refreshing breeze in our faces—I cannot help but mention the urban crisis and

Cleveland's great need for help from Columbus." He spoke directly to the governor: "When you get back to Columbus, we hope you remember that all kinds of problems remain here—housing, welfare, air and water pollution, education, law enforcement." The city would need state help, not just in the form of state tax dollars but also through the creation and enforcement of better state laws, especially regarding pollution.

The East 55th Street Marina was a particularly appropriate place to make this argument. Stokes said, somewhat awkwardly, that the city's problems were not "docked right here, except perhaps for water pollution, but they exist right behind that skyline." This phrase, "behind that skyline," was an odd choice, perhaps written the day before as he sat in City Hall nearly surrounded by sky-scrapers. But this morning, Stokes and the others were three miles from downtown, and even Erieview Tower was quite small in the distance and par-tially obscured by the smokestacks of the Municipal Light power plant, which sat just to the west of the marina. And the largest structure near the dedication ceremony was the massive coal-fired Lake Shore Plant of the Illuminating Company, looming over the lake just a few hundred yards to the east. Perhaps Stokes was being as careful as ever when he said "skyline," hoping that those gathered, including the governor, would take a moment to dwell on these two power plants, for their stacks took on considerable meaning in the polluted city, garnering outsized attention in the struggle for clean air.

And so here was Stokes, dedicating a new marina, praising the building of a new recreational city, looking out over a terribly polluted Lake Erie, while standing very nearly in the shadow of two notoriously smoky power plants, which themselves were inauspiciously nestled in a rapidly deteriorating indus-trial zone along the New York Central tracks and in close proximity to communities—Central and Hough—that constituted much of the city's "crisis ghetto," neighborhoods that had little use for slips to dock pricey sailboats and motor cruisers. The city planners who in 1949 had envisioned this facility, or something like it, and the planners who actually designed it in the 1960s, and Stokes, who oversaw its completion, all understood that the 274-berth marina had been built for people who lived some distance from 55th Street. With 270 parking spaces and easy access to the Shoreway, which engineers were busy upgrading to meet federal standards for interstate highways, the new marina would be convenient to boaters from around the region. On this day, a mayor so attuned to the needs of ghetto residents left unasked the increasingly obvi-ous question: who would be served by the new service city?

Three days before the dedication, Stokes received a letter of support from Willie L. Morrow, a former city resident who had moved to East Cleveland, one of the earliest suburbs to admit large numbers of African American residents. He still worked downtown, at the Central National Bank branch on Public Square, and he followed with great interest press coverage of the mayor. After quoting Martin Luther King Jr. on the issue of judging people on the content of their character and not on the color of their skin, Morrow encouraged Stokes to carry on. "Mr. Mayor keep up the good works you are doing and don't let no body turn you around. Keep on fighting for fair housing in the Lee Seville area and everywhere, keep on fighting for gun control laws, keep on fighting for air pollution control, but most of all keep on fighting for a fair and better government for the citizens of all races of Cleveland and this great nation of ours." The range of issues Morrow referenced spoke to the breadth of the mayor's agenda, but they all came down to one: fair and better government. Morrow knew that better policy and better enforcement would be critical to solving Cleveland's problems. At the marina that morning, politicians gathered to celebrate a small step forward—government cooperation and the completion of a long-planned project. Still, many Clevelanders, even many nearby, could be forgiven if they saw little reason to celebrate.[2]

THE FISH WILL LEARN

A year before the marina ceremony, Mayor Stokes had taken part in another celebration at the lakefront, one that received more attention from the press. On the last day of July 1968, Stokes took off his shoes, rolled up his pants, and waded into Lake Erie, smiling and frolicking with neighborhood kids at White City Beach on the far East Side. Clearly in a playful mood, Stokes joked with the press for the first time since the Glenville riots began the week before. With his spirits up and his guard down, he saw a young woman in a bikini and commented to a *Plain Dealer* reporter, "That's what we mean by Black is Beautiful." Commanded by their mayor, nearly the entire cabinet attended this event, a celebration of the beach's opening. Director of Public Utilities Ben Stefanski, whose department had charge of water pollution control, stripped down to a bathing suit and joined the kids in the lake, and at least one cabinet member was thrown in wearing his clothes. In keeping with the upbeat (and somewhat offbeat) events, Stokes cut a ceremonial fishnet and directed a student band for a couple of numbers. After a terrible week—seven people killed, three of them police officers, arson, National Guard patrols, and heightened racial tensions throughout the city—on this day the sense of relief was palpable. The violence had ended, and the city could cool itself in the lake, swimming at White City for the first time in more than a decade.

Months before, Stokes had sat with his cabinet brainstorming over how the mayor could keep his pledge that Clevelanders would once again safely swim in Lake Erie. Fouled by untreated sewage, city beaches had remained closed summer after summer because bacteria counts exceeded recommended levels. Stefanski decided that instead of cleaning the entire lake—a long-term and incredibly expensive proposition—the city could instead clean just a small part, keep it clean, and invite the public to swim. He hired Havens and Emerson, an engineering firm based in Cleveland and New York, to design what became known as "a swimming pool in the lake" at White City, a municipally owned beach that retained the name of a long-ago failed amusement park, which itself had taken its name from the Chicago World's Columbian Exposition of 1893. Using a $325,000 grant from the Federal Water Pollution Control Administration, the city hired a contractor to clear the beach of debris and soiled sand, build a protective crib, and hang weighted vinyl curtains from pontoons floating in a line out in the lake, separating the beach area from the rest of the lake. The city then doused the pool with chlorine to bring coliform levels down to the safe range. A week after the transformed beach officially opened, bacteria levels had dropped below the 1,000-count ceiling recommended for swimming, but just below. So Raymond Roth, the city employee overseeing the project, told the *Cleveland Press* that 4,000 gallons of liquid chlorine would be poured into the pool, supplementing the 350 pounds of powdered chlorine that had been added by hand each day. The liquid chlorine was donated by Dow Chemical, which hoped the White City experiment would allow it to measure the effects of this type of application. Meanwhile, outside the heavy vinyl curtains, discharges from polluted streams, sewer overflows, and the Easterly Sewage Treatment Plant—directly abutting the beach—kept lake waters filthy and unsafe.[3]

Lake Erie pollution had become a broad public concern by 1968. The *Plain Dealer* ran a weekly "Beach Bacteria" feature, a chart listing bacteria counts at the region's popular swimming spots. Headlands State Park, twenty miles northeast of the city, scored well below the threshold for safety. Huntington Beach, twelve miles to the west, was also safe. Bacteria counts along the city's shore were another story. Outside the pool at White City, the count could reach well above 5,000. In August, Edgewater Beach, just to the west of the Cuyahoga's mouth, scored an astounding 110,000.[4] Despite the fact that the lake remained terribly polluted along Cleveland's shore, Stokes was pleased with the results of the pool-in-the-lake experiment. The administration estimated that a thousand people used the beach each day in the summer of 1968—many more than would have defied the Beach Closed signs that had greeted visitors in previous years. Indeed, the pool in the lake worked well enough that the administration decided to repeat it the following year and even open an additional pool at Edgewater Park, where bacteria counts were astronomical.

Stokes described the pool in the lake in his testimony before a U.S. House Appropriations Committee on June 5, 1969, as Congress debated spending millions of dollars to clean up the Great Lakes. He also relayed to Congress a list of Cleveland's accomplishments in the effort to control its contribution to Lake Erie's pollution, focusing on the passage of a $100 million clean-water bond issue in 1968 and the passage of another $120 million state-level bond. Still, Stokes said that the lake's full recovery, a recovery that "will permit complete utilization of the water resources in our area for recreation, for commercial fishing and for all forms of light and heavy manufacturing and processing industries—will cost in excess of one billion." Given this price tag, Stokes, like his predecessor Ralph Locher, recommended federal involvement in sewage treatment plant construction modeled on the funding formula used to build interstate highways, in which the federal government paid 90 percent of construction costs. "Utilization of water resources," Stokes argued, "is as vital to our economy as a well-developed highway system."[5]

Knowing that the budget the Appropriations Committee was considering would not contain this much support, Stokes brought with him a list of small, discrete "demonstration projects" that might be funded and completed in short order. The list included creating diked areas for the storage of materials dredged from shipping channels, materials that had traditionally been dumped in the lake, where they continued to ooze pollutants. There was a scheme to combat pollution from sewer overflows by creating an impoundment area in the lake where untreated wastes could be stored and gradually cleaned. The city might even attempt "in-stream treatment techniques," such as adding chemicals to creeks and stream beds. Or perhaps the city could use federal dollars to install aerators in the lake, in the hopes of reducing blue-green algal blooms by improving oxygen levels. All these proposals shared a trait with the swimming pool at White City Beach: they projected engineering solutions out into the lake (or streams) instead of creating solutions closer to the actual sources of pollution—the city sewers and industries that let their untreated effluent run into waterways. If this list represented a failure of vision, it wasn't Stokes's. He knew how to solve the problem. Instead, the list of partial and temporary solutions represented a failure of funding. No one knew how the real solution would be paid for.[6]

At the congressional hearing, the mayor described the extraordinary swimming pool in the lake with pride, taking the time to praise the efforts of Stefanski, who sat next to him at the table. "None of us likes stop-gap or temporary measures when science and technology have provided us with the potential for solution of a problem," his prepared statement read, but "let me tell you what we did last year in Cleveland to make a portion of Lake Erie available once again for bathing by children and families, as it was when I was a youth." Stokes then joked for a moment before moving on. "That is a place where I have to apologize for because it is called White City. We are going to try to change that name, Mr. Chairman. It creates certain problems for me." In the coverage of the swimming pool's opening the year before, race had not been an issue, but clearly Stokes had not forgotten the desegregation battles earlier in the decade, when wade-ins forced communities to address discrimination at public beaches. Just days after the last fires of the Glenville riots had been doused, here was Stokes wading in the lake on the city's white far East Side. Perhaps even more memorable, however, a month after he testified before Congress, Stokes actually went swimming in the pool in the lake at Edgewater Beach on the white West Side. At a combined celebration of the pool's opening and the Fourth of July, the mayor overcame his modesty and joined Stefanski and dozens of children in the lake. That was one small step toward the creation of a recreational city, and a small step in the creation of an integrated city, too.

Unfortunately, that Independence Day would be remembered not because Stokes ensured that the beach would welcome both black and white swimmers, or because the beach welcomed swimmers at all after a long, polluted hiatus, but because a terrible storm rushed in from the northwest, catching thousands of people without shelter on the shore and hundreds of boaters unprotected out on the lake. The crowd at Edgewater, perhaps slow to give up prime seats for the evening's fireworks, dispersed too late to avoid debris thrown by gusting winds. Seven people died as the storm passed over Cleveland, most of them crushed by falling trees, including two who were running for the picnic shelter at Edgewater Park. The power went out in much of the city—and much of the region—and downed trees blocked streets, impeding rescue efforts. "The West Side was completely devastated as far as trees were concerned," Stefanski remembered two years later. He and his crews in the Public Utilities Department struggled with the cleanup, a long and arduous task, but Stefanski couldn't stop thinking about his pool in the lake at Edgewater Beach. When the storm hit, boats had streamed to shore as fast as they

Figure 7. Crowds gathered at Edgewater Beach on July 4, 1969, to help Carl Stokes and Ben Stefanski celebrate the opening of the pool in the lake and the nation's independence. Although the mayor was happy to talk to the press, his daughter Condi, clinging to his arm, was less comfortable with the crowd. Photo by John W. Mott. Cleveland Press Collection, Cleveland State University.

could, many of them running over the city's pontoons, sinking them. The vinyl curtain fell. The swimming pool in the lake had been breached.[7]

Two weeks later, another, smaller disaster struck the pool in the lake on the other end of town, when high winds and heavy chop continuously mixed the chlorinated and polluted waters over the pontoons and around the curtain wall. The city retaliated with more chlorine, which left beachgoers unhappy with the chemical smell and, the *Plain Dealer* reported, left fishermen even unhappier because the heavily chlorinated water had escaped the pool and caused a minor fish kill. Hundreds of perch, sheepshead, and carp floated on the surface. "White City Beach Fish Perish in Chlorine 'Flood,'" read the headline above a column written by Outdoor Editor Lou Gale. He described "super-bleached fish" and suggested that White City had taken on a new name, though not one Stokes would have approved: "Chlorine Beach." After the July 4th storm and now these high winds, one might begin to think that the lake didn't want to be treated this way.[8]

Later that summer, East Side Cleveland resident Annette Koman visited the repaired pool at Edgewater Beach with some friends. She was so put off by what she found that she typed up a letter of complaint to Mayor Stokes. "I am telling you," she wrote, "it was the worst beach I have ever went to! It was full of mud and a kind of mossy substance that was similar to quicksand." She also complained about the number of dead fish that had washed up on the shore. "The polluted water probably killed them," she concluded. The mayor's office directed the letter to Stefanski, asking him to respond, but it wound up on the desk of Edward Martin, who had arrived earlier in the year to direct the city's new Clean Water Task Force. Hired away from the Federal Water Pollution Control Administration, Martin was the city's highest-paid employee, charged with solving one of Cleveland's most pressing problems. As he mapped out a strategy for building new sewers and enlarging treatment plants, he took the time to respond to Koman, and not with a form letter acknowledging the threats posed by water pollution and reassuring her with a list of the city's actions—the typical bureaucratic reply to citizen complaints. Instead, he addressed her concerns one by one. "With respect to Edgewater Beach," he wrote, "we have taken steps to make the water safe for swimming. The water is treated with chlorine to kill the coliform bacteria that makes the water unsafe. The chlorine also kills the fish, unfortunately, which is why dead fish occasionally wash up on the beach." With this explanation made, Martin then asserted, "Eventually, the fish will learn to avoid this area."[9]

A PLEASANTER PLACE TO LIVE

Fish probably had trouble learning to avoid the chlorinated lakeshore, but Koman and her friends likely learned to stay away from Edgewater Beach. In a common trend in metropolitan America, natural amenities in and around cities suffered from abuse and neglect, and those who could afford to sought recreational opportunities beyond the core. In metropolitan Cleveland, this meant driving to cleaner suburban beaches, well away from the region's major sewer outfalls. Poorer city residents, especially those who didn't own cars, had a harder time avoiding polluted environments, of course. Inner-city residents, especially those in cash-strapped cities like Cleveland, learned not to expect much in the way of natural recreation. This was just one of the ways in which the environmental crisis and the urban crisis reinforced each other.

As Clevelanders learned to avoid polluted beaches, they also began to avoid other polluted areas of the city. In one of the most significant demographic trends of the late twentieth century, Americans increasingly moved away from polluted environments. This was particularly evident in the depopulation of industrial neighborhoods in the postwar decades. Although these neighborhoods had a variety of problems, such as poor housing quality, pollution—especially air pollution—was a significant contributor to discontent. Take for instance a June 1968 letter to Mayor Stokes from JoAnne Olszewski, a South Side resident, in which she expressed her support for the mayor but asked that he turn his energy toward air pollution. As a nursing student at St. Alexis Hospital on Broadway near East 55th Street, she attended "many patients (many are nonsmokers) needlessly suffering from chronic emphysema, carcinoma of the lungs and other respiratory problems." She had recently opened a hospital window to let in the spring air but instead was greeted by horrible pollution from the steel mills, which were just a half mile away. "I know the steel industry is vital to Cleveland's industrial wealth and power but certainly something should be done about this health hazard," she wrote. "I find it difficult to comprehend how patients can get well breathing in this foul air. St. Alexis is unfortunate to be located so near the steel mills, but its location is ideal according to the great number of patients she serves including many industrial workers and their families."[10]

Olszewski's letter nicely summarized the problem in Cleveland's most polluted neighborhoods, such as North and South Broadway, Central, Tremont, and Brooklyn. They were convenient to industrial employers and had filled with industrial workers, but they had never been especially desirable places to live. Despite strong ethnic neighborhood cultures, especially in North and South Broadway, the neighborhoods surrounding St. Alexis, families that could afford to move farther from the mills generally did. This was increasingly the case in the postwar era as the Jones & Laughlin and Republic steel companies made a series of investments in their riverside mills, some of which greatly increased the amount of pollution imposed on nearby neighborhoods.

Smoke from the mills was not a new problem, of course. Decades before Olszewski expressed her concerns to Stokes, Cleveland had participated in the Progressive Era smoke abatement movement, which gathered momentum after Charles F. Olney, an avid art collector, created the Society for the Promotion of Atmospheric Purity in 1892. Olney's Tremont home was not far from the industry and rail lines along Walworth Run and, nearly as close, the Cuyahoga flats. Olney began his antismoke crusade while constructing an art gallery attached to his home, and so his efforts were dedicated to the protection of his paintings. After the turn of the century (and Olney's death), the city took a number of steps to solve its smoke problems, from passing new laws to hiring prominent engineers as smoke inspectors, even hosting national air pollution control conferences and conducting major studies on the subject. All this effort had little effect on air quality, but it led to a major overhaul of the antismoke ordinance in 1947, when Cleveland created a Division of Air Pollution Control in the Department of Public Health and Welfare. The level of attention on the issue reflected the continuous public concern about smoke and the failure of the city and industry to effectively address it over these many decades. Even as technological advances led to periodic improvements, the city's industrial growth—especially in steel manufacturing—ensured that the city would remain smoky.

The problem persisted for one significant reason: the widely held belief that the expansion of industry was essential to the city's prosperity. In a typically tepid effort to limit smoke, the Regional Association of Cleveland formed a Smoke Abatement Committee in 1937. Using the letterhead of William Strong, chair of the Cuyahoga County Planning Commission, the committee sent out dozens of letters announcing its effort to draft a better ordinance. "We fully realize that in an industrial city all that can be hoped for is to minimize the amount of smoke in the air," the letter read. "We, however, feel that a great deal can be done to make Cleveland a pleasanter place to live in without in any wise interfering with the national operation and expansion of its industrial activity." Even this weak foray into antismoke activism elicited concern, however. Arch Klumph, a prominent businessman and Rotary Club leader, complained to Ernest J. Bohn, director of the Cleveland Metropolitan Housing Authority and a participant in the fledgling movement: "There is one thing we must not forget—that much of the smoke is due to factories providing work for men and women. I wish we had a lot more smoke in Cleveland today, if it meant more business." This last sentiment was no doubt commonly held in the depression-wracked city. "Furthermore," Klumph wrote, "I would rather see smoke than street walkers and cheap and unsightly hamburger stands such as you will find from one end to another along the street and allowed to be built right up to the sidewalk." Clearly opinions varied on the topic of how to make Cleveland a pleasanter place to live.[11]

While not all Clevelanders would have agreed with Klumph's concerns about hamburger stands, most would have agreed with his thoughts on smoke. Lax environmental regulation and heavily polluted air had become hallmarks of the industrial city—not just in Cleveland but around the nation. After the wartime boom and years of full employment, however, patience with industrial pollution grew thin. Beginning in 1946, Joseph Swatek, a Bohemian immigrant who sold and leased real estate from his office on Broadway near East 55th Street, took on the largest polluters of his neighborhood, Grasselli Chemical and Republic Steel, which sat side by side along the Cuyahoga. He wrote a series of articles complaining of smoke in the *Neighborhood News*, which served North and South Broadway. He also wrote a string of letters to Mayor Thomas Burke, in which he blamed "the two great plants" for "virtually destroying our neighborhood." Swatek claimed the companies "haven't hardly moved a finger to abate at least some of the smoke, dirt and acids, emanating daily from their plants in the Cuyahoga Valley." Indeed, the situation had deteriorated at Republic, where according to Swatek newly opened facilities "have been belching out volumes of fine red powder, which covers everything in reach." A month later, Swatek wrote to Burke again, noting that there had been no respite in the red dust. "I am trying to encourage the suffering people of the neighborhood to be patient as improvement is coming soon," he wrote, "but there is rumbling going on and unless this dumping of the red dust is stopped soon, you will hear from the masses direct." In another letter, sent in February 1947, Swatek reported to Burke that Republic had "sent forth tons and tons of that red ore dust, covering streets, roof tops and autos caught in the neighborhood." Then Swatek revealed how important this was to his livelihood in real estate, not just to his physical comfort and health. "We cannot lay down and have our properties damaged and people dissatisfied to the extent that they are threatening to leave the neighborhood as soon as possible. We all have too much at stake here and should this air pollution continue here much longer the exodus will surely result."[12]

Republic apparently took steps to reduce the pollution, which also periodically waned when production slowed. But that spring, Swatek reported more bad news to the mayor. "We, out here are fighting hard and doing everything possible and within the law, but this lawless smoke nuisance is getting the best of the neighborhood and is beginning to invite the kind of element that bespoiled other sections of our once fair town." In the continuing pollution, Swatek saw the seeds of his entire community's demise. Although he didn't mention race, the meaning of "the kind of element" to which he referred is clear. If current residents—Czech and Polish families primarily—put their homes on the market, they might find African American buyers. Air pollution was a periodically vexing problem, one to be taken seriously, but for Swatek, demographic transition represented a more permanent threat. And now he understood how the two were related.[13]

Swatek's campaign met with little success. The neighborhood's protests persisted into the 1950s, but the exodus many had feared only gathered momentum. In 1952, Louis Mikol complained about the air quality around his Nursery Avenue home to his congressman, Robert Crosser, who in turn asked Mayor Burke to explain why living in North Broadway was so unpleasant. As would remain common among Cleveland politicians for another decade, Burke offered little more than a defense of industry, claiming, "We think that conditions are gradually being improved" and that the conditions that led to Mikol's complaint had been corrected and "will not happen again." Burke's administration hadn't ignored the pollution problem, but by 1952 the mayor must have understood how intractable it really was. Eight years earlier, in the summer of 1944, police officer Henry Schroeder had investigated complaints of "smoke, dust, noise, and fumes" from Republic Steel. He walked along Eggers and Stillson Avenues, talking with residents and getting a sense of the problem. Many complained of the heavy red smoke, but others seemed to tolerate it fine. Schroeder interviewed residents at sixteen homes, among them Rosie Port, who lived along Independence Road, from which Eggers and Stillson ran west out onto a finger of land that overlooked Republic's Plant No. 5 before ending just above the company's dump. "She is an old resident," Schroeder reported, "and is trying to sell her place to get away from it all"[14]—just as Swatek feared.

Cleveland's economic elite had long argued for lax regulation so that industrial employers would add jobs and build the city. Now persistent and invidious industrial pollution was helping tear Cleveland apart. Over time the residents left, and the buildings did, too. None of the homes Schroeder visited in 1944 still exists; Mikol's home is gone, and so is St. Alexis Hospital, demolished in 2007. The neighborhoods of the industrial South Side have slowly disappeared—resident by resident and building by building—a process that has made clear how the environmental crisis and the urban crisis amplified each other.

SAVE LAKE ERIE NOW

Air pollution sparked a long, periodically intense public involvement in the politics of pollution control, while water pollution remained largely the concern of experts and officials charged with supplying potable water to a growing city. But in the mid-1960s, troubling signs in Lake Erie—polluted beaches and declining fish stocks—heightened public awareness and action in another pollution control battle. The broad movement that developed included some long-standing organizations, such as the League of Women Voters, which began studying Great Lakes pollution in the 1950s, and the Isaak Walton

League, a club of sportsmen active in protecting waterways since its founding in 1922. Organized labor, especially the United Auto Workers, had also taken up the issue, largely as it concerned workers' access to swimming, fishing, and boating. Olga Madar, of the UAW's Recreation Department, had become an important voice in the growing movement. But in Cleveland, the effort to save Lake Erie was led by one indispensable and unexpected activist: David Blaushild, a well-known Shaker Heights Chevrolet dealer.

On April 8, 1965, Blaushild sent a formal demand to Mayor Locher and his director of law, Bronis Klementowicz, that they take action against a list of industrial polluters, including Republic Steel, U.S. Steel, Sherwin Williams, and Harshaw Chemical Company, each of which dumped industrial wastes into the Cuyahoga. The city's laws required pollution control, Blaushild pointed out, and the administration had been derelict in its duty. Three weeks later, Klementowicz responded that the city had no basis for legal action and that all the companies on the list were complying with the law—this despite the fact that they were clearly dumping wastes into the river. Blaushild and his lawyers, Roemish and Wright, whose offices were in the National City Bank Building downtown, had anticipated this response, and they set to work on a lawsuit. Using a corporation he controlled, Bar Realty, Blaushild sued the city in the Cuyahoga Common Pleas Court, demanding a writ of mandamus, which, if the judge approved, would require the city to enforce the law. Blaushild's lawsuit, filed May 26, included the relevant sections of the city's sanitary code, which clearly outlawed the "discharge of offensive substances into public waterways" and even listed some of the offending substances: spent acid, spent alkali, petroleum, or "oily matter." Not coincidentally, these were just the types of wastes steel mills and chemical manufacturers were likely to drain into the Cuyahoga.[15]

The lawsuit wasn't the first volley in Blaushild's war on water pollution. His concern for the Shaker Lakes, just around the corner from his Shaker Heights apartment, had grown into a broader concern about water pollution every-where, but especially Lake Erie. In the spring of 1964, he had taken out ad-vertisements in both the *Cleveland Press* and the *Plain Dealer*. "Lake Erie is dying," one ad read. "Does anybody care?" That summer he bought a bill-board along the Shoreway: "Let's Stop Killing Lake Erie." He even used his clout as a major advertiser to influence Louis Seltzer, publisher of the *Press*, demanding that he step up his coverage of pollution issues. Seltzer responded by creating a fulltime environment beat for one of his reporters: Betty Klaric, who had been with the *Press* since 1955. Klaric had reported for the women's department and more recently served as a general assignment reporter, which

𝓕𝑖𝑔𝑢𝑟𝑒 8. Harshaw Chemical made colorful contributions to the Cuyahoga, making it a target for the antipollution crusader David Blaushild. Here calcium sulfate pours from the plant into the river in September 1969. Photo by Bill Nehez. Cleveland Press Collection, Cleveland State University.

had her occasionally filing stories on environmental issues. By the end of 1965, she reported exclusively on the environment, and her frequent water pollution stories appeared under a common logo that read "Save Lake Erie Now."[16]

Blaushild coupled the selling of Chevrolets with saving Lake Erie. He led a campaign to get Cleveland-area communities to pass resolutions addressed to Governor Rhodes demanding action on water pollution. As Blaushild pressed his lawsuit, more than thirty communities sent this resolution to Columbus, including Cleveland, Shaker Heights, Bratenahl, Maple Heights, and Parma Heights. Blaushild also led a campaign to gather individual petitions and letters of concern, even using newspaper advertisements that asked readers to clip, fill out, and send to him little coupons that read: "I share your deep concern about pollution of Lake Erie. I believe we need immediate action to save Lake Erie from destruction." More than two hundred thousand people signed his petition demanding that laws be enforced and that municipalities build proper treatment plants.

In August 1965, a few months after he had filed his lawsuit, Blaushild described his efforts at a downtown Cleveland conference sponsored by the federal Department of Health, Education and Welfare titled "In the Matter of Pollution of Lake Erie and Its Tributaries." Part of a series of federally organized meetings on the Great Lakes held throughout the region, and chaired by Murray Stein, the chief enforcement officer at the federal Division of Water Supply and Pollution Control, the conference featured testimony from a wide range of witnesses, from scientists to activists, who addressed a panel composed of officials from the federal government as well as the lake's watershed states—Ohio, Michigan, Indiana, Pennsylvania, and New York. Blaushild's blunt testimony made his frustration clear. "I am voicing the sentiments of hundreds of thousands of cynical, disillusioned residents of Northern Ohio, weary of the banalities and lethargy of our public officials in their attitudes towards the crucial problem of water pollution, and weary too of the negative, snide, condescending attitude of some of our major industries who keep wantonly infecting our waters, at the complete expense of an ever-angering public," he said. Calling for an end to surveying the problem and a start to solving it, he said, "For God's sake, let's get to work." And he expressed the urgency common of the era: "Unless something is done now, it can come to pass that the lake that made Cleveland and Toledo the great cities they are, will, in its own death, destroy its destroyers."[17]

A month after the Lake Erie conference, the city responded to Blaushild's lawsuit. Law Director Klementowicz made two arguments. The least effective claimed that Bar Realty and Milly Blaushild, David's wife, whose name also appeared on the suit, had "not suffered any irreparable injury or damage as a result of the acts complained of in the petition" and that they were "not the 'parties beneficially interested' in the relief sought." In other words, Klementowicz argued that the Blaushilds had no standing to sue because they had no special relationship to Lake Erie or the Cuyahoga, or, at least, that they had not claimed such a relationship. Since the suit argued that uncontrolled pollution affected the supply of potable water and access to recreation, this wasn't an especially strong argument. At a hearing on the issue, Judge Charles White asked the city's lawyer, "Does a person have to swim in Lake Erie and come down with a disease to claim personal interest?" He then dismissed this argument outright. The other line of argument, however, eventually proved successful. The state of Ohio, through the Water Pollution Control Board, had issued permits to each of the companies listed in Blaushild's suit. Those permits, included in the city's response, literally permitted the discharge of wastes into the Cuyahoga and, in Klementowicz's view, prevented the city from taking action against Republic, U.S. Steel, Sherwin Williams, or Harshaw Chemical.[18]

The pollution permits, certificates issued by the State Department of Health and bearing the Ohio seal and the explicit language "has been granted permission to discharge," seemed like powerful evidence. But Judge Merle Hoddinott, who ultimately heard the case in 1970, after a series of delays, including one caused by the change of city administration, concluded that state law did not preclude local enforcement. "Confusion should not result to the polluter," Hoddinott wrote. "The City should be more aware of local problems and possible economic dislocations than the State board." Hoddinott ordered the city "to manage and supervise the elimination, control or regulation of any matter relating to the pollution of watercourses, rivers, streams or lakes bounding upon or within the City of Cleveland." In other words, he ordered the city to enforce its laws.[19]

The city appealed, and Stokes found himself in the unenviable position of fighting a lawsuit filed because of the failings of the previous administration even while attempting to take on water pollution more vigorously. In the end, the city was more successful in fighting the pollution suit in court than fighting pollution in the Cuyahoga, appealing the case to the Ohio Supreme Court, which overturned Hoddinott's ruling in May 1972, months after Stokes had left office. In essence, the court argued that city officials had "discretion" in performing their duties, and only in cases of "abuse of discretion" should the court substitute its authority for that of the officials. The discharge of wastes into the Cuyahoga, the actual water quality of the river, the broader concerns about Lake Erie—none of this appears in the court's opinion. By the time it reached the Ohio Supreme Court, Blaushild's demand that the city protect its residents from water pollution had devolved into a case about regulatory authority and the relationship between city and state. Ignoring the needs of the lake, the court decided that the city need not enforce its laws because of "the apparent necessity for cooperation between state and local government."[20]

After seven years, almost to the day, Blaushild lost his suit, but he had made progress in the larger struggle. Forced to defend its own inaction, the city had made an issue of the state pollution permits, a system that made more and more Clevelanders scratch their heads. Among them was Charles Vanik, long-time congressman from Cleveland's eastern suburbs, who sat before the House Committee on Public Works in February 1969 and described the peculiar relationship between the city and the state. The state distributed all federally allocated pollution-control dollars, and Vanik provided the numbers to show discrimination against the largest counties, such as Cuyahoga. On a per capita basis, Ohio was much more generous to sparsely populated counties. More troubling, the state had dedicated none of its own dollars to pollution control. What's more, the federal Water Pollution Control Act of 1965 had granted states the authority to establish criteria for water quality in bodies of water inside their boundaries, even waters that flowed into other states or federally controlled waters, such as Lake Erie. Vanik complained that the Ohio Water Pollution Control Board had designated the Cuyahoga and other regional waters "industrial water supply," which allowed considerable pollution to persist. And, Vanik pointed out, the state then issued permits to individual polluters, allowing them to discharge wastes above even these lax criteria. One might imagine these permits to be a temporary system designed to give companies time to install better equipment, but the number of permits had held steady in recent years. In 1968, the state issued 1,371 permits to pollute the waters of Ohio, just nine fewer than in 1965.[21]

A week after his own testimony before the House committee, Vanik reappeared with six students from private high schools in Cleveland Heights and Shaker Heights. Each of them gave impassioned, urgent testimony about the crisis in Lake Erie. John Coventry, of the University School, said, "In my own lifetime I have seen the effects of the increasing pollution of Lake Erie. I have seen the fishing industry of Cleveland go out of business, and beaches where one could once swim closed." The students brought with them thirteen thousand signatures collected in less than a week on a petition that read in part, "We want prompt and energetic action in this session of Congress to clean up the waters of our nation." Like that day's testimony, the petition expressed urgency, demanding "a crash attack on the pollution that is killing Lake Erie." Several of the students also used the language of ecology, including Virginia Robinson of the Hathaway Brown School, who said, "Anyone can see and smell the flagrant abuse of the biosphere." Like many children of her generation, she expressed concern about the condition of the planet she would inherit from the previous generation, saying that "the accumulated debt of neglect and abuse must be paid."[22]

THE DIRT FACTORY

In the fall of 1966, in a not-so-veiled reference to Cleveland's racial tensions, the *Plain Dealer* ran the headline "Air Pollution Color-Blind" between two large photos of smoking stacks. One was a nearly beautiful image of white plumes rising from the five stacks of the Cleveland Illuminating plant along the Shoreway; in the other, dark smoke issued from the six stacks of the Municipal Light plant about twenty blocks to the west.[23] The two sets of stacks, both rising from coal-fired electrical plants, had become familiar symbols of the city's air pollution problem, especially among East Side commuters who drove in and out of downtown. In the previous two decades, Cleveland's first limited-access highway had gained a new name—Memorial Shoreway, in honor of Americans who had died in World War II—and a series of improvements that made it increasingly useful for suburban residents driving into the city. This was Cleveland's early effort to create what in 1947 urban economist Mabel Walker called a "fluid city," one less reliant on railroads and more accommodating to automobiles. As a result, the two plants, both right up against the highway, had gained special visibility. Just that summer the *Plain Dealer* had run a front-page photo of the Muny Light plant, showing a depressing row of five stacks, each one issuing dark smoke. Although the photo accompanied a short article about the city's plans for equipment upgrades that would reduce the smoke, improvements, if they occurred, were short-lived. At the same time, officials in the Locher administration pointed out that the plant did not violate the antismoke ordinance, but most likely not with the intention of suggesting that perhaps the law—just four years old—was as out-of-date as the plant.[24]

Although somewhat smaller than the Illuminating Company's facility, the Muny Plant became the greater magnet for attention. Some of this attention came because it was owned and operated by the city, and so by the mid-1960s the plant symbolized government hypocrisy and ineptitude. How could the city expect industry to reduce air pollution when the city couldn't even clean up its own stacks? As early as 1961, as City Council considered an antismoke ordinance, Cleveland Air Pollution Commissioner Albert Locuoco joked that the new law might put the Muny Light plant "out of business." Like other parts of the municipal bureaucracy, Muny Light didn't always run effectively, and with a power plant inefficiencies are visible for all to see—in the form of smoke. In 1966, Mrs. Alan Loden of Shaker Heights wrote to the *Plain Dealer* that her four-year-old son called the Muny plant "the dirt factory," a designation that might have sparked a chuckle among Clevelanders but also a knowing shake of the head.[25]

The smoke notwithstanding, Municipal Light itself had long been a source of pride among some Clevelanders. Created by Mayor Tom L. Johnson as part of his assertion that cities can and should provide basic services to residents, Muny Light had been expanded by Mayor Newton Baker, and in 1914 the city opened the largest municipally owned power plant in the nation on the lake at East 53rd Street. Since then, nearly continual improvements and expansions had allowed the plant to serve a growing customer base while Cleveland retained its reputation for inexpensive electricity. With this in mind, it is worth pausing to consider why the Muny plant gained so much negative attention in the 1960s. It was a nuisance, surely, but nothing compared to the major polluters—the steel mills and chemical factories to the south, where prevailing winds pushed smoke and fumes over North and South Broadway and other working-class neighborhoods, creating both chronic and acute threats to residents' health. The focus on the relatively small contributions of the Muny plant might suggest a reluctance to take on the steel mills, but more likely it had to do with location. Fewer and fewer Clevelanders lived in and around the industrial Cuyahoga Valley—or traveled there for any reason—and middle-class residents, so important to the developing environmental movement, were more likely to see Muny's smoky stacks than those of the mills.

And then too the Muny plant's smoke symbolized municipal decline itself, in a way that factory smoke never could. In April 1969, the popular *Plain Dealer* columnist George Condon wrote a scathing piece that appeared under the headline "A City Goes Down the Hill," in which he took aim at Cleveland's "drab and dreary downtown." Part of Condon's object was to explain why bars in the flats—down the hill—had gained in popularity. There was something charming and attractive about old, industrial Cleveland and its residual working-class pubs. But Condon also claimed that the problems of downtown had driven Cleveland to drink along the Cuyahoga. "It will take nothing less than an angry city to rout the dirt and check the decay of downtown," he wrote. Among the many problems of downtown was air pollution. And the one source of air pollution that gained Condon's attention: Municipal Light. This despite the fact that the Muny plant was three miles from Public Square and downwind as well.[26]

The Stokes administration was well aware of the Muny plant's special role in the air pollution debate. The difficulties in keeping it running efficiently and the chronic bad publicity were among the reasons Stokes had pledged to sell the plant to the private Illuminating Company, which had the capital to upgrade the facility and run it well. But by the summer of 1969, as City Council discussed yet another new air pollution ordinance, Stokes had made no progress toward the proposed sale. The *Plain Dealer* hoped the new law would finally force the city to purchase cleaner coal for the plant, an easy but expensive step that would have solved much of the problem. That summer's attention to air pollution in turn heightened scrutiny in the mayor's office. Bob Bauerlein, an assistant to Stokes, discussed Muny's operations with relevant personnel throughout the city's complicated bureaucracy. Tom Kinder, an engineer with the Division of Air Pollution Control, reported that a new boiler with a working precipitator was improperly run and in need of maintenance. Kim Wald, in purchasing, reported that the plant superintendent had consistently accepted deliveries of coal that did not meet contract specifications. Most troubling, John Fakult, who had charge of the city's Light and Power Division, seemed to be unreceptive to making changes, nor did he appear concerned about air pollution.

Sensing that the problem at Municipal Light had as much to do with management as with dated technology, Bauerlein visited the plant himself in October 1969, just as City Council scheduled a vote on the air pollution ordinance. Bauerlein was so troubled by what he saw that he filed a letter with John Little, the mayor's executive secretary. "I would like to go on record as stating that in my opinion, it is only a matter of time before someone at the plant is either killed or seriously injured," he wrote. "The plant is generally filthy; graph papers on many gauges have not been changed for quite some time and thus are unreadable; in many areas the coal dust and sulfur gas is so heavy that breathing is difficult; and there is a water leak at the base of the new boiler pouring out gallons of hot water every minute." No wonder the plant smoked. The staff managed the equipment poorly, and there had been no timely repair of existing problems, let alone a program of preventative maintenance. "To allow this situation to continue can only cause untold injury," Bauerlein concluded, "not to mention our usual amount of political trouble."[27] The dirt factory was chugging along.

WE STAND ANKLE DEEP IN SEWAGE

Not surprisingly, many of the speakers at the August 1965 conference on Lake Erie were from Cleveland, including Vincent DeMelto, who was then the director of Public Utilities. DeMelto offered a succinct history of Cleveland's attempts to control its sewage, beginning with the 1905 construction of a large intercepting sewer that diverted wastes from downtown and the length of the East Side to East 140th Street, where they drained into the lake. Not until 1922 did the city provide sewage treatment, when the Easterly plant opened at the end of the intercepting sewer and the Westerly plant opened near the mouth of the Cuyahoga. Meanwhile, most of the city had been built with combined sewers, meaning storm runoff and sanitary wastes mixed in the same pipes. During rains or snowmelts, volumes in the pipes quickly outran treatment plant capacity, and the excess passed over weirs into overflow pipes that led to the lake or its tributaries. Even though significant upgrades in 1938 increased the capacity of the two lakeside treatment plants and the Southerly plant on the Cuyahoga, the combined sewers ensured that the city could not always contain and treat its own sewage.

DeMelto's report to the conference emphasized Cleveland's long and evolving relationship with water pollution control. Over the decades, the city had made continuous investments using current technology—improvements that should not be overlooked. Still, DeMelto could not hide the fact that Cleveland remained a major contributor to Lake Erie's pollution problem, even without considering the industrial effluents that didn't enter the city's system but instead flowed directly into waterways, especially the Cuyahoga. One notable failure was the design of Westerly to serve as only a primary treatment facility, meaning that the plant removed solid wastes but did not otherwise reduce the organic content of the effluent. "The plant is intended to relieve the load of pollution on the shore waters of Lake Erie," DeMelto reported, "and at the same time prevent the discharge into the lake of floating solids which are offensive to the sight, and of settleable solids which may form sludge banks, and which due to putrefaction become offensive to both sight and smell." As foul as this must have sounded to many observers, it was of even greater concern to those who used Edgewater Beach, directly adjacent to Westerly. To protect swimmers, the city treated the plant's effluent with chlorine to reduce coliform counts, although this step clearly didn't solve the problem.[28] Although the Easterly plant provided more complete treatment, it still posed problems to the neighboring White City Beach, and the city had taken to treating effluent from that facility with greater amounts of chlorine.

Given that a considerable amount of sewage bypassed the plant through large sewer overflows, the chlorine treatments had a limited effect.

The 1965 Lake Erie conference in Cleveland ended with the adoption of a series of recommendations. Among them: "Combined storm and sanitary sewers are to be prohibited in all newly developed urban areas, and eliminated in existing areas wherever feasible." Although the recommendation carried no weight of law, it matched federal goals as described by the Public Health Service and echoed the state of Ohio's policy prohibiting the construction of combined sewers in newly developed areas and in urban renewal zones. Despite the widespread recognition that combined sewers were a significant contributor to water pollution in Cleveland, the city proposed to build new combined sewers in the University-Euclid urban renewal project. In a classic case of federal bureaucratic stalemate, the Public Health Service demanded that the Housing and Home Finance Agency (HHFA), which distributed money for urban renewal projects, withhold funds for a project that clearly ignored water quality goals set at both the national and state level. The conflict inspired an investigation by Congress's Committee on Government Operations and a lengthy report in June 1966 that revealed shocking disregard for pollution prevention in the HHFA and the Locher administration, which was willing to perpetuate the errors of the past simply to save money in the short term. The report called the local position on water pollution control "apathy." The media wove the sewer affair into the general story about the Locher administration's mismanagement of urban renewal. A scathing *Press* editorial in the fall of 1965 ran under the title "Hypocrisy in Sewer Plans." With the bad press and congressional pressure, which forced both the Federal Urban Renewal Administration and the Ohio Department of Health to review the University-Euclid approval process, the city had no choice. It revised the project to include separate sewers, adding $425,000 to the projected costs.[29]

"Hypocrisy" wasn't too strong a word to describe the city's original position on renewal zone sewers. After all, Locher also addressed the Lake Erie conference, where he described at length the steps Cleveland had taken to reduce its contributions to the lake's pollution. But he began with a familiar theme: his city would need federal dollars to solve this problem. "Everyone in this room knows how water pollution can be stopped, but, likewise, everyone in this room recognizes, I believe, that it will cost a great deal more to restore our waters to their original quality than any local government can afford." In Cleveland's initial University-Euclid plan, of course, federal dollars would do nothing to restore the waters. Still, Locher sounded genuine when he admitted, "We have been bad stewards of what God has provided for us." And then, turning to the great technological promise of the moment, Locher pressed the irony: "This age could well be known as the one in which America is shooting rockets to the moon, while we stand ankle deep in sewage."[30]

If Locher was a miserable administrator, he was surely a skilled politician. He talked passionately about the city's problems and sounded sincere when describing progress. At the conference, he touted the city's development of a master plan for pollution control, which would appear three years later, and the city's ongoing $19 million investment in upgrades to the Easterly and Southerly sewage treatment plants. But real improvement would take hundreds of millions of dollars, and thus far Cleveland had received no external aid, not even from the state. This had to change, Locher argued, not just for the sake of the lake but also for Cleveland, which relied on the lake for its water supply and for recreation. Pollution threatened both of these uses. "The city of the future must be made livable, bright and appealing," Locher said to the conference. And then, borrowing a phrase from the struggle to improve urban neighborhoods, in which he was simultaneously engaged, Locher noted, "Such negative factors as air pollution and water pollution are a blight upon our very lives." To emphasize the growing importance of quality of life in cities, Locher described Cleveland's effort to develop two new marinas on the lakefront, which had been projected by the 1950 city plan. "At my insistence," Locher said, "fishing piers are to be provided, because more and more of the elderly, in their leisure hours, and the young people, desire fishing as one of their diversions." Unfortunately, Locher reported, "it is common knowledge that the fishing is not good. I hear it from my neighbors and my friends." Commercial fishing data confirmed that stocks in Lake Erie had plummeted. Blue pike, for instance, had until recently been caught in the millions of pounds per year, but it had largely disappeared from the lake. Also known as blue walleye, this fish has not been caught in the Great Lakes since the 1970s and is probably extinct.

Four years after Locher's testimony, as Mayor Stokes stood with Governor Rhodes at the dedication of the East 55th Street Marina, his staff presented the press with a fact sheet describing the city and state investments in the project and the services the facility would provide. In addition to the berths, there were restrooms and showers in the marina headquarters building, retail space for boat-related items, and "a first class restaurant facility." The marina did not include the fishing pier Locher had insisted on, but at Gordon Park, just to the east of the Illuminating Company's plant, the city had added a long pier, which doubled as a protective breakwater for the smaller, older marina there, at East 72nd Street. Construction of the pier had begun with the scuttling of two massive ore vessels several hundred feet from shore. The city then bridged the gaps with crushed cars. For over two years, beginning in 1967, the city used the site as a landfill, dumping up to 230,000 pounds of rubbish a day, using only riprap to separate the waste from the lake. In October 1969, a federal inspection of the site found an abundance of rats (a sign that considerable organic wastes were present), as well as grease, paint, motor oil, and other wastes that would seep into the lake. Eventually the city covered the wreckage and the waste, and one would hardly guess the origins of the peninsula today. But the symbolism of the construction is evident, not just in the literal burying of the old ore-steel economy to make a more recreational city but also in the failure to account for the ecology of the lake. Even as Cleveland struggled to save the lake, as late as the fall of 1969 the city couldn't stop thinking of it as an inexpensive dump.

WITHIN REASON, THE PRICE MUST BE PAID

On April 10, 1969, Stokes released a statement announcing "an important step in fighting the problem of air pollution." Recognizing that current staffing would not allow effective regulation, the city would use a $222,000 federal grant from the National Air Pollution Control Administration, combined with $423,000 in local money, to create a larger Division of Air Pollution Control in the Department of Public Health and Welfare. The revamped division would have five new engineers, four additional technicians, two chemists, a full-time attorney, and a deputy commissioner. Stokes also announced that the Law Department was at work on a new air pollution ordinance, noting that since the current law had been passed in 1962 not a single violator had been brought to court. The statement ended, "Cleveland has taken the forefront nationally in the battle against water pollution and with this announcement today we are making significant steps to match that effort in our desire to control air pollution."[31]

A month later, Stokes proposed the new, tougher air pollution code to City Council, which then held a series of hearings on the ordinance. In selling the proposed law, Director of Public Health Frank Ellis called it a modern code, modeled after others that had been adopted around the country. The code limited emissions of particulates and sulfur dioxide, setting standards for concentrations of both inside smokestacks. The standards would force industries to adopt the best control technologies available and in some cases switch to lower-sulfur fuels. The code set out a compliance date—the end of 1972—and set up a system for granting variances for businesses that had yet to meet their goals. Companies would have to get city approval for their control plans and allow city inspection of both smokestacks and abatement equipment. Companies out of compliance would be subject to fines. In its extensive coverage of air pollution that summer, the *Plain Dealer* used the terms set out by Ellis and federal air pollution control officials, continuously referring to the proposed law as a "modern" code, indicating on which side the newspaper would fight as the council considered the ordinance.[32]

On May 23, Bailus Walker Jr., deputy commissioner of health, spoke before the council's Air and Water Pollution Committee in support of the proposed regulations. Standing in for his boss, Ellis, Walker said, "The overriding reason for controlling air pollution is because it is responsible, wholly or in substantial part, for unnecessary deaths and unnecessary illness, disability, and discomfort in this country." To be certain that council members understood the gravity of the situation, Walker emphasized that evidence "demonstrates beyond any reasonable doubt that air pollution is guilty of killing and disabling people." He listed disasters in Belgium's Meuse Valley in 1930; the Donora, Pennsylvania, smog of 1948; and episodes in London in 1952 and in New York City in 1966, all of which led to a significant number of deaths during acute pollution events. Less well known, of course, were the consequences of chronic exposure to air pollution, although studies had shown that residents with heart or lung conditions were at elevated risk of death when exposed to high levels of pollution.[33]

Walker's testimony linking air pollution and health made the *Press*, published just hours later, but it appeared under the headline "Air Code Seen Closing Factories." Several opponents of the proposed law testified during the hearing, perhaps most effectively Richard DeChant of the Greater Cleveland Growth Association, who reminded the council that Cleveland's industrial plants employed three hundred thousand people, including eighty thousand in primary metal manufacturing. "All Cleveland citizens must be aware of the industrial nature of their city," he said, "a pattern which was established many years ago and has provided the impetus for our economic growth and present enviable position among our nation's industrial centers." DeChant then warned, "In its present form the code would force some of our foundries and metal fabricators to close down permanently." Echoing an argument that had been made repeatedly in the defense of the underregulated environment that had encouraged industrial development, DeChant, the son of a steelworker, said that should the ordinance pass, "there would be a temporary or permanent loss of employment for many Greater Clevelanders." This was clearly the most powerful statement of the hearing.[34]

Supporters of the proposed code had a chance to rebut industry on June 6, when a variety of citizens—a union official, a doctor, a teacher, and a chemistry professor—testified before the council committee. They emphasized health and justice and decried industry's attempt at economic blackmail, surely a reference to DeChant's testimony two weeks earlier. But industry had interests to protect, and so a few days later their representatives came before the committee's next hearing with a variety of concerns. On June 13, as Stokes stood with bankers celebrating the new Central National Bank tower and the building of the new service city, just three blocks away officials from the old economy testified against the proposed air pollution code at City Hall. That hearing was dominated by coal, railroad, and steel industry executives who cast the ordinance as severe and unrealistic. R. Thomas Schoonmaker, of Penn Central, the year-old corporate combination of the Pennsylvania and New York Central railroads, reminded council members that his company employed 2,500 people in Cleveland and paid approximately $3 million in taxes to the city. Reducing air pollution would be expensive, he said, allowing that "within reason, the price must be paid." But he emphasized that "careful consideration must be given to the cost-benefit relationship"—an important theme in the go-slow mantra of industry's battle against increased regulation. Because the coal economy was essential to Penn Central, Schoonmaker was there specifically to speak against a transition away from Ohio's high-sulfur coal, nearly all of which would become unusable in the city under the code's strict limits on sulfur dioxide concentrations in smokestacks.[35]

The next morning, the *Plain Dealer* ran a story on the Central National Bank's time capsule ceremony next to an article recounting the air pollution hearings, a useful if unintentional juxtaposition of the consequences of the city's shifting economy. The old economic powers demanded the maintenance of a policy structure that had benefited them greatly. For more than a century, manufacturers had passed on nearly all the costs of air pollution to citizens, and now they argued that ending that arrangement was simply unreasonable. At the same time, however, new economic powers were building a gleaming downtown. In a sign that the old regime was faltering, the ordinance, slightly amended, passed unanimously after eight months of consideration. It came into effect on October 27, 1969.

THE ULTIMATE METHOD OF POLLUTION CONTROL

In June 1968, Havens and Emerson sent Ben Stefanski the *Master Plan for Pollution Abatement, Cleveland, Ohio*, an impressive two-volume report that detailed the water pollution control system as it existed and recommended a series of upgrades to meet demands for improved water quality. The plan described shortcomings in the city's three treatment plants, some of which the city had already begun to address, and it outlined steps that would be necessary to connect growing suburban areas to the sewer system, since most suburbs had not and would not build their own treatment facilities. But the largest problem facing the city stemmed from the 45,000 urban acres that were served by combined sewers—those that accepted both sanitary wastes and street runoff. Cleveland, like many older cities, had constructed these sewers under the guidance of an older engineering philosophy that prized the efficiency of running a single pipe through neighborhoods and tolerated the discharge of untreated sewage into waterways. Now a substantial reduction of waste discharge into Lake Erie and its tributaries would require separating sanitary sewers, an incredibly expensive proposition. The process was already under way, since large urban renewal sites, like Erieview, included the construction of new, separate sewers. The building of the region's highways also provided the opportunity to create new drainage systems. The vast majority of the suburban areas, including Shaker Heights, Cleveland Heights, and Lyndhurst, were served by separate sewers, but most of the city, including all sixteen thousand acres served by the Easterly plant, was still drained by combined sewers.

Havens and Emerson assumed that the work of disentangling the sewers would continue, but it envisioned no broad or immediate steps to force this solution. Instead, the firm picked up a plan that had been proposed by John Wirts, superintendent of the Easterly plant, three years earlier, about the time Havens and Emerson began working on the master plan. Wirts imagined the construction of a huge basin in the lake, formed by sheet metal walls protected by fill. As Wirts described it, the basin would act as an expansive sewage treatment plant, collecting all the waste runoff from the city's troubled streams and sewer overflows, along with the effluent from the Easterly plant. Once in the basin, the wastes would receive treatment, and solids would be allowed to settle out.

Although Wirts's idea was very expensive, costing as much as $75 million, it was featured in the Locher administration's grand plan for the lakefront, announced in June 1966. Locher's fantastic vision, with a total cost of $385 million, included a seven-mile highway running through the lake via a combination of causeway, tunnel, and artificial island. For part of its length, the highway would top the breakwater that protected Cleveland Harbor and pass along a new jetport built entirely on landfill out in the lake, beyond the harbor wall and thus well beyond the existing airport built on landfill along the shore. On the other side of this new jetport, Locher's plan envisioned Wirts's "settling basin," where storm runoff and sewer overflow could be held in a five-thousand-acre pond carved from the lake. As a bonus, the solids that settled in the basin could be pumped out to help form the landfill necessary to support the new jetport. All this, Wirts assured the *Plain Dealer*, would not smell. It would be the first storm water basin built in a body of water any-where in the world, he said.[36]

Since none of the Locher lakefront plan came to fruition, it is easy to sug-gest that it had no hope of becoming reality. True, the highway on the lake must have been dreamed up by someone who had never spent a winter in Cleveland, where north winds regularly blow freezing mist off lake chop. Perhaps the vision of ice-covered traffic jams a half-mile from shore, or the bills from the near-constant salting that would have been necessary to keep the road passable, forced the city to rethink this aspect of the plan. Still, the settling basin and jetport concepts remained alive, the latter into the 1970s, when an engineering study found that an island airport would survive lake currents. The settling basin, in an altered form, became the central feature of the *Master Plan for Pollution Abatement*.

In 1967, the Federal Water Pollution Control Administration hired Havens and Emerson to conduct a feasibility study of a "stabilization-retention basin in Lake Erie." The study concluded that the basin would provide "a higher degree of pollution abatement than would separation of sanitary and storm sewers, at about one-third the cost." The report also said, "No major objec-tions or obstacles which would prevent its construction have been found," al-though the firm considered only engineering objections, ignoring potential aesthetic and ecological concerns. The report described at length how pol-luted waters would pass through three areas of the basin: the first would pro-vide aeration; the second a long, still period for the settling of solids, which "would form a sludge blanket at the bottom"; and in the third stage, just be-fore the water was to be released into the lake, the city could add more aera-tion and chlorine if necessary. To minimize cost, pontoons holding neoprene fabric curtains would separate the three areas of the basin.[37]

Using its own feasibility study for justification, Havens and Emerson's *Master Plan* recommended that the basin "be adopted as the ultimate method of pollution control for the area east of Cleveland Harbor." The firm deter-mined that a nine-hundred-acre basin in the lake, with an average depth of thirty-four feet, would be large enough to take all the effluent from Easterly and the other troubled East Side sources. The plan even touted secondary benefits of the basin, which would stretch southwest from the Easterly plant

OFFSHORE   STABILIZATION   BASIN   HAVENS & EMERSON · CONSULTING   ENGINEERS

Figure 9. The stabilization basin imagined in 1968 by Havens and Emerson mixed sewage treatment in an expansive impoundment in the lake with recreation along the retention walls. Although never built, the basin was at the heart of Cleveland's *Master Plan for Pollution Abatement* from the same year. Havens and Emerson, *Feasibility of a Stabilization-Retention Basin in Lake Erie at Cleveland, Ohio* (May 1968).

toward the outlet of Dugway Brook in Bratenahl. As the feasibility study announced, "The project would create a sheltered bay about 1.2 miles long which would be an invaluable recreational asset, suitable for swimming, boating, fishing, and other water-based recreation. This bay would be protected physically, and water quality could be readily controlled to bathing water standards."[38]

Unlike the swimming pools in the lake, also designed by Havens and Emerson, the stabilization basin was no temporary, stop-gap measure. It was by far the most expensive project proposed in the master plan—roughly a third of the entire cost of the program. The basin shared important traits with the pools, however, even beyond the use of heavy plastic curtains strung from pontoons. The engineering firm had taken a rather narrow view of its task. Harmful bacteria and suspended solids would be removed from waters

139

draining into the lake, but the lake itself seems not to have won much attention, at least not beyond the idea that it provided inexpensive space for a new sewage treatment facility. Following typical modernist thinking, Havens and Emerson had compartmentalized space, even space in the lake, just as planners had separated land uses in downtown Cleveland a decade earlier. In essence the engineers treated the lake as fully malleable space, not as a valued ecosystem, where connections mattered most. For several years, activists had been demanding that the city "Save the Lake," without describing the path to salvation. With its stabilization basin, "sludge blanket," and "readily controlled" bay, the master plan represented a half-step toward a new kind of city, one that prized recreational spaces but held on to segregated thinking. Walls, even plastic ones, could not contain the fluid city, and they certainly couldn't contain the lake.

Whether or not the particulars of the master plan came to pass, everyone knew that addressing the pollution problem would take lots of capital. The Stokes administration proposed a bold step—a $100 million bond issue, to be paid back through property tax, specified as just over two mills, or about $20 per year for a $10,000 home. The bond campaign in 1968 didn't dwell on the specifics of sewer construction and treatment plant upgrades. Rather, the theme became "Don't let a Great Lake die," a phrase that appeared in a number of newspaper ads, including atop a full-page ad the afternoon before Election Day 1968. The phrase ran above a photo of two children playing on a beach. "Vote 'yes' for Clean Water," it read below. On a different page the same words appeared in an ad paid for by Blaushild Chevrolet, accompanied by a photo of David Blaushild.[39]

Voters approved the bond by a two-to-one margin. *Press* reporter Betty Klaric, now writing articles accompanied by a new symbol—an oblong globe with the phrase "A Better World Around Us"—called the passage "something of a personal victory for Mayor Stokes' youngest cabinet member," Ben Stefanski. In a lengthy interview, the "jubilant" Stefanski thanked all those who worked on the clean water campaign, making certain to give special praise to the *Press*, by which he really meant Klaric, and Blaushild, who together did "the spade work" of making the public aware of the problem. He claimed the passage would allow the city to put pressure on the state and federal governments, asking them to ante up, to pay their fair share. He also said, "If the people in the neighborhoods are willing to spend money, then industry, too, should be willing to spend the money necessary to get rid of deleterious wastes going into the Cuyahoga." In other words, the money wouldn't just help build a cleaner Cleveland; it would help Cleveland pressure others to join in the investment. "The people have given a mandate and a challenge to the city government," Stefanski said. "Now it is the responsibility of the city to do the job."[40]

YOURS FOR A SAFER, CLEANER, PRACTICAL, MORE ECONOMICAL CITY

In early March 1969, East Side resident Laverne Amory wrote to Mayor Stokes with a list of serious complaints. "As a native Clevelander, I am appalled and quite disgusted and exasperated by what is happening to my town." She was concerned about high taxes, which she mentioned early in the letter, and a proposed Cleveland Transit System fare hike was the impetus for her lengthy letter. The letter makes clear, however, that other aspects of the city troubled her more, especially dangerous streets. Her sense of danger was at least partly driven by the ongoing racial transition, as more and more whites fled to the suburbs, even from the comfortable Mount Pleasant neighborhood where Amory and her husband—a city employee—lived in a tidy duplex. She assumed the mayor's Cleveland: Now! program would help only blacks and certainly wouldn't "make a white person feel any safer on the city streets." Amory told Stokes, "Schools, parks, and other institutions are being closed because of your inability to control the black community. The phrase 'Concrete Jungle' is most apropos for this city." Despite the racist overtones, Amory didn't simply blame blacks for Cleveland's troubles. She asked, "Mr. Mayor, what is being done about *other* health hazards. We hear plenty of talk about studies of air and water pollution; but we continue to breathe and swallow poisonous chemical fumes, smoke, dust and waste matters. It makes one wonder if perhaps there is a payola bribery involved that the public is not aware of." Amory worked downtown, where she had seen lots of construction in recent years—although she had seen even more demolition. "It is ironic to see skyscrapers, great educational institutions and cultural centers going up in a city that is slowly becoming a *ghost town*," she wrote. Amory understood that Cleveland faced a crisis, and for whatever reason—racial divisions, corruption, misplaced policy priorities—the city simply couldn't find solutions. She felt so strongly about the trajectory of her city that she sent copies of her letter to each of the city's councilmen, the directors of several city departments, members of the Transit Board, the president of Case Western Reserve University, and fifteen corporate leaders from Cleveland's largest companies, including Republic Steel, Standard Oil, and Central National Bank. For good measure, she also sent copies to Thomas Burke, who served as mayor in the late 1940s and early 1950s (perhaps what Amory considered Cleveland's golden age), and Seth Taft, Republican candidate for mayor that year. She signed the letter, "Yours for a safer, cleaner, practical, more economical city with more sensitivity to the things that will keep Cleveland a great city."[41]

In the summer of 1969, disagreements persisted about what policies might keep Cleveland great, but Clevelanders increasingly agreed that controlling water and air pollution would have to be part of the solution. People with options rarely choose to stay in polluted neighborhoods. As Amory wrote her letter to Stokes, the Clean Water Task Force was putting the finishing touches on its "action program." Devised by Edward Martin, the action program used the master plan as a working base, but its main feature was completely new. Instead of a settling basin in the lake, the heart of the master plan, Martin envisioned the creation of a great water recycling system. All the water used by the city and its industry would go through advanced waste treatment and then be pumped up, away from the lake, and emptied into the Cuyahoga, from which it could be drawn out by industry and reused. In short, Martin envisioned a system "with ultimately no discharges to Lake Erie." The fifty-seven-page plan, delivered to Stokes on May 13, promised to "restore maximum recreational activities to the Cleveland area" and bring about the improvement of the water supply through "the elimination of the taste and odor-bearing pollutants." Lake Erie's condition would improve through "the removal of nutrients which contribute to algal blooms."[42]

Martin focused largely on personnel in the action program, listing new position titles and enumerating tasks and responsibilities. But the program also included a schedule of specific projects, with $33 million in immediate spending, mostly on sewer upgrades and improvements at the Southerly and Westerly treatment plants. In the months that followed, contract by contract the money flowed into these projects, but progress was very slow, especially when measured in water quality improvements. The state of Ohio continued to invest little of its own money in pollution control, but the Water Pollution Control Board increasingly expressed concern about how little Cleveland had accomplished. In April 1970, just a week before the first Earth Day, Stokes issued a statement about the growing conflict between city and state. Reacting to rumors that the state was about to issue a building ban in the city of Cleveland, using its power to block permits for sewerage connections, Stokes angrily defended his administration's "meaningful effort" and "leadership, energy and dedication to the task of meeting the crisis in the environment." The statement described how devastating a building ban would be to the city. "The impact on employment would be terrible. The impact on city income tax revenues . . . would be terrible. The setbacks to school building programs would be horrendous. The setback to Cleveland State University's building program, the state of Ohio's own program would be awful." In 1968, the city had issued permits for $154 million in construction, a record, and then broke that record by $5 million the next year. Stokes feared that a halt in building permits would break the city's movement toward the construction of a new city, with glass towers, educational institutions, and public housing. "I plead with the board," he wrote, "to permit Cleveland to continue moving forward to meet our problems of housing, school construction, urban renewal, as well as water pollution control." The service city would require progress in all these areas and more.[43]

5 The Burning River

On Monday, June 23, 1969, Carl Stokes led the local press on a pollution tour of the Cuyahoga River at the southern end of the city's industrial flats. About a dozen people—reporters, cameramen, and government officials—joined the excursion, which stopped at four sites, all of them near the Harvard Road bridge beyond the river's navigable channel. At one stop, they stood and watched sewage pour from the defective Big Creek Interceptor, a large pipe designed to deliver waste and runoff to the nearby Southerly Treatment Plant. It had been malfunctioning for over a month and emptying directly into the Cuyahoga. Just around the corner, the group peered into the forty-nine-acre facility of Harshaw Chemical Company, which for more than sixty years had produced a variety of acids and salts—sulfates, carbonates, chlorides, nitrates—to meet the needs of the region's industry. Here, tainted by chemicals, including Harshaw's sodium sulfate, the river changed colors. Downstream, it passed between the great steel mills and turned ruddy from the iron wastes. At another stop on the pollution tour, Stokes pointed to a sewer pipe that emptied wastes from suburban Cuyahoga Heights directly into the river because that community had not connected the pipe to the nearby Southerly plant. The featured stop on the tour, however, was a mile downstream, where Stokes stood on one of the two railroad trestles that had been damaged by a fire on the Cuyahoga the day before. Here the group stood and spoke about the long-standing and complicated problem of pollution in the river. This is why they had come.

The administration had organized the tour quickly, having heard of the previous day's fire only that morning. Here was a chance to define the problem, to describe what the administration thought needed to be done to solve it. Putting together the list of stops on the tour wasn't difficult. Crusading car dealer David Blaushild had named Harshaw Chemical in his lawsuit against the city four years earlier, in part because it had been a notorious polluter of the river for decades, even before it had refined uranium for nuclear weapons at its Harvard Road plant in the 1940s and 1950s. The Big Creek Interceptor had been dumping sewage since May 20, although the story didn't make the papers for another six days. By then, it had spilled over 150 million gallons of sewage, in a failure that had real consequences for the river and symbolic implications for the city's inadequate infrastructure. As the *Cleveland Press* reported, this was "at least the fifth break in the sewer in the past six years."[1] And the city had been in a long, fruitless negotiation with Cuyahoga Heights and other suburbs regarding cost sharing for sewer development, attempting to determine how suburbs should be charged for new sewers that would connect to the city's Southerly treatment plant.

The highlight of the tour, of course, was the site of the fire. Out on the damaged trestle, Stokes was in crisis management mode. But unlike when he traveled the overheated and roiling streets of Glenville the previous summer, he wasn't trying to calm the situation as he walked from pollution site to pollution site on this Monday morning. Rather, he was trying to fan the flames, to draw attention to the fire. At his side stood Betty Klaric, the *Press* reporter who had taken on the environment beat and covered the polluted city since 1965. "This is a long-standing condition that must be brought to an end," Stokes said to her. "There may be some wry humor in the phrase 'the river is a fire hazard' but it's a terrible reflection on the city surrounding it when it does indeed become one." Stokes wasn't willing to accept full responsibility for the fire, claiming, as he did frequently, that because the state continued to issue permits to polluters, the city could accomplish little. Now he determined that the courts should settle the issue. To Stokes, pollution wasn't a technical problem so much as a political one. Who should be responsible, and how should they find the resources needed to build the solution? "We'll file the lawsuit on behalf of all the citizens of Cleveland and let the courts decide," Stokes told Klaric.[2]

Reflecting back on that day in an interview in 2008, Klaric said, "To us it was just another fire . . . we all knew that the river was an open sewer used by industry which was dumping all this oil and all kinds of chemicals in the river, so we took it as a matter of course." Just another day in the polluted city, or so she thought.[3] But the fire began to take on greater meaning, even in the days that immediately followed. During the pollution tour, Stokes attempted to assign meaning to the fire. He argued that the city was not in a position to control the pollution within its borders. His administration had inherited a

Figure 10. On the Monday after the Cuyahoga blaze, Mayor Stokes led the media on a tour of critical spots near the fire. Here Stokes talks with the *Cleveland Press* reporter Betty Klaric on one of the railroad trestles damaged by the fire. Photo by Herman Seid. Cleveland Press Collection, Cleveland State University.

flawed infrastructure, including the faulty Big Creek Interceptor. Cleveland had no power over its suburbs, such as Cuyahoga Heights, and the city had failed to find an acceptable metropolitan solution. And it had no control over state regulations and the pollution permit system. Harshaw Chemical could pollute with impunity. Altogether, Stokes must have felt powerless on that charred trestle, looking down on the foul waters making their way through his city.

Stokes needed allies, and he sought them in the press, the federal government, and the environmental movement. If Cleveland was going to change, the Cuyahoga could no longer be an open sewer, let alone a fire hazard.

146

Changing the river would take years and millions of dollars. It would also take a change in thinking about the Cuyahoga. It was not irredeemable; it could be reclaimed, and perhaps even become a living river again. Over the previous century, industry had made itself comfortable on the riverbanks, but now citizen demands for environmental quality were reaching even this most diminished of environments. In 1969, the city was in the midst of a long transition, as industrial plants shrank and closed—along the lakefront, along the rail lines, even on the industrial flats. But right where the 1969 fire began, capital investments had intensified in the postwar decades, as the steel mills modernized. Industry's commitment to that spot helped the burning river become an especially meaningful battleground in the transition from industrial to service city. For his part, Stokes hoped that if his administration could stop the burning here, maybe the burning would stop elsewhere in the city, too.

THE OIL-SLICKED RIVER BURST INTO FLAMES

The Cuyahoga River caught fire just before noon on Sunday, June 22, 1969. An oil slick and accumulated debris burned intensely for less than half an hour, damaging two railroad trestles, the Newburgh & Southern slightly and the Norfolk & Western more seriously. Firefighters arrived in time to douse the blaze before it could do more damage; photographers arrived too late to catch the flames on film. And so the next day, Cleveland's newspapers both ran front-page photos of the twisted Norfolk & Western tracks. The *Plain Dealer* photo, run with the caption "River Fire Damages Trestle," showed a fireman soaking a charred pier with a water cannon from the deck of the *Anthony J. Celebrezze*, the city's fireboat, which was stationed down the river. The caption reported that the fire had caused about $50,000 in damage. Battalion Chief Bernard Campbell said that in addition to the *Celebrezze*, the department had responded with fire trucks, which helped break up the burning slick from the shore.[4]

The damaged trestles crossed the Cuyahoga at a critical juncture, where the river jogs east, wedged between the long rolling mills of the Jones & Laughlin Steel Company on the west bank and the towering Republic Steel blast furnaces on the east. The trestles marked the end of the navigable stretch of the narrow river, and the wooden bridges held their tracks just a dozen or so feet above the water. The bridge piers trapped tree limbs and other debris, which accumulated in great piles that dried above the slow-moving current. Soaked in the oily sheen that covered much of the lower river, wooden debris gathered in many spots like this along the winding Cuyahoga, behind piers and pilings, in eddies and still corners, creating fire hazards awaiting a spark. Neither the city nor the state could determine the immediate cause of the fire, but nearly everyone assumed that the two massive mills were at least partly to blame. In its brief Monday morning coverage, the *Plain Dealer* asserted, "Flames leaped up from floating oil wastes dumped into the Cuyahoga River by waterfront industries." And that afternoon the *Press* announced on page 1, "Oily industrial waste on the Cuyahoga River caught fire." Both papers apparently relied on the conclusions of Battalion Chief Campbell, who didn't need to conduct an investigation before blaming waterfront industries that had dumped oil wastes into the river for decades.

Both Cleveland papers ran photos on Monday, but only the *Plain Dealer* included an article, which appeared on page 11C and was so clumsily handled that it contained two typographical errors in the lead paragraph. Under the headline "Oil Slick Fire Damages 2 River Spans," the un-bylined article began: "An [*sic*] burning oil slick floating on [the] Cuyahoga River caused $50,000 damage to two key railroad trestles at the foot of Campbell Road Hill SE about noon yesterday, closing one to traffic." At first neither Stokes on his pollution tour nor the papers that reported on it suggested that the fire represented an ecological disaster. Clevelanders were not ready to think of a burning river as an apocalyptic symbol of the developing ecological crisis. That symbolism would be learned slowly, over time. Instead, initially the story was about the damaged trestles, not the burning river. If the Cleveland papers made little of the incident, the national press initially ignored the blaze altogether. Apparently neither the Associated Press nor any other wire service produced a story about the Cuyahoga fire that June, since nothing about the fire appeared in the *New York Times*, the *Chicago Tribune*, the *Cincinnati Enquirer*, or the *Columbus Dispatch*, although the *Dispatch* carried a story two weeks later about the fingerpointing between Cleveland and the state over who was to blame.[5] The mild initial reaction to the burning Cuyahoga suggests that Clevelanders, and Americans generally, still had limited expectations for urban, industrial environments.

Most of the slight newspaper coverage in the weeks after the fire involved the back-and-forth between the city and state, but the *Plain Dealer* published a sharp editorial on Tuesday, the day after Stokes's pollution tour. Under the headline "Cleveland: Where the River Burns," the editorial opened with a "joke that isn't a joke": "Cleveland, eh? Isn't that the place where the river is so polluted it's a fire hazard?" Clevelanders apparently didn't find this amusing because, as the editorial pointed out, the river *was* a fire hazard and it did "catch fire from time to time." The *Plain Dealer* expressed anger toward industry in the flats: "So much heat should be put on industrial polluters that they will cease forever dumping oil and other wastes into the river." And the piece expressed frustration with the jurisdictional conflicts between the state and the city and the city and its suburbs. But the paper considered the burning river a problem because of what it meant to the city's reputation rather than its ecology. The *Plain Dealer* lamented that the "oily gunk" in the Cuyahoga had "given the river and the city a bad name for years."[6]

The *Press* had a noticeably broader take on the situation, at least by Wednesday, three days after the fire, when it published its first editorial on the topic. By then the *Press* had reason to hit a different tone. On Tuesday a major chemical spill on the Rhine River in Europe had initiated a still-unfolding ecological disaster. Pesticides were floating downstream, killing millions of fish and causing German and Dutch cities to shut off their water intakes and prohibit swimming. The *Press* editorial, under the headline "And Now—the Rhine," despaired that "the mighty Rhine has fallen to the level of the filthy Cuyahoga." The German spill was "one more painful manifestation of human beings poisoning their environment." And then, linking a series of environmental stories in a way that more and more Americans—and Europeans—were doing, the *Press* gave a sense of a larger unfolding environmental crisis. "As the Cuyahoga burns with its industrial wastes; as the Rhine flows majestically with its toxic insecticide; as the U.S. Army threatens to dump nerve gas into the ocean; as the Ohio Legislature refuses to ban Lake Erie oil drilling, United Nations Secretary U Thant warns in a report that mankind is destroying himself through pollution of land, sea and air." The last entry on this list, a reference to a UN document created in preparation for the 1972 Stockholm Conference on the Human Environment, connected the Cuyahoga to a crisis that stretched around the world.[7]

And so slowly the burning river became part of a much larger story, not just of the polluted Cuyahoga, or of a terribly polluted Cleveland, or of industrial pollution generally, but of a global environmental crisis. This transformation accelerated after a short essay appeared in *Time* magazine in early August. Under the headline "The Cities: The Price of Optimism," the un-bylined piece listed several troubled urban waterways, including the Potomac, which entered the nation's capital "as a pleasant stream, and leaves it stinking" from untreated sewage, and the Missouri, fouled by meatpacking wastes in Omaha. The Hudson, Milwaukee, Buffalo, and Monongahela were all terribly polluted by the cities through which they flowed. "Among the worst of them all," *Time* reported, "is the 80-mile-long Cuyahoga." "Some river!" the essay exclaimed. "Chocolate-brown, oily, bubbling with subsurface gases, it oozes rather than flows." After repeating a joke about how people who fall into the river decay rather than drown, the essay quickly told the story of the fire. "A few weeks ago, the oil-slicked river burst into flames and burned with such intensity that two railroad bridges spanning it were nearly destroyed." Perhaps that one sentence about the fire would have had less influence had it not appeared above a dramatic photograph of a boat nearly engulfed in flames on the water, dark smoke filling the sky, streams of water from bridge-bound firefighters feebly spraying the tug. "Boat Caught in Flaming Cuyahoga" was the only caption.[8] *Time* failed to note that the photo had been taken seventeen years earlier, when another fire swept across the Cuyahoga's waters. It's not clear whether the editors at *Time* mistakenly used the older photo or did so deliberately, perhaps thinking the more dramatic scene would grab readers' attention. Either way, *Time* created a new story for the 1969 fire, connecting an old image with a new interpretation. When combined with the essay, the photo suggested that the river's pollution had finally gotten so bad the river simply and spectacularly "burst into flames," seemingly for the first time.

Time published another photo with the "Price of Optimism" essay, in which Carl Stokes stands next to Ben Stefanski during the pollution tour the day after the fire. Reporters stand in a semi-circle around the mayor, who seems to be gesturing toward the sewer outfall over his shoulder. Appearing next to the photo of the flaming Cuyahoga—burning in 1952—the image of Stokes and Stefanski heightened the sense that the administration might not be up to the task at hand. The essay emphasized the "archaic sanitary storm system" and the broken Big Creek Interceptor, which was still spilling "a gray-green torrent" of sewage into the river. *Time* gave Stefanski credit for successfully leading the campaign to approve the $100 million bond issue. "No one could be against clean water," he said modestly in explaining the broad support for the bond. Still, the essay ended on an ominous note. "The Cuyahoga can be cleaned up in Cleveland, but as long as other cities keep dumping wastes upriver, it will remain exactly what it is today—an open sewer filing Lake Erie with scummy wavelets, sullen reminders that even a great lake can die."

After the *Time* coverage, the 1969 Cuyahoga fire evolved into one of the great symbolic environmental catastrophes of the industrial era. In November, *Audubon* featured the Cuyahoga on its back cover, in a short, poetic piece labeled "Counterpoint." At the top of the page was an aerial photograph of an ore ship winding its way up the river with downtown in the background. "Cleveland, take pride in your river. Cuyahoga. The very name flows as mightily as this great torrent of Midwestern capitalism." Cleveland should feel no shame, for this is a river that had made so much. "The river of orange.

The burning river. Unique to America, famous to the world." *Audubon*, tongue in cheek of course, urged Cleveland not to clean its waters, which painted Lake Erie in hues that would make Picasso proud. "Let the West have its National Wild and Scenic Rivers. Dedicate your stream as a National Industrial and Urban Waterway, a tribute to progress." The burning river and industry should be forever forged, *Audubon* said, a "monumental landmark" in the "shadows of towering factories."[9]

By the end of 1970, the river's infamy was secure. By then, political crusader Ralph Nader had formed a water pollution task force, one of many study groups made up of college students—commonly known as "Nader's Raiders"—eager to investigate the nation's many pressing problems. The water pollution study group focused on the federal government's failure to prevent water pollution despite significant engagement with the issue over the previous decade. The results of the nationwide study appeared in a four-hundred-page book, *Water Wasteland*, published in 1971 as Congress was putting together what would become the first Clean Water Act. Task force leaders David Zwick and John Esposito wanted to open the book with an image that would grab people's attention, and so they began, "On June 22, 1969, the Cuyahoga River burst into flame." Zwick would later recall that the Cuyahoga fire was an obvious choice. "When a river catches on fire in one of your major cities, it's obviously something of a problem," he said in 1999. "Any uninitiated person would say that."[10]

If the river fire had begun to influence the political debate concerning environmental regulation, it was gaining even more influence in cultural conceptions of the industrial Midwest. *National Geographic*'s stark issue in December 1970, under the cover "Our Ecological Crisis," prominently featured the Cuyahoga, using a foldout image of the industrial river. The dark photo showed the smoking stacks of the Republic Steel blast furnaces, but no flames leapt from the shadowed waters. Next to a small headline, "Sad, Soiled Waters: the Cuyahoga River and Lake Erie," a four-paragraph caption described the fire and its industrial setting: "Along this six-mile stretch, before emptying into Lake Erie, the river receives the wastes of steel mills, chemical and meat-rendering plants, and other industries." An additional caption on the same page described tests using minnows and the cyanide-laced waters of the Cuyahoga. Shown in a small photograph, the fish, belly up under the watchful eye of a federal water pollution control biologist, died in less than seven minutes. As with the initial coverage of the river fire, the connection between industry and fire was assumed here, but in other ways the story had changed dramatically. The Cuyahoga was now part of a larger, troubled ecology, one that included more than just the great lake into which it flowed. The "Ecological Crisis" issue described—and illustrated—a wide variety of environmental problems: air pollution in Montana, DDT in weakened birds' eggs, heat pollution from nuclear plants, raw sewage in the Hudson River, and the visual pollution of sprawl in North Miami. By clustering images and descriptions of a variety of environmental problems, from oil spills to overpopulation, *National Geographic* was making a larger point about the "fragile beauty all about us" and the "threat to man's only home," phrases that appeared on the issue's cover. As the caption concluded after describing the Cuyahoga's troubles, "Thus man disrupts the ecology, the delicate interrelationship of organisms—including him and their environment." The Cuyahoga, in its foldout magnificence, had become the poster child of the ecological crisis.[11]

THE RIVER IS GOING TO BLAZE UP AND DESTROY US

In the summer of 1969, Clevelanders knew, or ought to have known, that their river caught fire "from time to time," as the *Plain Dealer* editorial had phrased it. It is impossible to know how many times flames spread over the river, simply because press coverage was inconsistent, but at least ten times the Cuyahoga burned intensely enough to catch the attention of the press. The first fire may have occurred in August 1868, when a spark from the stacks of a passing tug apparently ignited an oil slick on the river. The *Plain Dealer* noted then that the fire could have been far worse had it spread to the vast lumber stores along the banks. Further, the *Plain Dealer* heightened its crusade to force oil refiners along the river to clean up their businesses. "We have called attention to the fact that along the whole length of the river, under the wharves, and even under the warehouses, there are deposits of this inflammable stuff," the paper reported, "and in some places to the thickness of several inches." Just the year before the 1868 fire, John D. Rockefeller had cobbled together five refineries within the firm of Rockefeller, Andrews & Flagler, already the largest oil refiners in the world. Still, the *Plain Dealer* had little patience for the relatively new business, seeing oil along the water as a threat to the already complex economy of the flats. Above the floating oil there were "millions upon millions of property in warehouses, elevators, flouring mills, machine shops and railroad freight depots, and extensive lumber yards, all liable at any moment, by the merest carelessness, of the use of a match or a lighted cigar, to be set on fire producing a conflagration that no human efforts could stop." The newspaper's reaction, along with that of Mayor Stephen Burhrer, who encouraged City Council to take further action to outlaw oil discharges, made clear that the problem revealed by the burning river was that the flames threatened shipping and riverfront businesses, which were at the heart of the city's prosperity.[12]

In 1883, a spectacular fire raced across the high waters of Kingsbury Run during a dramatic late-winter flood. Oil leaking from a still at the Thurmer and Teagle refinery was ignited by a boiler house standing in the rising water. The *New York Times* described the horror of burning water moving downstream toward Standard Oil's massive refinery. Although the heroic efforts of firemen and employees saved much of the plant, several Standard tanks exploded and buildings burned. Men jumped into the high water to dam up the culvert that separated Kingsbury Run from the Cuyahoga, successfully keeping the fire from the flooded flats along the larger river. Nearly thirty years later, in 1912, another horrific blaze threatened Standard Oil's Refinery No. 1, when gasoline leaking from a barge at Standard's docks covered the river and then caught fire. This time no floodwaters threatened to push the fire deep into the city, but the rapidly spreading flames killed five men caulking a boat at the Great Lakes Towing Company near Jefferson Avenue. "Without warning," the *Plain Dealer* reported, "a shriveling blast of blue flame from the water beneath them wrapped the drydock in fire." The deaths and the extent of the fire, which destroyed five tugs, a yacht, and three dry docks, heightened fears about the river as a fire hazard. The *Press* reported one tug captain as saying, "We don't know at what moment the river is going to blaze up and destroy us." Although the Cuyahoga remained critical to the city's economy, "The Menace of the River," as the headline of a *Plain Dealer* editorial called it, was unmistakable.[13]

These two fires became national stories because the loss of life and the scale of the damage warranted reporting. That the fires occurred on bodies of water was significant only because the waterways themselves were important as industrial thoroughfares. Along the Cuyahoga (and its small tributary, Kingsbury Run), businessmen developed the city's most valuable properties—the properties that drove the economy. In Cleveland, like other successful industrial cities, land uses and water uses could conflict. Different interests—steel making, oil refining, shipbuilding, paint manufacturing among them—asserted their demands on the river. The Cuyahoga's modest flow would cool the steel, dilute the wastes, and float the massive ships that moved to and from Lake Erie. In the first half century of Cleveland's rapid industrial development, the city hardly regulated the use of the river. Wastes that emptied into the stream were problematic only if they threatened some other industrial use. Government and the Chamber of Commerce worked to balance the interests of those in the flats, but just the economic interests. There were no other considerations.

To some degree the industries worked in concert. Steel manufacturers made the materials that helped build the ships (and dozens of other products); chemical manufacturers supplied the acids needed to wash the steel; oil refineries supplied the lubricants and some of the fuel. Altogether, industrial Cleveland was an impressive, well-oiled machine. But it lasted only so long. American Ship Building Company, formed in 1899 through the consolidation of three Cleveland firms, was one of the mainstays of the lower Cuyahoga, with slips and dry docks along the Old River Bed near the mouth. After building a series of ships for service in World War II, however, the company closed its hometown yards, moving manufacturing to other Great Lakes ports and eventually south to Tampa, Florida. Likewise, Standard Oil, founded in Cleveland in 1870, had a shifting relationship with its hometown. Founder John D. Rockefeller moved to New York in the 1880s, and although he kept a home in Cleveland for many years, the Rockefeller wealth accumulated mostly in other places. The breakup of his company in 1911 left Standard Oil of Ohio (known as Sohio after the 1930s) based in Cleveland, and for decades refining, research, and corporate jobs remained in the area. As late as 1944, Sohio employed eleven hundred people at its Refinery No. 1 on Kingsbury Run. With the development of new sources of oil far from Ohio, however, eventually it no longer made sense to refine along the Cuyahoga. Sohio stopped refining oil there in 1966, when it cleared the site of its Refinery No. 1 and laid off or relocated the employees who worked in the flats.[14]

Tellingly, when Sohio announced the closure of the plant in 1964, the *Plain Dealer* ran the story under the headline "Closing of Sohio Works Will Help Clear the Air." The first paragraph concluded that when the plant closed, "some of Cleveland's air and water pollution problem will vanish."[15] Sohio gave a portion of the Kingsbury Run property to the city, along with a cluster of buildings. Among them was the company's water pollution control facility, built to skim the oil off the company's wastes before they emptied into the Cuyahoga. Although part of the land once occupied by the refinery remains vacant and overgrown, much of it became a truck terminal, built just after the dismantling of the refinery to take advantage of nearby Interstate 77. Undoubtedly the terminal's construction eased concerns about the loss of jobs and suggested how land use would evolve in the new fluid city.

THE RIVER WILL BURN

In February 1936, the Cuyahoga caught fire under the Erie Railroad bridge that spanned the river between Gulf Oil's storage tanks and the American Steel and Wire Company's central furnace, just south of the Kingsbury Run outlet. The fire burned away the wooden piers of the bridge, temporarily closing the line and forcing a rerouting of trains. A worker who was operating the torch that ignited the oil suffered minor burns. The *Press* announced in a headline that the "Long-Feared River Peril" had arrived, indicating that the greatest consequence of the fire was "in its practical demonstration that the river will burn." The real fear that day was that a fire on the river would ignite Gulf's stored gasoline. Fire Chief James E. Granger concluded that the city needed to reacquire a fireboat. A series of fireboats had plied the river before 1932, when the last had been decommissioned in an effort to save money.[16]

In February 1948, another major fire made the papers. The *Press* coverage of the fire opened with the telling phrase, "Industry in the Cuyahoga River Valley is constantly menaced by fires." The Saturday night blaze had caused $100,000 in damage, but the three-alarm "slop oil" fire had threatened much greater damage in the flats. The *Plain Dealer* ran the front-page banner headline "River Oil Fire Perils Clark Bridge" and reported that more than thirty hoses had trained water on the fire before it was extinguished. By then, the fire had buckled parts of the Clark Avenue Bridge and burned through a bundle of electric cables, knocking out power in the nearby Brooklyn neighborhood. The jackknife bridge of the River Terminal Railroad was inoperable; hot-burning railroad ties caused serious damage to the bridge itself, and the spreading fire destroyed the controls. According to the *Press*, the economic impact of the fire included a 10 percent "reduction loss" at Republic Steel because the railroad bridge linking two parts of the steel plant had been disabled.[17]

That August, the skipper of the city's fireboat, The *Mavret H.*, told the *Press* that his boat had patrolled the Cuyahoga the entire previous winter "because there is not enough water in the river to freeze." The headline on the story read, "Fire Hazards Peril Cuyahoga Shipping." In December, the *Plain Dealer* reported that chemical company representatives told the city's port and harbor commission that "all-out war on the fire-hazardous oil slicks in the Cuyahoga River calls for more heroic measures than the mere spraying of chemicals." Instead, skimming the oil from the surface "is the most important tactic in keeping the five river-miles of docks, bridges and industries safe from slick-fed fires, the commissioners were told."[18] Through all the press coverage in the late 1940s, it remained clear that the major problem of the burning river was its threat to transportation, both of shipping on the Cuyahoga and across the many bridges that spanned the water. References to the plight of the river itself were few. A 1948 editorial in the *Press* that focused on fire prevention also included a reminder that "while not entirely related to fire prevention, the whole question of sewage and industrial waste in the Cuyahoga River remains unsettled." It noted, "Raw sewage continues to be dumped in the river today," a problem that needed to be resolved, though perhaps not as urgently as the replacement of wooden pilings with nonflammable concrete.[19]

Coverage of the river fires in Cleveland's newspapers was undoubtedly influenced by local economic interests, but these fires garnered essentially no coverage outside the city. The *New York Times*, the *Chicago Tribune*, and the *Columbus Dispatch* did not run a word about the fires of 1936 and 1948. Further, a *Cleveland Press* article in early 1941 suggests that fires that caused no significant damage may have escaped media attention altogether. The last paragraph of a March 17, 1941, story in the *Press* referred to a "recent" river fire that caused $7,500 in damage to an ore carrier. The *Press* files don't contain a story about the fire itself, however. It's likely that the paper's editors thought to mention the fire only after the Coast Guard threatened to prosecute "industries which pollute the Cuyahoga River with refuse which may impede navigation in the Cleveland harbor," which was the subject of the story. The article also noted that insurance underwriters and "shipping interests" had often appealed to city officials to stop the pollution. "The oil-covered Cuyahoga River long has been classed by marine fire underwriters as one of the worst fire hazards on the Great Lakes." Tellingly, the Cuyahoga was only "one of the worst," an indication that other ports also had difficulty controlling flammable pollutants.[20]

The fires in the 1930s and 1940s didn't spark a broad movement to clean the river, but they helped spur the construction of an improved sewer system that would—for the first time—serve the industrial valley. In early 1941, the state approved a general plan for sewering the valley, which in turn required the city to conduct studies concerning waste volumes and contents so the treatment plants could be adequately enlarged and improved. Consulting engineers Havens and Emerson conducted a 1944 study of "trade wastes" in the Low Level District—the industrial flats. It reviewed existing and planned sewers, including intercepting sewers that would redirect wastes from outlets on the river to the Westerly and Southerly treatment plants. But the heart of the study was data from twenty-eight industrial establishments within the city limits that released wastes directly into the Cuyahoga, data gathered to determine how much effluent would flow to each of the city's treatment facilities if all wastes entered sewers rather than waterways. Havens and Emerson concluded that the large steel mills, which contributed nearly 10 percent of all wastes emptied into the river, should construct their own treatment facilities, given the acidity and metal content of their discharges, both of which would have posed problems for municipal facilities. The study advised that the Sohio oil refinery, which contributed a bit more than 10 percent of the valley's wastes, should do the same.

As Havens and Emerson conducted its study, City Council created a special committee on stream pollution to gather facts and issue policy recommendations. The committee took a wide view of the problem, noting in its 1946 report: "The damages caused by stream and lake pollution are related to public health, domestic and industrial water supply, recreation, navigation, plant and animal life, and aesthetic values." Using data gathered by Havens and Emerson, the council committee asked three critical questions: How much and which of the Low Level wastes should be treated in city plants? What wastes, if any, should be discharged directly into the river? And which industries should treat their own wastes? The committee also determined that legal questions concerning suburban wastes, some of which flowed into the Cuyahoga directly south of the city boundary, in Cuyahoga Heights, would have to be resolved before any solutions could be implemented. The report concluded that jurisdictional uncertainties had led to a failure to act. "The overlapping and divided responsibilities of authorities lead to a do-nothing attitude or to futile and scattered efforts to ameliorate bad conditions." In 1946, Cleveland was just beginning a very long process of determining how to clean up the river.[21]

Beyond the committee's policy and administrative recommendations, the report included an expansive table containing the Havens and Emerson data from the Industrial Wastes Survey of Principal Cuyahoga Valley Industries, conducted in 1944. The data reveal the employment value of the twenty-eight major industrial firms in the flats and give a sense of the relative pollution loads the industries contributed to the river. Harshaw Chemical was a fairly small employer—325 men worked at its riverside plant—but it produced over 700,000 gallons of wastes per day. Standard Oil's Refinery No. 1, employing over 1,000 men, created 18 million gallons of process waste every day. These wastes contained oil residues and a host of other chemicals. The steel mills were larger still, with Jones & Laughlin's 4,000 employees creating

57 million gallons of wastewater per day, much of it cooling water, contaminated only by heat. U.S. Steel's American Steel and Wire coke works and furnaces employed 800 men and produced more than 80 million gallons of waste per day. The largest employer, Republic Steel, with over 5,700 employees, didn't provide complete data, so the actual waste total is unknown, but all told, industry along the river employed more than 16,000 workers and produced more than 170 million gallons of daily waste. These totals didn't include the Aluminum Company of America and U.S. Steel's Cuyahoga Works, both major plants just outside the city limits in Cuyahoga Heights. Even without including these plants, the Havens and Emerson data made clear that industry was more than the central feature of the flats; it was also central to the region's economy. Just as clear: the millions of gallons of process and cooling wastes posed an incredibly difficult engineering problem, one that would take years of study—measuring, calculating—before anyone did much in the way of building the solution.[22]

After the damaging 1948 fire, the Chamber of Commerce, which fought most regulation, became concerned enough with the condition of the river that it gathered together key players to discuss potential solutions. In addition to lobbying the city to rehabilitate the fireboat, the group hoped to persuade Clevelanders who worked with flammable liquids not to dispose of them in a way that might take them to the river. The committee would even study whether enough oil accumulated in the river to make its reclamation profitable.[23] A few months later, the River and Harbor Committee of the Chamber of Commerce, headed by Gifford F. Hood, president of the American Steel and Wire Company, announced a four-part plan to prevent further fires, involving several responsibilities to be taken on by the city: employing a fire tug or the harbormaster's yacht to patrol the river several times a day in search of slicks; purchasing equipment to remove slicks; and analyzing the river's water quality at "various locations." The committee also recommended a broad public campaign to discourage the draining of flammable wastes into the river through sewers. Unsurprisingly, the chamber's plan was modest, required essentially nothing of industry, and failed to consider the Cuyahoga as anything other than the proper place for industry to dispose of its wastes. Taking a stunningly narrow view of the problem, the chamber had focused completely on oil slicks. For the chamber, the river's only real problem was that it caught fire from time to time.[24]

Cuyahoga pollution studies continued to roll out; another major one appeared in 1960, conducted by the Sewage and Industrial Wastes Unit of the Ohio Department of Health. At the same time, some progress was made in controlling wastes. The state's 1954 survey of wastes had found that Sohio was putting 782 gallons of oil into the river every day. That revelation forced Sohio to change production procedures, which halved the amount of oil reaching the river, and by the end of the decade, Refinery No. 1 had gained a new oil-skimming facility that reduced releases even further. Sohio was a major consumer of water, and oil was a visible pollutant, the one most directly related to the river fires. In part to be a good corporate citizen, to avoid bad press, and to keep ahead of state regulations, Sohio made it company policy to reduce its oil discharges. All this was achieved by 1960, when a lengthy *Plain Dealer* article described the company's efforts under the headline "Sohio Spends Millions to Cut Contamination of Streams." Unfortunately, other industries, including the steel mills and Harshaw Chemical, were less concerned about keeping ahead of the regulatory curve.[25]

CLEVELAND HAS BEEN EXCEEDINGLY LAGGARD

The day after the pollution tour, two days after the fire, Mayor Stokes wrote a letter to Governor Jim Rhodes demanding that the state investigate pollution entering the Cuyahoga from outside the city limits, review its permits for industrial polluters along the river, and establish a water pollution enforcement office in the area. The next day, state engineers patrolled the river, searching for the source of the unknown pollutant that fueled the fire, and Dr. Emmett Arnold, director of the Ohio Department of Health, defended the state's role in water pollution control. In an interview with Betty Klaric, Arnold speculated that a spill of some volatile substance might have been at fault, although no company had reported such an accident, as required by law. Sounding like a politician, Arnold asserted that the state had the power to solve the problem since it had the authority to issue daily $500 fines to companies out of compliance with their permits. To his knowledge, no such fines had ever been issued, but, he told Klaric confidently, "We can usually get these industries to be good boys."[26]

The visit by Arnold and the state engineers provided an initial response to Stokes's letter, but a week later the state issued a fuller and more aggressive rejoinder, written by John Richards, engineer-in-charge at the Sewage and Industrial Waste Unit of the Department of Health. Richards claimed that the fire had focused "critical attention on the failure of the City of Cleveland to meet its schedules for pollution abatement." Ignoring the riverside industry, Richards claimed that "Cleveland has been exceedingly laggard" in carrying out its sewer system improvement program, citing the combined sewers, which regularly emptied untreated wastes into the river, and the breakdown of the Big Creek Interceptor, which was still discharging twenty million to thirty million gallons a day into the Cuyahoga. He was also critical of the city for discontinuing its operation of a scavenger boat, which had plied the river to remove debris that posed a fire hazard. More important, Richards claimed the city had not made the promised progress on its three treatment plants, each of which still discharged only partially treated wastes. Noting that the state had already taken action to freeze all construction in five suburbs until they moved forward with plans to treat their sewage, Richards threatened to do the same in Cleveland.[27]

Stokes sent Richards's letter on to Edward Martin, director of the Clean Water Task Force, who issued a thorough reply, which he also provided to the press. Point by point, Martin refuted the state's claims about the "laggard" city. He wrote that the city's investigators had determined that a highly volatile material had caused the fire, not "accumulated small quantities of oil 'drippings' originating in Cleveland's combined sewer system." He noted that the city's scavenger boat had indeed been in operation before the fire, and had been "in continuous operation" since, but because the fire began on the upstream side of the bridges—the exact spot where the river's navigable channel ends—the boat never had the ability to remove debris from beneath the trestle. Martin also defended the city's slow response to the Big Creek Interceptor, noting that planning for a thorough reconstruction had been delayed by state highway construction in the area—Interstate 71 and the Jennings Freeway. Most important, the city had been slow to advance work on the treatment plants because it had yet to receive matching funds from the federal or state government. The *Press* correctly summarized the letter with the headline "City Rejects Blame for Fire on River."[28]

The city-state conflict wasn't playing well in the press, and Governor Rhodes must have recognized that it didn't serve his purposes to continue the back-and-forth. He instructed Richards to respond to Martin's letter. With a much more conciliatory tone, Richards made some concessions and found some common ground. He even praised the "leadership that Cleveland is providing in endeavoring to get an interceptor sewer installed up the Cuyahoga River." He was not willing to move any of his personnel to Cleveland—his engineers were stationed in Cuyahoga Falls, twenty miles to the south—but he attempted to close his letter on a positive note: "It is our hope that cooperative efforts can help to speed a solution to your problems." Still, calling the polluted Cuyahoga "your problem" reasserted the city's primary responsibility for cleaning up the river.[29]

The Stokes administration and the state hadn't exactly patched up their relationship by mid-July, but at least the Big Creek Interceptor had been fixed. After pouring 1.4 billion gallons of sewage into the river over the course of fifty-six days, the interceptor was now sending its wastes to the Southerly Treatment Plant. The repairs were not over. Longer sections of the pipe would have to be replaced over the winter, but the river got a reprieve. After hundreds of thousands of dollars in unplanned expenses, the city had at least ended the immediate crisis. Broader structural problems remained.

THE RAPE OF THE CUYAHOGA

On April 28, 1970, Carl Stokes was back in Washington to support legislation before Congress, this time bills introduced by Edmund Muskie that would increase federal spending on water pollution control. Muskie, the Democratic senator from Maine, had become a champion of environmental causes in Congress. He had strong allies among the nation's mayors, including Stokes, with whom he had a good working relationship. On this occasion, Stokes came on behalf of the National League of Cities and the U.S. Conference of Mayors, organizations created to help press the priorities of cities in Washington. His prepared statement was filled with statistics about municipal investments in sewage infrastructure and the indebtedness of the nation's cities. He painted a convincing picture of the need for greater state and federal help, especially in the building of sewage treatment plants. But when Muskie asked him to make any remarks he would like, Stokes opened, "Frankly, on Earth Day, just a few days ago, I was not particularly impressed with the Congressmen and Senators and mayors and legislators and members of the administration who fanned out across the nation giving speeches about the terrible threat to the continuity and longevity of this nation, because there is no question in my mind but that those same Congressmen, those same Senators and legislators and very often the mayors will be reluctant to try to face what it would cost to do something about that which they were speaking so pointedly and so brilliantly on the various podiums throughout the nation." This was a long-winded way of saying that on Earth Day many politicians were frauds.[30]

Stokes was careful to describe water pollution as a national problem and the difficulty of financing pollution control as a universal one, but he noted that Cleveland was a good example of the predicament in which cities found themselves. "We in Cleveland sit on the banks of a river and lake which has become almost legendary, not only in the United States but abroad." Stokes said that during his February 1970 trip to Europe he "got very little humor out of the fact that the Cuyahoga River was being used as an example . . . of how bad rivers are. It just so happened that this followed not too long after our Cuyahoga River had realized its potential of actually catching fire." In November 1969, the British Broadcasting Corporation had labeled Cleveland the pollution capital of the world, the burning river serving as irrefutable evidence. The story of the fire had spread, and now Mayor Stokes used his troubled river as the most moving evidence in the case for increased federal spending on sewer construction.

Significant revision to federal water pollution control law would await the passage of the Clean Water Act in 1972, but Congress was willing to take smaller steps in the meantime. In the fall of 1970, Carl's brother Louis Stokes, who represented part of Cleveland in Congress, introduced a bill in the House to empower the Army Corps of Engineers to "investigate, study, and undertake measures in the interests of flood control, recreation, fish and wildlife, water quality, and environmental quality" on the Cuyahoga River. In supporting the bill, passed as part of the broad Rivers and Harbors and Flood Control Act of 1970, Congressman Stokes spoke at length about the Cuyahoga, noting that it would "live in infamy as the only river in the world to be proclaimed a fire hazard." "In June of 1969," he added, "the river actually caught fire, causing almost $100,000 damage to two railroad bridges. A continuous and vigorous cleanup program could have prevented this shameful occurrence." As he continued, it became clear that the problem of the river fire was not the damage to the two bridges, as the newspapers had originally suggested. Stokes resented the stigma the fire had attached to Cleveland, the negative press his city had received, even in Europe. He noted that the lower Cuyahoga had "virtually no fish life" and that recreational uses of Lake Erie had decreased because of the river. Sport fishing had diminished and swimming had been disallowed in several areas "because of the hazardous levels of bacterial contamination." "In short," Congressman Stokes concluded, "the rape of the Cuyahoga River has not only made it useless for any purpose other than a dumping place for sewage and industrial waste, but also has had a deleterious effect upon the ecology of one of the Great Lakes." He spoke the evolving language of environmentalism, helping to change the meaning of the story. Louis Stokes had found a new way to talk about an old problem.[31]

Congressman Stokes was successful in his bid to direct federal funds toward the cleanup of the Cuyahoga, and over the next several years the Army Corps conducted the study and even made some improvements to the river. But the corps focused on flood control and largely disregarded broader water quality issues. It issued a series of interim reports on what it called simply a

"Flood Control Study" of the Cuyahoga, in which it described efforts to curb upstream erosion, trying to prevent high waters from cutting banks and sending silt and debris downstream into the navigable channel. The corps did not report on sewers or industry or water quality at all, beyond the problem of silt buildup. Congressman Stokes had been moved by the language of environmentalism, by the vision of a river that could serve as more than an industrial sewer. The Army Corps retained its narrower view. Its object: keep the river in its banks and keep it clear for shipping.

DANGER IN THE HEART OF CLEVELAND

Despite the considerable political attention to the economic threat posed by the polluted river, fires on the Cuyahoga had peaked in the late 1940s and early 1950s. Another railroad trestle was destroyed in June 1949, and a spectacular oil slick fire sent clouds of heavy smoke over the lakefront in March 1951. In October 1950, a year-long survey by the fire department concluded that, with some notable exceptions, most industries were cooperating with the city's requests to stop dumping flammable liquids into the Cuyahoga. But the river "still presents a serious fire hazard to the community," fire officials reported. In May 1952, *Press* reporter Maxwell Riddle took a fireboat tour of the river with city fire officials, who pointed out two-inch-thick oil slicks. "In many places, the river was bubbling like a beer mash," Riddle wrote. Fire officials told Riddle that the worst spot on the river was near the mouth of Kingsbury Run, the creek that ran through the Standard Oil refinery before joining the Cuyahoga at the Great Lakes Towing Company boat repair yard. "A fire here would wipe that company out in a hurry," a lieutenant with the fire prevention bureau said.[32] Six months later, it happened. The 1952 fire was large enough to warrant another front-page banner headline, "Oil Slick Fire Ruins Flats Shipyard," in the *Plain Dealer*. The fire damaged the Jefferson Avenue Bridge and came perilously close to the Standard Oil refinery; at the Great Lakes Towing Company, it destroyed three tugs and the dry docks. Firemen battled the blaze from the bridge and from a fireboat, attempting to prevent the fire's spread. A series of photos snapped for the *Plain Dealer* included one of a tug "enveloped in flames," which accompanied the story on page 1—and would appear in *Time* magazine years later.[33]

Local coverage of the November 1952 fire and the subsequent crackdown on polluters was still framed in economic terms. City leaders fretted over pollution not for the river's sake but because it put others at financial risk. Under the headline "Danger in the Heart of Cleveland," an editorial in the

Figure 11. Firefighters fought the 1952 Cuyahoga fire from the Jefferson Avenue bridge. The fire, among the worst on the river, caused serious damage to the Great Lakes Towing Company dry docks, hidden here by the smoke. Photo by James Thomas. Cleveland Press Collection, Cleveland State University.

Press on November 4, 1952, said the big fire underscored the cost of inaction. "Well, somebody had better get busy. The oil slick menace is bound to affect fire insurance rates. Vessel owners are not going to use the river for winter mooring if they feel that the ships will not be safe there. That would be an economic loss."[34] As with the fire four years earlier, the 1952 blaze attracted essentially no press attention outside Cleveland. The *Columbus Dispatch* ran part of an Associated Press story on the fire, but the *Cincinnati Enquirer* failed to mention it at all. The *Wall Street Journal* also did not refer to the fire, though three days later it reported that Cleveland had reached a long-time low in unemployment, having apparently shaken off the effects of a recently re-solved steel strike. According to a Federal Reserve Bank report, the Cleveland region had topped records in both steel and automobile production, suggesting that all was well in the industrial metropolis.[35]

164

In 1952, Cleveland was still obviously an industrial city. This central fact was most evident at the upper reaches of navigation on the Cuyahoga, where two massive integrated steel mills crowded along the narrow channel. To the west, the Jones & Laughlin's Cleveland Works, formerly Otis Steel and Cleveland Furnace Company, handled limestone and ore delivered by tug-guided ships. Its sintering plant prepared the ores for two blast furnaces; coke ovens baked thousands of tons of coal, delivered by rail, using some of the thirty-eight miles of standard-gauge track that laced the property. The plant consumed oil delivered by pipeline from a nearby refinery, as well as natural gas, used in the finishing mills, where steel took on the various shapes buyers demanded. On the opposite bank of the Cuyahoga, Republic Steel's facilities were equally impressive. Sprawling across twelve hundred acres, these mills revealed industrialism's productive genius and offered thousands of high-paying jobs.[36] The 1950 census found roughly 42 percent of the city's workers employed in manufacturing, many of them in the industries that filled the flats and the neighborhoods around the river.

Not all of Cleveland's industries thrived in the 1950s, but steel industry investments continued. Jones & Laughlin invested more than $300 million in its physical plant in the twenty years after World War II, and improvements kept coming—new rolling mills, pickling lines, an electric furnace shop, and a basic oxygen steelmaking shop, the last completed in 1960. Modernization of J&L's Cleveland Works was so extensive that it even required the straightening of the river—moving the channel to create a ten-acre site for a new hot strip mill in 1962. At its annual meeting in 1964, J&L described its new production units along the Cuyahoga, assuring shareholders that market studies "indicate that Cleveland is strategically located and is in the center of the geographic area that is the primary flat-rolled steel market in the world."[37]

Republic Steel also made significant investments along the Cuyahoga. In the mid-1960s, Republic built new cold strip and hot strip rolling mills, investing $200 million in its flat-rolled steel plant. In 1969, Republic's assistant vice president, John Lowey, called the hot strip mill "the largest single capital spending project ever undertaken in this city." Like any good politician, Carl Stokes helped celebrate investments in his city. He and Ben Stefanski were especially eager to attend a ceremony in the Republic Building, part of the Terminal Tower complex near Public Square, for an announcement that the company was set to construct a new wastewater treatment plant at its Cleveland works. The plant would treat more than 100 million gallons of water a day, approximately equal to the waste created by a city of 500,000 people—an

indication of just how much water steelmaking consumed. At the brief ceremony, Republic announced that the plant would be completed by the spring of
1970. Although pollution control facilities represented a small fraction of
total capital investments, they added up. By its own accounting, Republic invested more than $27 million in wastewater treatment facilities in its Cleve-
land plants during the 1960s, including the construction of a sanitary sewer
system to stop the dumping of waste from its 8,500 employees directly into
the river—a practice ended in 1965, when the new sewer connected the
plants' toilets to the Southerly Treatment Plant.[38]

No wonder the state was accustomed to treading lightly when it came to
regulating the steel industry. The hundreds of millions of dollars invested in
Cleveland plants encouraged the development of a cooperative relationship
between industry and the state. Just how cooperative this relationship had
become was on display in the fall of 1969, when U.S. Secretary of the Interior
Walter Hickel asked the Federal Water Pollution Control Administration to
hold informal hearings with Cleveland's three major steel companies: Jones &
Laughlin, Republic, and U.S. Steel, whose major regional plant was south of
the city in Cuyahoga Heights. In calling for the October hearing, Hickel had
taken everyone by surprise—the companies, the state, and even the press.
"People of America have made it abundantly clear they will no longer tolerate
pollution of their environment," Hickel said in an attempt to explain the
hearings.[39]

Steel industry executives gathered at the Pick-Carter Hotel in downtown
Cleveland on October 7 and listened to their unlikely champion, Emmett Arnold, chairman of the Ohio Water Pollution Control Board, defend the performance of the companies to Murray Stein, chief enforcement officer at
the Federal Water Pollution Control Administration. Arnold set the tone for
the gathering, calling it "a waste of time and money" and stating flatly that the
state resented federal interference. Arnold assured Stein that Republic Steel,
the first company to address the gathering, was under state permit orders and
not in any violation of the law. Further, the company had agreed to the recommendations and conclusions of the Lake Erie Conference, announced in June,
and had set out a schedule to make the necessary plant improvements. Arnold's defense of the status quo was even more vigorous than that of Republic
Steel, which offered a lengthy statement—essentially a long list of the company's investments in water pollution control at its Cleveland facilities. At the
end of the statement, however, John Lowey reminded Stein that Republic had
invested a huge sum "so that we may continue to be competitive with the best
flat-rolled steel available anywhere in the world. . . . This is our way of

REPUBLIC STEEL CORP.
CLEVELAND DISTRICT STEEL PLANT

Addition to air cleaning systems presently serving the basic oxygen furnace shop (A) and open hearth shop (B).

Cost: $1,250,000.

Ⓐ

Ⓑ

CLARK AVE. BRIDGE

INDEPENDENCE RD.

DILLE RD.

Figure 12. Republic Steel's massive plant along the Cuyahoga, just out of the picture to the right, was among Cleveland's most conspicuous polluters, which brought unwelcome attention and forced expensive alterations to its mills. As Republic attempted to limit the costs of regulation, it touted its investments in pollution abatement equipment, as with this photo supplied to the *Cleveland Press* in April 1970, a week before the first Earth Day. Cleveland Press Collection, Cleveland State University.

protecting the jobs of roughly 8,500 employees of this district.'[40] After the statement, Republic officials refused to answer Stein's questions. The only consequence of the hearing for Republic—and for Jones & Laughlin and U.S. Steel, which were more cooperative in that their representatives answered questions and pledged compliance in the near term—appears to have been a few days of bad press, nothing they hadn't suffered through already, especially since the fire.

Republic pushed back after the hearings, using former U.S. senator from Ohio John Bricker to lobby Secretary Hickel, a fellow Republican, in the hopes of stalling the sudden federal urgency concerning water pollution control, or at least in the hopes of shifting more of the heat away from industry and toward municipal sewage and agricultural runoff. In an internal document, Republic's assistant counsel, J.W. Mills, offered guidance to Bricker, noting that the aggressive approach to enforcement announced by Hickel "could have a divisive effect and could be detrimental politically." According to Mills, "radical political elements," including Students for a Democratic Society, which was helping to organize "a national teach-in on pollution for next spring" (the first Earth Day), were trying to discredit the Nixon administration by keeping pollution in the news. "These groups foster an atmosphere of emotionalism," Mills wrote in his November 19 memo, "whereby pollution is approached on the basis of general allegations rather than scientific proof." He hoped that the Republican administration would give greater consideration to the problems industry faced in trying to meet the new pollution standards, especially in view of the engineering difficulties and the size of the capital investments required. And Mills reminded Bricker, "Industry has been a leader in the efforts to solve water pollution problems and has often been considerably ahead of both municipalities and agriculture."[41]

In addition to the work of its own lobbyists in Washington, the steel industry could count on the support of the Greater Cleveland Growth Association (formerly the Chamber of Commerce) in working against greater federal involvement in water pollution control. The association was a consistent foe of increasing environmental regulation, especially at the federal level. Earlier in the year, it gathered members that had interests along the Cuyahoga, including the three steel companies, out of concern over new dredging guidelines being developed by the Army Corps of Engineers. The mill owners and other industries dredged the river in front of their docks every year, a task that was essential to their operations. The Army Corps had proposed banning the dumping of dredge spoils in open water, the common practice, since spoils were contaminated and contributed to the pollution of Lake Erie. Sensing that this new rule would greatly increase the costs of dredging, the association sponsored a series of meetings, including a breakfast meeting in March, three months before the river fire. Those gathered discussed ways to combat the proposal, including offering the argument that "there is no technical support for the theory that lake dumping causes pollution of the water." However, the members recognized that "a strong public relations issue compels industry to seek an alternative" to open lake dumping. The compromise that the association proposed, and Cleveland congressman Charles Vanik supported, involved free private access to dump sites created by the federal government. In Cleveland, these sites eventually included an area behind a dike adjacent to Burke Lakefront Airport and a larger site adjacent to the pier at Gordon Park, where the city was gradually filling in around scuttled ore boats. This solution eased tensions on this particular issue, but the Greater Cleveland Growth Association, and the steel companies particularly, surely recognized that they were losing control of the regulatory process. The era of easy waste disposal was at an end.[42]

Industry lobbied against new regulations, strict enforcement, and quickened timelines in an effort to keep control of a process that it had long had well in hand. Since entering into the permit arrangement with the Ohio Water Pollution Control Board in 1953, Republic had invested heavily in pollution control equipment, with the concern that quality was a moving target. Republic and other industrial polluters worked to manage the rising expectations of residents and regulators. As Republic's supervisor of water management, Louis Birkel, said to the control board in May of 1968, "the magnitude of the municipal and industrial complex served by the very small Cuyahoga River is truly astounding and the quality objectives should be correspondingly related."[43] Republic's position was always that people should have realistic goals for the Cuyahoga, and realism was clearly at the core of industry's relationship with state regulators. That relationship had led to discrete and identifiable improvements. Even Betty Klaric had noticed, reporting in January 1969 that things were improving along the river, where the discharge of pickling acid from the three largest steel mills had dropped from 150,000 gallons in 1963 to just 1,500 gallons. The discharge of iron had taken a similarly precipitous fall. She noted that the actual effect on the quality of the river was unknown, however, and after the river burned, it became more difficult for Republic and other companies to claim progress in pollution control.[44]

TO SWIM OR NOT TO SWIM?

After the 1969 Cuyahoga fire, the press remained alert to the troubled river. Fire Lt. Donald Pahler remained alert, too. Commanding the *Celebrezze*, Pahler and his men, alternating with two other fireboat crews, patrolled the Cuyahoga, motoring upstream to the end of navigation, where the river had caught fire, and making their way back down to the river's mouth, breaking up oil slicks and piles of debris as they traveled. This was daily work. "There's always the possibility if they burn, they'll spread to another boat or even to shore," Pahler said of the oil slicks. The *Plain Dealer* featured Pahler in a mid-August Sunday magazine article, illustrated by the same photo the paper ran the day after the fire, the one of the *Celebrezze* hosing down the trestle. The article emphasized the hazards these men faced—diluting a radioactive cobalt spill from a paint plant one day, trying to suck up a 200,000-gallon gasoline spill on another. And there was the constant threat of fire. Pahler, a twenty-four-year veteran of fireboat duty, took it all in stride. "I guess the Cuyahoga is an industrial river. It's not pleasant but I really can't point the finger at any one person or company for its condition. Look, water beauty to some people is a fat paycheck." Pahler hadn't seen anything living in the river since the end of the 1951 steel strike, but to him the best the city could expect from the Cuyahoga was that it not catch fire. Anything short of flames was okay. *Plain Dealer* reporter Edward Whelan spent the day with Pahler and his crew out on the water, Pahler's last tour before taking a vacation on Lake Erie near Sandusky. As Whelan wrote, "Lt. Pahler went pleasure boating far from the gas tanks, paint plants and oil slicks."[45]

Like Pahler, Klaric kept up her vigilance. Even before the fire, she had become part of the expanding Cleveland environmental story. In May, the *Press* began a series in which her stories appeared under a new byline: Betty Betterment. In a clumsy attempt to take advantage of her growing reputation in environmental reporting, the stories featured Klaric's own activities, including her "campaign against blight," which began at Gordon Park. There she took up a push broom "ready to tackle the litter," an act that was captured in a large photo. She didn't mention the fill operation—the dumping of rubbish into the lake—but she noted that the city provided too few garbage cans. She reported that lakeside open burning, an old municipal practice, had returned to Gordon Park, but it turned out to be a temporary effort to dispose of diseased elms. Next Betty Betterment tackled unkempt lawns in Tremont, where she helped plant grass and publicized a budding neighborhood beautification effort. In an article under the headline "Young Blight Fighters Need Tools," she described how the Cleveland: Now! program might supply volunteers with rakes, shovels, and even a truck to facilitate the cleanup of Tremont, the aging ethnic neighborhood perched over the industrial flats. And then, just like that, the series in which Klaric played the conservative role of middle-class "municipal housekeeper," a tradition that stretched back into the 1890s, ended, apparently cut short by the fire. Betty Betterment dropped her push broom and headed down to the filthy river to join Stokes on the pollution tour.[46]

But Klaric wasn't finished being part of the story. A month after the fire, she and a half dozen of her *Press* colleagues decided to take a midday swim at Edgewater Beach. Braving the smelly water, the seven *Press* staffers ran through the shallows holding hands, a moment captured for the next day's paper. "To Swim or Not to Swim in Lake?" the *Press*'s headline asked. Klaric answered "yes." A sidebar listed bacteria counts at the city's beaches, including Edgewater and White City, both of which had seen their numbers improve dramatically after the installation of the plastic barriers and the use of chlorine. Klaric even suggested that bathers need not concern themselves too much with the numbers, since, she wrote in an unfortunate phrase, "engineers have been pooh-poohing bacterial standards." It seems that the greatest impediment to swimming in the lake was the smell.[47]

Klaric stayed on the environment beat through 1972, attending government meetings, press conferences, court proceedings, and hearings. She churned out hundreds of articles before the *Press* folded in 1982, after which she earned a law degree and embarked on a second career. She donated her clippings file to the Cleveland Public Library, where they have since been put on microfiche. Although there were real moments of crisis and movement—the river fire and Earth Day, for example—when read all together Klaric's articles give a sense of treading water. The same issues crop up, the same names, the same companies—not because Klaric didn't do her job or couldn't uncover the real story. The story simply remained remarkably consistent.

Harshaw Chemical saw its share of press over the years, some of it good, including when the company and the city announced an agreement that would prevent 300,000 pounds of calcium sulfate from reaching the river every day, instead sending it to Southerly, where it would help precipitate phosphates in the sewage. This October 1969 agreement was rare in that it pleased both business and environmental interests.[48] In early 1970, Harshaw was back in the *Press* after Klaric traveled to San Diego to report on an American Management Association meeting. There Paul Pine, a retired Harshaw vice president, spoke at length about pollution control. Pine had headed up the Committee on Industrial Wastes for the Greater Cleveland Growth Association, and he had been an active opponent of increased federal involvement in pollution regulation. He opposed the creation of the Federal Water Pollution Control Administration (which happened in 1965) and the development of federal water quality standards, arguing, as he did in 1963, that the "proper federal role is in the field of research, consultation, advice and promotional education efforts." He thought the state was the appropriate governmental body to oversee pollution control. Unsurprisingly, then, while in San Diego, Pine praised the relationship that industry had built with state regulators in Ohio. "I cannot say enough in appreciation of the attitude, the patience and the competence of the Ohio Water Pollution Control Board and its staff of engineers," he said. He praised at length the working relationship between understaffed regulators and the state's industries, which had "stepped into the gap" and conducted the necessary research on pollution control. This cooperative relationship had been a success, Pine said, noting, somewhat optimistically, that "the Cuyahoga is no longer billed by the news media as the only river in the world that is a fire hazard." Problems remained to be solved, Pine conceded, especially controlling household dumping of oil in sewers, the use of phosphate detergents, and the littering of waterways—all issues related to individuals, not industries. Klaric's article on this positive appraisal of water pollution control ended with Pine's thoughts on the Stokes administration's creation of pools in the lake at White City and Edgewater beaches: "probably the most expensive swimming water in the nation."[49]

Just two days after Stokes's October 1969 announcement of the city's agreement with Harshaw, which came on the same day the steel companies began the hearings before the federal regulators, the *Press* ran an editorial, "For a Cleaner River," in praise of federal involvement in water pollution control. After eight paragraphs on the Cuyahoga, a smaller headline added " . . . And Cleaner Air," after which the *Press* demanded that City Council pass the new air pollution ordinance. Just below the editorials on pollution, the *Press* ran another, which to most readers probably seemed unconnected. "This has been a bloody week in Cleveland," it began. Five homicides—and it was only Thursday. The city's homicide total had reached 212—61 more than the previous year at that point. After repeating Mayor Stokes's call for the passage of a gun control ordinance, "bottled up" in council since May, the *Press* asked, "How many more must die?" The juxtaposed *Press* editorials remind us that Cleveland was dealing with the environmental and urban crises at the same time, and both were wreaking chaos and sparking calls for greater regulatory control. While standing on the charred railroad trestle earlier that year, Stokes had talked of remaking the city, moving away from the industrial past. He knew this would not be an easy task.[50]

6 From Earth Day to EcoCity

"Stokes Fears Poor Lose Priority to Pollution War," read the *Plain Dealer* headline—not exactly the type of press that organizers of the first Earth Day were hoping for. Appearing on Thursday, April 16, 1970, the story covered the ceremony announcing Cleveland's "Crisis in the Environment Week," scheduled to begin that Saturday. Mayor Stokes had invited a number of environmental activists to City Hall for the occasion, where he indicated that his administration was supporting the event and then, surprisingly, announced concerns. In a statement that appeared in the *Plain Dealer* the next day, in the African American weekly *Call and Post* the next week, and in the *New York Times* the next month, Stokes said, "I am fearful that the priorities on air and water pollution may be at the expense of what the priorities of the country ought to be: proper housing, adequate food and clothing."[1] Suddenly the administration's support for the growing environmental movement seemed in doubt.

Plain Dealer reporter Robert McGruder captured some of the discussion that took place in City Hall after Stokes expressed his reservations. Rev. Earl Cunningham pushed back, quoting statistics about how many people would die that week because of the effects of pollution. Cunningham was the white pastor of the all-black Mt. Pleasant Methodist Church on Cleveland's East Side—the church the Stokes family attended. He was no stranger to the problems of urban poverty, but he must have been taken aback by Stokes's sudden skepticism about the "glamour" of the ecology movement. "If you cannot breathe and there is no water it doesn't matter what kind of house you live in," Cunningham said. Stokes would have none of it, retorting with his own statistics about how many babies would die because of poor prenatal care and adding that hungry children in Biafra, Mississippi, and Hough needed food today. Then, after conceding that air and water pollution were important issues, Stokes revealed his growing frustration with suburban leaders, with whom he had reached an impasse regarding sewage treatment. "It is a lot easier to get the people in Parma and Shaker Heights and Lakewood, and even the President of the United States concerned about pollution than about hunger," he said, according to the *Plain Dealer*. Perhaps this back-and-forth was inadvertent—a momentary lapse for a mayor who usually stayed on script—or perhaps Stokes was making a calculated political stand, one that might serve him in the future.

No doubt Stokes's position played well on Cleveland's East Side, especially after a longer piece on the issue appeared in the *Call and Post* under the head-line "Poverty Gets Top Priority over Pollution from Stokes." In the article, German-born poet, photographer, activist, and reporter Ulf Goebel included many of the same quotes as McGruder, and he added his own pointed analysis about the suburban/urban divide. "Even environmental problems that lack the glamour of air and water pollution control tend to be forgotten about," he wrote. "For example, there is in the ghetto a substantial rat problem. Subur-ban idealists have no experience or knowledge of this. So they don't worry about it." Goebel, like Stokes, understood that the crisis in the urban environ-ment involved more than just polluted air and water.[2]

Stokes's position didn't play as well in the *New York Times*, which usually treated the mayor with admiration. A month after Earth Day, a *Times* edito-rial, titled "Ecological Backlash," noted that the people of Cleveland had seen "with their own eyes their river go up in flames" and then chided Stokes for his position. "It is sad to see so fine a Mayor as Carl B. Stokes of Cleveland succumbing to the notion that the fight against pollution can only be waged at the expense of the poor." The *Times* argued, "Far from being competitive, these two vital sets of demands are interwoven aspects of the same environ-mental problem." Stokes understood this, of course, and had made that argu-ment himself, but now, with the federal budget under pressure from the seemingly endless Vietnam War, and an obvious pullback in the War on Pov-erty, Stokes also understood that the political winds had shifted, along with the nation's priorities. Cleveland was struggling through an increasingly bad budgetary situation and could no longer hope for greater support from the federal government. Since the state legislature was an unlikely savior, Stokes knew something would have to give.

After the initial encounter at City Hall, Environmental Crisis Week proved a great success. A long roster of events, many of them organized by city em-ployee Laurence Aurbach and Cleveland State University student Larry Tom-scak, garnered good attendance and positive press. The Sierra Club led a cleanup of Edgewater Beach, where chapter vice president Grant Thompson explained that the club wanted to "dramatize the tragic condition of Cleveland's water recreation areas."[3] At the same time, Boy Scouts and Girl Scouts planted seedlings in the park. Stokes missed these events and others, as he traveled to Tulsa with his family to visit his sister-in-law, but his absence didn't seem to matter. Ralph Nader roused a crowd of eight hundred at Cleveland State, arguing that it would cost corporations only a fraction of their profits to control pollution. "The way to do it is known and it would not cost any jobs," he said, singling out Republic Steel for his criticism. According to the *Cleveland Press*, after the talk some of those in attendance picketed the Republic headquarters, a mile from campus. The previous day, April 22, more than a thousand students and faculty participated in a "March of Death" from the Cleveland State campus down to the river where Moses Cleaveland had disembarked and founded the city. *Press* reporter Betty Klaric kept busy during the week, reporting on events from the "March of Death" to the activities of Lakewood sixth-graders, who gave presentations to younger students and picked up litter around the Roosevelt School. The *Call and Post* also offered positive coverage of the events, noting that congregations made plans for "Save Our Environment" services at the beginning of the week and that many East Side schools had plans for cleanup activities, educational posters, skits, and, at Glenville High School, even chemistry experiments to demonstrate the consequences of water pollution.[4]

The enthusiastic participation of East Side schools and the positive coverage in the *Call and Post* didn't reflect the ambivalence of the African American community about the growing influence of the environmental movement. Some prominent African Americans, including Stokes, were concerned that the environmental reform would be too narrow. As prominent civil rights leader Whitney Young Jr. wrote in his widely read syndicated column, "I get the uneasy feeling that some people who have suddenly discovered the pollution issue embrace it because its basic concern is improving middle-class life." Like Stokes, Young knew that African Americans suffered from severe environmental degradation, but pollution wasn't their only concern. As he put it in his Earth Day column, which appeared in the *Call and Post* on April 25: "Air pollution isn't such a hot topic in the ghetto today. The pollution of racism and poverty is a bit more relevant." He concluded his column with a powerful message for the environmental movement: "The choice isn't between the physical environment and the human. Both go hand in hand, and the widespread concern with pollution must be joined by a similar concern for wiping out the pollutants of racism and poverty."[5]

ᚠigure 13. Cleveland State University students organized a march on the first Earth Day, April 22, 1970, which passed through Public Square and down to the Cuyahoga. Large numbers of Clevelanders participated in Environmental Crisis Week events, but not Mayor Stokes, who was out of town that week. Photo by Bill Nehez. Cleveland Press Collection, Cleveland State University.

Young wasn't the only African American leader who used Earth Day as an opportunity to offer a broad definition of, and broad goals for, the environmental movement. Nathan Hare, founder of *The Black Scholar*, similarly argued that African Americans had environmental concerns distinct from those of suburban whites. His essay, titled "Black Ecology," which appeared in the April issue of his journal, argued that "black and white environments not only differ in degree but in nature as well," and that "the causes and solutions to ecological problems are fundamentally different in the suburbs and ghetto." Writing in San Francisco, Hare described the nature of the ghetto's environmental crisis. "Three of every ten dwellings inhabited by black families are dilapidated or without hot water, toilet or bath," he wrote. "Many more are clearly fire hazards."[6] In other words, the environmental movement could not forget the fundamental human environment: housing. Stokes might have said all this, or something like it, but he stayed quiet during Environmental Crisis Week, missing his chance to help define a movement that continued to gain influence in American politics over the next decade.

Instead, a week later, Stokes decided to decry the hypocrisy of politicians who spoke about the urgency of environmental problems but failed to take meaningful steps in their offices. Stokes even called out Nixon for making "a mockery of Earth Day" by authorizing the construction of the Trans-Alaskan Pipeline on April 23. Several city officials, quoted in the *Call and Post* as they reflected on the week's events, held to what had become the administration's position. Port control director Kiely Cronin said, "My concern is that the basic problems of society are not ignored. The problems of hunger, housing and discrimination have not been met and have not been solved." Law director Clarence James: "We are still sending astronauts to the moon. What about the problems that affect all of us, like air pollution, water pollution, nutrition deficiencies, and so on? We are still fighting in Vietnam when we should be fighting on the urban frontier." Public properties director Edward Baugh voiced a more common concern: "I hope general clean-up efforts continue without the benefit of a special day."[7]

Clean-up efforts indeed continued, from periodic neighborhood trash sweeps to the passage of major federal legislation, the Clean Air Act later that year and the Clean Water Act two years later. Earth Day helped educate and energize a generation of environmental activists, and over the next decade their gains were significant. At Cleveland's City Hall, however, the wave of environmental letters sent on Earth Day was followed by a mere trickle of such correspondences over the next two years. Among them was a November 1970 letter from St. Peter High School, signed by student Pat Ryba. The letter opened with a quote from the *Press*: "Ecologists are agreed that callous indifference to the delicate balance of nature has brought mankind to the brink of disaster." Thereafter the letter sounded very much like the Earth Day letters, even echoing the essentially defunct Cleveland: Now! program with "We must act *now*!" The letter, like so many others, was inspired by personal experience with the polluted city. St. Peter was in downtown Cleveland, just beyond the boundaries of the Erieview urban renewal plan, and many of its students commuted from other neighborhoods. "Coming to school each morning is one of many encounters with visible air pollution," Ryba wrote. "What about the air pollution we cannot see?" But Lake Erie was her primary concern. "When we visit the lake in certain areas (Edgewater for one), we find junk floating all around. The lake is filthy looking. The smell is almost overpowering. It's enough to make one sick!" (Clearly the "pool in the lake" couldn't solve the odor problem at the beach.)[8] At the end of the letter, Ryba politely asked Stokes or someone from the administration to come to the school to discuss environmental policy and what students could do to help.

The administration's replies to such letters sometimes went beyond the we're-doing-everything-we-can responses you'd expect from a politician. In April 1971, just a few days before announcing that he would not seek a third term, Stokes signed a response to John Chambers, who had written about Cleveland's pollution problem from Mentor, a distant eastern suburb. The letter thanked Chambers for his concern, said a bit about the administration's efforts and accomplishments, and asked for his continued support for environmental improvement. But the letter closed with what had become Stokes's caveat: "I feel very strongly that dealing with matters of pollution, although very important, must not keep us from dealing with more important problems such as providing decent housing for those who are forced to live with rats and cockroaches, and seeing to it that the children of Cleveland have adequate food, clothing, and medical care. We must also assure Clevelanders that our city is a safe place for them to live in." In a world of increasingly scarce resources, and with just seven months left in office, Stokes had decided to make poverty, not pollution, his priority.[9]

From the spring of 1970 through the end of the Stokes administration in the fall of 1971, the language of ecology and its philosophy of connectedness permeated the broader society. In those years and the ones that followed, legislators at all levels of government passed a torrent of environmental legislation, and Americans expressed concern, took action, and improved their environment in a number of significant ways. But from where Stokes sat, in the City Hall of a crumbling city, the barriers of the American metropolis remained visible and strong. The meaning of the municipal boundary in particular became ever starker, as it increasingly overlapped with class divisions. In a nation pulled apart by the war in Vietnam, a racial divide as disruptive as ever, and growing suspicions in suburban and rural America about the fate of urban communities, breaking down barriers to create regional solutions to pressing environmental problems simply wasn't politically viable.

FORWARD TO OBLIVION?

College campuses were alive with activity on the first Earth Day, as students and faculty engaged in the national teach-in on ecological concerns. Universities had long been central to ecological research and teaching, of course. Just eighteen months earlier, Kent State had hosted a symposium on the Cuyahoga watershed, during which half a dozen scientists shared their water quality research. Eugene Odum, the leading figure in American ecology, gave a talk titled "The Watershed as an Ecological Unit," concluding, "If we 'tell it like it is,' as our young people would have us do, then we must own up to the fact that our agriculture and our cities are grossly inefficient in terms of the basic ecological necessity for recycling of materials." Although he was an academic superstar, Odum wasn't a particularly political figure, unlike other scientists, such as Barry Commoner and Paul Ehrlich, who had dedicated their efforts to popularizing ecological ideas. Still, Odum's ideas permeated national discussions about the need for a holistic approach to studying the environment—the need to understand entire ecosystems, which had both living and nonliving components.[10]

Scientific symposiums held on campuses are commonplace, but the range of discussions and the numbers of participants made Earth Day a singular moment. Case Western Reserve University got a head start, holding its environmental teach-in a week early, on April 10 and 11. The student newspaper, *The Observer*, called these activities "Project: Survival." It began with a series of talks, many of them from visiting scholars, most of them scientists. Up first was Dr. Eugene V. Perrin, a Case pathologist, who spoke on the need for a "radical ecology." Scientists and physicians from Johns Hopkins, the University of Kentucky, and Washington University followed. They spoke about radioactivity, the biological hazards of chemical pollutants, and air pollution and young citizens, among other things. The last speaker was Murray Bookchin, the radical environmental activist whose *Our Synthetic Environment* (1962) and *Crisis in Our Cities* (1965) had made urgent pleas for fundamental changes in American society, emphasizing decentralization and the return to human-scale agriculture and urbanism. The latter book, which concerned the mental and physical health costs of living in cities, included a *Plain Dealer* aerial photograph of Cleveland Harbor, in which the relatively clean, dark water of Lake Erie resists mixing with the highly polluted, gray Cuyahoga discharge. At Case, Bookchin spoke about political action.

The following day, Case sponsored a series of workshops on a remarkable range of topics. Students could join conversations such as "Chemical and Biological Warfare," "Labor and the Environment," "Life or Death for Lake Erie," "Legal Aspects of Pollution," and "Surplus People and Instant War." All these sessions, and a score more, would be staffed, *The Observer* reported, "by coordinators and 'Experts.'" The quotation marks around "experts" provided just a hint of the growing tension between the younger generation's desire to challenge authority and the environmental activist's need to accept knowledge created by scientists. As the range of topics that day and the range of speakers the day before made clear, understanding the environmental crisis required at least a basic understanding of ecological science.

On April 10, *The Observer* published a special supplement on the environment, with articles on a range of topics that nearly matched the workshops for their diversity. Most of the articles read like student reports on assigned topics—"The Problem of Solid Waste," "Air Pollution," "Women's Liberation and Birth Control." An editorial called "Forward to Oblivion?" introduced the supplement, asserting that environmental issues "united all of our futures." "No one can escape the effect of the environmental crisis, nor can the concern for the quality of the environment lie with a few selected intellectuals or a group of 'radicals'—it is everyone's problem." And like so many of the talks and articles, the editorial implicitly linked the environment to other concerns of the day, including crime and disorder. "Air and water pollution, noise, pesticides, etc., are forms of violence perpetrated on the American people." Another editorial ran in *The Observer* that day, making even more overt links to another pressing issue. "Polluting Vietnam" connected the problems in metropolitan Cleveland, such as air and water pollution, with destruction in Vietnam, saying, "While we must be concerned with our own polluted environment, we must realize that we are the primary polluters of Southeast Asia."[11]

The peaceful, thoughtful, and earnest campus events around the nation on Earth Day served as a reminder that universities were indeed still primarily places of teaching and learning, despite the fact that the conflicts surrounding the free speech movement, civil rights demonstrations, and anti-war protests had dominated media coverage of college campuses in recent years. The

Earth Day events suggested ways in which diverse communities might come together around a unifying cause, but most observers of college campuses couldn't help but notice the development of yet another boundary in American society—the generation gap.

WHO GETS HELPED AND WHO GETS HURT?

On October 11, 1971, the *Plain Dealer* ran an especially rancorous column by one of the mayor's fiercest critics, Wilson Hirschfeld. Under the headline "Freeway Fantasy at City Hall," Hirschfeld lambasted Stokes for a recent "anti-freeway manifesto," which, among other things, demanded that state and federal governments compensate the city for any costs associated with continued highway building—a proposal which Hirschfeld assumed would bring to an end the building of highways within the city and which he called "an invitation, loud and clear, for more factories and office buildings to move away."[12] In addition to the financial compensation, Stokes and his city planning director, Norman Krumholz, who joined the administration in 1969, proposed a new way of siting highways. Instead of pushing freeways through neighborhoods or parks, Stokes and Krumholz proposed building elevated highways above rail lines, especially on the East Side, where the controversial Clark Freeway would link Interstate 90 near the steel mills with the Outer Belt Freeway (Interstate 271) in the far eastern suburb of Pepper Pike. The Clark Freeway and the north-south Lee Freeway, which would have linked the Shoreway in the north to the Outer Belt Freeway in the south, bisecting Cleveland Heights in the process, had been part of the county's highway plan since the mid-1950s, but a detailed location study only appeared in late 1963. The Clark Freeway would have sliced through the beautiful, planned city of Shaker Heights, but engineers, following common practice, decided to minimize the destruction of homes by running the highway through parkland—in this case Shaker Lakes Park, which belonged to the city of Cleveland. Opposition was fierce, especially in Shaker Heights, where seventy-five homes would have to be destroyed despite the use of parkland. In his objection, Shaker Heights Mayor Paul K. Jones asked, "Have we become so callous that we can disregard the value of irreplaceable parks and historical landmarks?"[13]

Freeway opposition grew and organized after the Cuyahoga County Engineer's office, headed by Albert Porter, announced its expansive plan in late 1963. Most important, a number of garden clubs joined forces in a new Park Conservation Committee led by Mary Elizabeth Croxton, and their rhetoric and action swirled around the park itself, not the communities the highways would disrupt. "To exchange this park of irreplaceable beauty for a mass of concrete roadway would be an unthinkable act of vandalism," Croxton said. The women proposed to build a nature center at the site where the Clark and Lee freeways would intersect, in part to draw attention to Shaker Lakes but also to add another layer of protection to the park. Given the strength of the opposition, and the wealth and position of those who organized it, the Clark and Lee freeways were in trouble even before more detailed engineering studies appeared in 1966. (Interestingly, the Clark Freeway would have cut along the Cleveland–Shaker Heights border and directly in front of the home Carl Stokes purchased in 1968, after having been elected mayor, although this seems to have played no role in the highway's fate.) After years of protest, in 1970 Governor Jim Rhodes removed the Clark and Lee freeways from the state's highway plans, effectively ending the threat to Shaker Lakes and Shaker Heights.

By the time Shaker Heights got a reprieve from the governor, the women who led the opposition to the Clark Freeway were part of a national movement that had significantly slowed, diverted, or stopped highways, saving neighborhoods in New York, San Francisco, Milwaukee, New Orleans, Baltimore, and many other cities. A.Q. Mowbray, contributor to *The Nation*, summarized the rationale of the nation's anti-highway movement in his 1969 book *Road to Ruin*, in which he argued that throughout the country "the body of the city is being destroyed by freeways," through a process he called "auto-erosion." Not everyone was as observant as Mowbray, but by the late 1960s it should have been clear to urban residents that highway construction did not serve cities well, as they lost residents, structures, and character, while gaining noise, pollution, and a new set of physical barriers.[14]

In this context, Hirschfeld's attack on Stokes for opposing continued highway building takes on greater meaning. Claiming Cleveland needed a good laugh "after Stokes' four years at City Hall," Hirschfeld wrote, "Whether or not the Clark Freeway is built, it is a joke for City Hall to come up with some impractical, unachievable, elevated expressways which will not serve present or future auto, truck and bus traffic flows." Stokes fired back, sending a lengthy letter to the editor the next day, which ran on the editorial page two days later. Stokes wondered why Hirschfeld thought that "citizens of Cleveland, through their taxes and displacement, should be delighted to subsidize the destruction of their own community for the convenience of regional and highway interests." Noting that he wasn't opposed to all future highways, he clarified his administration's position. "We have done two things: 1) attempted to minimize freeway destruction to the city and its people by carefully locating future routes and 2) merely asked the question (which I heartily suggest to Mr. Hirschfeld and other fire-breathing members of the highway lobby) 'Who gets helped and who gets hurt by the freeway?' "[15]

Despite Hirschfeld's reference to the Clark Freeway, the timing of this exchange was driven by concern for a different road, the Parma Freeway, a proposed north-south highway on the West Side. Stokes claimed that this freeway would cost Cleveland $10.6 million in construction costs, force the demolition of 932 homes in the city, and require the taking of 123 industrial and commercial properties. Because highways pay no taxes, the taking of land would cost the city $352,000 annually in lost property taxes, and because of the loss of housing, cost nearly $50,000 in lost annual income taxes. According to Stokes, all this urban destruction would primarily serve suburban commuters. But to make his point Stokes went further, well beyond the Parma Freeway. "To date, the City of Cleveland has suffered the loss of more than 6,000 housing units and is slated to lose 3,500 more," Stokes wrote, referring to the number of homes expected to be demolished by highways still on the drawing boards. He added that the Ohio Department of Highways estimated that nineteen thousand Cleveland residents had already been displaced by highways, and another eleven thousand could be forced out of their homes if all the proposed freeways were built. Stokes argued, "The freeway program has disrupted and sometimes utterly destroyed whole neighborhoods by ripping through them with total abandon." He cited one obvious example: Tremont, the West Side ethnic neighborhood just above the Cuyahoga, which had been "quartered" by I-90 and I-71, and where residents had complained bitterly about their treatment at the hands of city and state officials as their properties plummeted in value. And although Shaker Lakes might have been saved, highways had already destroyed precious urban parkland. On the West Side, I-71 had sheared parts of Brookside, Emery, and Gunning parks, while the Edgewater and Gordon lakeside parks had lost acreage to the Shoreway. Not surprisingly, Stokes also made an argument about the injustice of the nation's highway-only transportation policy. Freeways had "improved the mobility of many people with cars," but ridership of public transportation had declined, meaning "higher fares and restricted service to those too poor, elderly or infirm to own or drive a car—which is about 30% of our population!" Finally, Stokes noted that if all the highways proposed for the city were built, they would cover about 10 percent of the city with "non-taxable concrete."

The anti-highway movement in Cleveland coalesced around the effort to save Shaker Lakes and the wealthy communities of Shaker Heights and Cleveland Heights. But in all the noise about the Clark and Lee freeways, little was said about other proposed highways that would have carved up the East Side and the small, integrated city of East Cleveland. The Clark's impact on Shaker Heights would have been significant, but in Cleveland the freeway would have destroyed 810 homes and 75 businesses. In communications to the Ohio Department of Highways, which had ultimate authority over federal highway spending in the state, Stokes and Krumholz demanded "fair and equitable" treatment for Cleveland. As the controversy over the Parma Freeway heated up, Stokes wrote to state highways director Philip Richley, "We are unwilling to continue merely to supply the body upon which the transportation surgery is performed without any compensatory benefit." Throughout the highway planning process, however, Krumholz and Stokes couldn't help but sense that city interests garnered little attention at the state level or from the Northeast Ohio Areawide Coordinating Agency, the regional body created in 1968 to coordinate federal grant applications.[16]

The Clark Freeway would have been just the start of the demolition on the East Side, as three other highways, with a series of interchanges that linked them, would have brought even more destruction. A series of route location studies conducted by Howard, Needles, Tammen & Bergendoff, consulting engineers, and published in 1966 and 1967 described the destruction in detail. One study issued in March 1967 placed the east-west Heights Freeway running from East 55th Street out to the Lee Freeway. It would replace dozens of blocks of housing in Hough, south of Superior, then cross over Rockefeller Park, separate Glenville from Wade Park and the cultural center, and enter East Cleveland adjacent to the area where the Glenville Shootout would take place one year later. A month earlier, the route location study for the Bedford Freeway showed a north-south highway connecting the Heights Freeway with the Clark Freeway, running along the eastern edge of Hough, and demolishing blocks and blocks of housing. A third freeway, Central, was mapped two months later. It would have run from the Inner Belt (I-90) to the Lee Freeway, mostly replacing the small factories, warehouses, stores, homes, and apartment buildings in the blocks between Cedar and Carnegie as they ran from downtown toward the Cleveland Clinic. The amount of demolition imagined in these designs is staggering, but as the introductory letters to the various reports make clear, the goal was to increase access to urban renewal sites, especially around University Circle and downtown. Demolition in surrounding, troubled neighborhoods was tolerable, if not actually desirable.

𝓕igure 14. In the mid-1960s, Cuyahoga County planned a web of highways that would cover Cleveland's East Side. This planning map showed how Bedford Freeway would link the Outerbelt with the Clark Freeway and eventually the Central and Heights freeways. None of these were built as planned. Howard, Needles, Tammen & Bergendoff, *Route Location Studies: Bedford Freeway, Outer Belt South Freeway to Clark Freeway* (1967). Courtesy of Cleveland State University.

IN THE INTEREST OF TRULY BRINGING US ALL TOGETHER

On April 14, 1970, Mayor Stokes issued a statement encouraging "all members of our community to endorse the April 15th march against the war in Vietnam." The statement urged orderly and peaceful participation, clearly an indication that Stokes feared violence, but he also took the opportunity to assert that the war had begun to affect domestic spending. "Our nation, and particularly our cities, cannot tolerate a conflict which saps our national resources and divides our people. Our government can no longer neglect its grave domestic needs. The wars we must wage are those against hunger, woefully inadequate medical attention, lack of housing, pollution of our air and water, and inflation." Ironically, given the growing divide over the war, Stokes wrote, "In the interest of truly bringing us all together, I urge everyone to join in this peaceful quest for an end to this war."[17]

Of course, Cleveland and the nation didn't come together over the war, and just two weeks after the march, when President Nixon announced that American forces would enter Cambodia, the nation further fractured on the issue. College campuses, the site of so many peaceful events on Earth Day, erupted in demonstrations, some of them violent. At Case Western Reserve, about fifty students occupied the Air Force ROTC offices on campus, demanding that the program be dropped. At Kent State University, even more disruptive protests forced the city of Kent to call in the Ohio National Guard, which used tear gas and fixed bayonets to disperse students who had moved their protests into the town on May 3, two days after Nixon's announcement. About fifty students were arrested that night. The next day, a weekend of protests and violence culminated in the guardsmen firing fifty rounds into a crowd of students on Kent's campus, killing four. The community, state, and nation were shocked—and fearful of more violence. Kent canceled classes and sent students home, and other Ohio campuses followed suit. Mayor Stokes, like other public officials, decried the violence, demanded an investigation, and called for calm. Although none of the dead was from Cleveland, Kent was just forty miles from City Hall, and many of its students came from the metropolitan area. "Now, more than ever before," read Stokes's May 5 statement, "Clevelanders and Ohioans must put aside their differences and personal hostilities and by reasoned and rational behavior bring some order to this grave situation."[18]

The Ohio National Guard had been busy that spring. On April 8, Stokes put the Guard on alert because of spiking racial violence at the integrating Collinwood High School on the city's far East Side. The school board, on the principal's advice, had kept Collinwood closed for two days after white demonstrators had broken windows and damaged furniture in the school, but Stokes demanded that it reopen. While more than one hundred fifty police officers kept the peace at the school that morning, seven hundred soldiers stood by at nearby Forest Hills Park and the Shaker Heights Armory. (About the same number of students did not attend school that day—30 percent of Collinwood's student body stayed home.) Meanwhile, addressing the Cleveland Foundation at a luncheon downtown, Stokes said, "It is going to take a bigger man than I am" to solve the problems of race, adding, "But I appeal to you businessmen to help solve problems in the schools and in housing, jobs and food and clothing for the inner city residents. I am going to do all I can within my powers to see that those who want to use clubs, bricks and violence to achieve their ends do not do it."[19] This was a message of nonviolence, but also of steadfastness. Fortunately, Collinwood remained peaceful over the remainder of the week, and the Guard stood down after school on Friday.

Just two weeks later, on April 30, Stokes and other mayors asked Governor Rhodes to call up the Guard to patrol interstates in northeast Ohio during an intensifying wildcat teamsters' strike centered on Cleveland, Chicago, and St. Louis. Up to six thousand drivers, many of them independent steel haulers, had been on strike for most of April. Hoping to prevent attacks on drivers ignoring the strike, guardsmen took up positions along Interstate 71, stationed on bridges and patrolling in military trucks. Some even escorted convoys to their destinations. For their part, the strikers set up response teams, vowing to stop any truck that wasn't carrying food, drugs, or beer. By late April, the strike had taken its toll, with nearly forty thousand other workers idled in Cleveland alone, and now Republic Steel, its products piling up outside its riverside plants, was warning that it might have to idle ten thousand employees. Fortunately for the city's economy, the teamsters voted to end their strike on Sunday, the day before the shooting at Kent State.

Three days after the shootings in Kent, Stokes appeared on the local NBC affiliate, Channel 3, with students from four local colleges—Case Western, Cleveland State, John Carroll, and Cuyahoga Community College—to talk about the war, the protests, and the deaths at Kent State. In his opening remarks that evening, Stokes said:

> We must understand each other. If there is a generation gap, we should bridge it with dialog and discussion, with knowledge and understanding of differences, rather than with violence and recrimination which contribute nothing. My whole public life has been dedicated to making government responsive to people's needs and legitimate aspirations. It has been dedicated to eliminating

barriers between people and groups, and if I can be of any help in this present crisis on our campuses and in the community generally, I do not shirk that responsibility, heavy as it may be and surely of no personal or political advantage whatsoever to me.

Stokes closed his opening statement with questions for the students: "Do you think society has failed you? Has government failed you?"[20]

NO LONGER STOPPING AT THE CITY LIMITS

In late August 1971, Ruth Sicherman of University Heights wrote an especially vehement letter of complaint to Mayor Stokes, even though his term would expire in three months. She claimed that Muny Light and the city asphalt plant "discharge more pollutants into the air than human beings can survive in health, but they refuse (1) to repair death-dealing waste elimination processes, and (2) to accept community warnings and fines for that destruction." She concluded, "It is bad enough that private industry breaks the law (with government's collusion) but municipal government must not be allowed this corruption."[21] Sicherman's complaint was part of a letter-writing campaign organized by the Air Conservation Committee of the Tuberculosis & Respiratory Disease Association of Cleveland & Cuyahoga County, led by Ann Felber of Shaker Heights. Felber's activism had made her well known at City Hall, and although she was a valuable ally in the effort to improve air quality, the Stokes administration had grown tired of the attention to Muny Light. Stokes had long ago proposed to sell the municipally owned system, with the expectation that the private power company, Cleveland Electric Illuminating Company, would operate it more efficiently. That proposed sale tinged the mayor's relationship with employees at the Muny plant, which remained an albatross around the administration's neck through Stokes's four years in office. Although the city had upgraded the facility, spending $6 million, the stacks continued to smoke, and the administration blamed the incompetence or ill-will of the workers. After a power outage during Memorial Day in 1970, Stokes even suggested—publicly—that failures during holidays (there had been outages the previous Christmas and New Year's, too) were acts of sabotage perpetrated by disgruntled employees.

The administration hoped to redirect the energy of the Air Conservation Committee to the county, as the city attempted to create an air control district that stretched beyond municipal boundaries. In May 1970, Stokes sent a letter to Hugh Corrigan, one of the three county commissioners, asking him to engage in collaboration to create a county-wide air quality program. Stokes argued that since Cleveland's air pollution problems were not confined by the corporate boundaries, "effective control can only come about through a regional program." In 1969, the state of Ohio expended just $250,000 on air pollution control, and although state law allowed the creation of county-wide programs, none existed. In other words, municipal governments were forced to take the lead on air pollution control. Cleveland's program cost $400,000, and Akron, Canton, and Lorain also spent local dollars on air pollution control. The day after Stokes sent the letter to Corrigan, his assistant Robert Bauerlein sent a note to Ann Felber. "Here is your big chance to aim in another direction many of those wonderful letters the Mayor has been receiving from misinformed suburbanites," he wrote, enclosing a copy of the previous day's letter. "I would hope that the Air Conservation Committee will get behind this proposal with as much enthusiasm as was exhibited in other recent activities," he continued. Despite the belligerent tone of the letter, or perhaps because of it, he signed his name under the closing "Peace."[22]

The Air Conservation Committee was already engaged in the effort to set up an effective regional approach, backing the short-lived effort to create the Greater Metropolitan Cleveland Intrastate Air Quality Control Region. The federal Air Quality Act of 1967 required that states create regulatory regions, but as of 1970 none existed in Ohio. As the 1967 law dictated, the National Air Pollution Control Administration was charged with creating the regions, and then the states would set standards, with the approval of the U.S. Department of Health, Education and Welfare. Finally, states would create and implement plans to meet those standards. Not surprisingly, progress was painfully slow around the nation, and Congress recognized the difficulty of creating regions, since boundaries would have significant consequences for industry and potentially for future economic growth. To rectify the problem, the Clean Air Act of 1970 did away with the regional approach, substituting states for regions, and initiated the creation of federal standards and enforcement.

In sum, the federal government's regional approach was short-lived and ineffective. It was also just a part of a broader discussion of the proper boundaries of government authority. Along with air pollution, issues of transportation and watershed management were central to the national discussion about proper planning, regulation, and, perhaps most important, appropriate funding sources. Cities argued vehemently that they needed financial support in environmental regulation—support that could come through the creation of a regional regulatory approach. As Patricia Smith of the Air Conservation Committee noted in 1972, as the state of Ohio continued to debate the proper role of local governments in environmental regulation, "city boundaries are not large enough to cope with the air pollution problem in this area." Although she and the other members of the Air Conservation Committee had worked to expand pollution control regulation, either to a new regional authority or to the county, nothing had come of it. At a committee meeting concerning the revision of the Ohio constitution, Smith said, "The one main argument that we have for going county-wide rather than remaining within city boundaries is that, even though most of the industrial complex is contained within the city, we feel that we needed the larger tax base to cope with the problem. It is ridiculous to ask the City of Cleveland residents to cope financially with the problems created by this industrial complex from which the whole county benefits."[23]

Smith's argument relied on a logic similar to that used by Stokes when he discussed the funding of government services: since everyone in the region would benefit from improved air quality, everyone in the region should contribute to the cost of regulation. Other observers expanded this argument for fairness to one of justice. At the same 1972 meeting concerning the Ohio constitution, W. O. Walker, the long-time editor of the *Call and Post* and a trusted adviser to Mayor Stokes, argued for regional government to coordinate transportation and pollution control, to help spread the cost of improvements. He maintained, as had Stokes, that transportation policy focused on highways had hurt the city—it had taken land off tax rolls, forced the reduction of support for public transportation, and left inner-city communities stranded because automobile transportation was more expensive. Walker asserted that regional authority must expand to match reality because "people are living in a region now, not just in a small community or not just in one county." Lives had sprawled along with the metropolis, but government had not kept pace. "So we finally admit that services and the attendant cost that follows, that we are going to have to approach some regional form of government on many of the things that people are demanding service," Walker said, "like pollution, transportation, garbage disposal, water and a lot of other things that are no longer stopping at the city limits of any community."[24]

Wayne C. Dabb, assistant director of law under the new mayor, Ralph Perk, agreed with Walker and Smith on the fundamental issues, noting at the 1972 meeting, "There has to be some change in the city, a broadening of what we know now as a city, if we are going to solve many of the problems and revitalize local government." But he was realistic: "Everyone likes their little kingdoms. These do not fall easily." As Dabb well understood, the suburbs—fifty-six municipalities in Cuyahoga County alone—had created local control intentionally, and they would defend it vehemently. Watershed management, air quality regions, and metropolitan governance all sounded like improvements in an age swimming in ecological thinking, at least to those who struggled to solve urban problems, but for many Americans, municipal boundaries served a purpose: local control, especially of tax rates, schools, zoning and housing policy. Some "little kingdoms" might fare well enough, but the boundaries that ran through metropolitan Cleveland impinged on the making of the service city, restricting resources, impeding effective regulation, and speeding economic decline—for the entire region.[25]

THE WATERSHED IS A COMPLEX POLITICAL SYSTEM

On April 15, 1970, the day Stokes simultaneously introduced Cleveland's Crisis in the Environment Week and expressed concerns about putting pollution ahead of poverty on the nation's priorities list, the Ohio Water Pollution Control Board held a hearing at the Hotel Sheraton-Cleveland. Several industries and communities were called to defend their progress, but the primary focus of the hearing was the city of Cleveland, which the state had already warned because it had been so slow to act on water pollution. As Stokes feared, the state took a firm position and, for the first time ever, imposed a ban on new sewer connections, effectively prohibiting the city from issuing new construction permits. Stokes was irate, and while the city didn't fully comply with the order, the mayor spoke frequently about the fundamental injustice of the state bringing the city to a halt without having spent any of its own money on the water pollution problem.

Although the city had been making incremental improvements in its sewage system, real progress awaited the construction of major intercepting sewers that would gather wastes for delivery to expanded and improved city treatment plants. These intercepting sewers would traverse municipal boundaries, in many instances moving into communities that did not yet have an agreement with the city to treat wastes. Not surprisingly, suburban communities balked at having the city maintain control over the spreading system for fear that it would impose excessive rates. Most suburbs argued for a county-run system, but the city countered with a proposal to create an independent sewer authority, run by a board to which the city and suburbs would appoint members. The long delay in water pollution control, then, was not technical or even economic, but political, as suburbs and city struggled for control.

Sporadic negotiations dragged on for months, outlasting the Stokes administration, and Cleveland suffered through the building ban all the while. Even after Common Pleas Judge George McMonagle, empowered by state law to oversee the process, extended the ban to an additional twenty-nine suburbs, giving everyone at the table a sense of urgency, the parties could not reach an agreement. Finally, in April 1972, two years after Cleveland's building ban began, McMonagle imposed a regional sewer plan from his bench. The Cleveland Regional Sewer District represented a compromise for both sides. The city gained the independent agency structure it favored, along with majority representation on the board, while the suburbs gained a relatively low price for the city's extant treatment plants, which would be purchased by the regional district. Nearly three months later, after the details had been worked out, the judge lifted the building ban on both the city and the suburbs. The *Plain Dealer* cited unidentified local officials who claimed the ban had cost the region $500 million in economic development and seven thousand jobs.[26]

While the political wrangling about metropolitan sewage treatment was under way, technical planning for an upgraded system continued, seemingly oblivious to political realities. In 1966, the state created the Three Rivers Watershed District, a powerless board charged with overseeing water resource planning in the region. The three watersheds—the Cuyahoga, Chagrin, and Rocky rivers—drained most of Cuyahoga County and land in six other counties. With a tiny budget and no real authority, the district merely served as an observer of city, county, state, and federal planning, but its chairman, Wendell La Due of Akron, became a cheerleader for more comprehensive planning. "The Watershed is not only a complex ecosystem; it is also a complex political system," he wrote in 1970, in recognition of how difficult it would be to bring the various political entities into an accord on resource management.[27]

One of the planning processes the Three Rivers Watershed District observed was the Army Corps development of sewage treatment plans. In late 1971, Congress authorized the Army Corps of Engineers to create a variety of viable plans for the district. In 1973, the corps provided preliminary data on twelve different plans based on the use of two very different technologies. Most of the plans relied on building advanced biological and physical-chemical treatment plants along the region's rivers and lakeshore, mostly through the improvement of existing facilities. Other plans involved land disposal of sewage sludge, which would require the construction of aerated lagoons to provide preliminary treatment, a large effluent tunnel to transport this waste beyond the county, and perhaps 160 square miles of farmland on which the lightly treated sludge would be sprayed. The Army Corps imagined this disposal taking place mostly in Huron, Seneca, Crawford, and Richland counties to the west, well outside the Cuyahoga watershed. All the plans involved combinations and variations on these two approaches, with some adding the piping of sludge to the coal mining region of eastern Ohio, where the waste would be an important ingredient in the restoration of strip-mined land.

The Army Corps had long been involved in local projects—from dredging the Cuyahoga River to creating and maintaining Cleveland Harbor—and it had planned and completed its work without much public engagement, beyond communication with local business leaders, and it had historically ignored the ecological consequences of its work. But 1970 initiated a new era for the corps. The National Environmental Protection Act, signed into law in January 1970, required that any project receiving federal money create an environmental impact statement. Later in the year, President Nixon created the Environmental Protection Agency to serve as a stronger, centralized bureaucratic force at the federal level, and the Water Pollution Control Act, passed in late 1972, would set quality standards. In sum, the Army Corps could no longer operate without public involvement or without concern for ecological outcomes.

In this new context, as the corps worked on its Three Rivers Watershed plans in 1972, it organized a series of public meetings, held workshops, and gave presentations to interested groups, including chambers of commerce, the League of Women Voters, and some environmental groups, such as the Sierra Club and the Izaak Walton League. The corps also issued a newsletter, "Purewater Press," beginning in April 1972, and distributed a feasibility report that outlined the twelve alternatives. Altogether the corps engaged in a great deal of teaching of fundamental science, especially ecological principles. This was particularly true as it attempted to explain the value of land disposal of sewage. Corps programs and materials emphasized that land disposal allowed for the recycling of nutrients and the natural filtering of waste, what the corps called "a living filter," which meant that land disposal required far fewer chemicals than traditional sewage plants. This system would be especially valuable in eastern Ohio's coal lands, where hundreds of square miles had been stripped of topsoil. The corps clearly favored land application, not just because it brought considerable savings in capital investment but because it struck the engineers as the more ecologically sound approach.

Public participation quickly revealed flaws in the corps' thinking, however, and the universally negative reaction of local officials in the affected counties revealed how much ecological thinking they were doing as well. They raised questions about the millions of gallons of water used to transport the sludge through the pipeline that would leave the Three Rivers Watershed. Would all this water swamp the lands in the disposal counties? And what about heavy metals contained in the sludge? In January 1973, Dr. George Linn, Huron County health commissioner, expressed his concern about the disposal of wastewater in his area in a letter to the Ohio Department of Health, which he copied to the Army Corps and many other officials. Sounding very much like an ecologist, Linn asked a series of useful questions: "What new kinds of organisms would find this a desirable habitat? Bacteria? Other micro-organisms? Parasites? Insects? What kinds of changes might occur in the weather itself? What effect on stream water quality due to erosion?" In addition to these sensible ecological concerns, Linn revealed the primary issue, which had to do with justice. "Needless to say," he wrote, "this proposal has our entire farming community in an uproar, to say nothing of the senses of the rank and file citizens who are offended by the thoughts of having Cleveland's dirty water dumped on our greatest asset—our land."[28] Striking a similar tone, the Huron County Regional Planning Commission commended "the idea of the local recycling of wastewater through the soils for the benefit of ecology and environment, as well as economic gain," but like everyone who responded, it was simply unwilling to accept metropolitan Cleveland's waste.[29]

Despite the consistent opposition to the land disposal proposal, in August 1973 the Army Corps ended the process by publishing three potential plans. Plan A (which had two variations) relied on advanced sewage treatment plants, essentially an extension of existing practices. Plan B combined new plants with the transportation of sludge to eastern Ohio strip lands. Plan C would pipe the majority of metropolitan Cleveland's sewage and storm water runoff to 147,000 acres in Huron and surrounding counties. By keeping—and in fact favoring—the land disposal plan, the Army Corps had badly misjudged the situation. It had underestimated the power of certain boundaries, especially the line on the map indicating "Land Treatment Area," and the boundary between city and country, which might appear blurred within metropolitan Cleveland but was remarkably clear from the fields of Huron County. The people of north-central Ohio rejected Plan C, and the state of Ohio dismissed it immediately. And so the Army Corps planning process revealed more than just the growing influence of ecology in government planning. It showed that science and engineering simply could not offer a single best solution to sewage control. Acceptable solutions could be derived only through politics, and political negotiations required a very different skill set than the Army Corps possessed in 1972.

Clearly the early 1970s push for regional environmental management had a limited impact on local government, but the spread of ecological knowledge continued along with calls for a regional approach. This effort reached a new

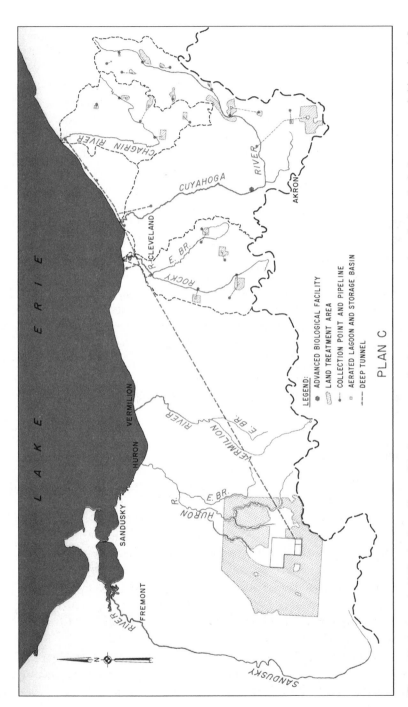

LEGEND:

● ADVANCED BIOLOGICAL FACILITY
▨ LAND TREATMENT AREA
—•— COLLECTION POINT AND PIPELINE
□ AERATED LAGOON AND STORAGE BASIN
——— DEEP TUNNEL

PLAN C

Figure 15. In the early 1970s, the Army Corps of Engineers attempted to become more responsive to both ecological concerns and citizen input. In planning improvements to Cleveland's sewage treatment system, however, the corps failed to hear the unified opposition of those who lived beyond the metropolitan region but were targeted to receive the city's waste. Army Corps of Engineers, *Wastewater Management Study for Cleveland-Akron Metropolitan and Three Rivers Watershed Areas Summary Report* (August 1973), 148.

apogee in 1993, when freelance writer and editor David Beach published the first issue of *EcoCity Cleveland*, a sixteen-page newsletter with articles about brownfields, PCBs, wind farms, sustainable development, and "the Cuyahoga River Suffocation Zone," concerning the lack of oxygen that prevented fish from inhabiting the shipping channel through the flats. The cover story appeared under the headline "Thinking Bioregionally in Northeast Ohio" and opened by asking readers to "start by erasing the artificial lines on the map. Block out all the human-drawn boundaries—city limits, county lines, census tracts, roads. Then look at what's left—the land, water, plants, wildlife, people—and think again about where you live." A Cleveland Heights resident, Beach proposed calling this unbounded area the "Cuyahoga Bioregion," using the watershed to help define the place in which he lived. This reconception of place would be critical to creating "a more ecologically-healthy region," Beach's fundamental goal.[30]

Erasing the artificial lines on the map, thinking more bioregionally, was closely akin to removing other archaic structures of the industrial era—the hulking warehouses, empty factories, unused rail lines—and creating a more fluid city, as Mabel Walker had described nearly fifty years earlier. Creating a just and effective governmental system that kept pace with the demographic and environmental changes in the region should have been part of the process by which Greater Cleveland worked its way through its urban crisis. But Cleveland failed to overcome its jurisdictional fragmentation, ensuring that it would continue to be held back by the carcass of its past.

THE STOKES YEARS

In the fall of 1971, as Stokes prepared to leave office, his staff created a nicely illustrated, boosterish summary of his administration's accomplishments, which appeared under the title *The Stokes Years*. In an introductory letter, Stokes expressed pride in what they had been able to accomplish, especially in enlarging "the vision and understanding of the role of local government." He admitted to "some mistakes and failures," but he also noted the special obstacles his administration had faced. "As the first Negro Mayor of Cleveland—in fact, of any major American city—my administration faced heightened resistance and sometimes outright hostility from some members of City Council, from many suburban officials bent on exploiting the central city and from the old-line political establishment unwilling to accept change," he wrote. The nearly forty pages that followed listed a wide range of accomplishments grouped around nine themes. The order in which these accomplishments appear give us some sense of how the administration prioritized its goals, or at least how it ranked its successes.

Stokes emphasized his communication with residents, listing "Citizen Participation and Involvement" first among his accomplishments. In his four years in office, Stokes held twenty-one town-hall meetings, some of them on very difficult topics. One of those contentious issues was the construction of public housing, which Stokes listed second among his accomplishments. His administration had resuscitated the public housing program, which had stalled during the previous administration, and had built 4,206 housing units in four years. Third, Stokes listed "Jobs and Small Business," emphasizing the expansion of equal employment opportunities, despite the fact that the employment picture remained bleak in the poorest sections of town. The city had lost eighty thousand jobs in the previous decade, and the concentration of poverty was evident not just in statistics but in wide swaths of the city. Next, under "Health," Stokes stressed the acquisition of state and federal grants, the construction of new clinics, and the initiation of new programs, mentioning the rat control program specifically—even though rat infestations remained common in the city's troubled neighborhoods. In 1970, Director of Public Health Frank Ellis wrote in an internal memo: "Complaints continue to come to my office as well as to the mayor about vacant structures which are rat infested and demolished, with resulting disturbance of the rat colonies. On several occasions our community hygiene staff has verified the existence of active rat burrows on these premises."[31]

In the fifth section of *The Stokes Years*, "Pollution Control," Stokes touted the new air pollution code and the passage of the $100 million clean water bond, although these were but small steps on the road to a cleaner environment. Under "Downtown Development," Stokes claimed that $223 million had been invested in Erieview, although he clearly counted some buildings that had been completed before he took office. Seventh, Stokes listed advances in public safety before turning to "Recreation," a section in which he emphasized the pools in the lake, claiming, "Thousands and thousands of Clevelanders enjoyed the recovered opportunity for safe swimming and bathing at the two beaches." Indeed, the "swimming pools in the lake" had become so popular that when budget cuts threatened their reopening in 1971, an anonymous benefactor donated the money to install the plastic barriers, purchase the chlorine, and even pay the lifeguards. *The Stokes Years* also praised the administration's acquisition of the nation's largest federal grant for the purchase of open space, used to create new parks, including a number of "vest pocket parks," which largely replaced abandoned and unkempt lots. Finally, in the ninth section, Stokes described his administration's participation in urban renewal, including the federal Model Cities program, although even by 1971 the results of these programs could at best be described as modest.

All this rhetoric, putting the happiest face on Cleveland's not-so-happy fate, gave a sense of hope even while Stokes admitted that his administration had made only a start in all these areas. In reality, the Stokes administration was limping toward its finish line. As in all American cities, Cleveland's budget was reliant on property taxes, but falling property values, property abandonment, and tax delinquency cut into the city's income. By 1970, 15 percent of city property tax bills went uncollected and 28 percent of property in the city was tax-exempt. Stokes pleaded with voters to approve an income tax hike (from 1 percent to 1.8 percent) to help compensate for flagging property taxes, but the issue failed badly in November, having gained wide support only in the heavily African American neighborhoods. The administration responded quickly by slashing its budget for 1971, actually shrinking city spending at a time when the national inflation rate approached 6 percent. The city stopped hiring immediately and initiated plans to lay off one thousand workers. The administration attempted to pass a smaller income tax hike (to 1.6 percent) in a special election in February, but that also failed. Although *The Stokes Years* praised advances in recreation, the administration relied heavily on the Recreation Department for cuts, taking millions from parks and playgrounds. The Health Department saw significant cuts, too. In what would become the norm for struggling cities facing shrinking tax revenues, police and fire budgets remained intact while quality-of-life spending plummeted.

Two years removed from office, Stokes published a more honest assessment of his time in City Hall. Unlike *The Stokes Years*, the book *Promises of Power: A Political Autobiography* was a frank exposition of the headwinds into which Stokes sailed as a progressive black politician and as a city leader in the age of suburbia. Although largely tactful, as he tended to be, Stokes occasionally revealed his bitterness about the forces lined up against reform: the conservative ethnic bureaucrats inside City Hall who "had held their jobs so long that their control was impenetrable"; the conservative white leaders outside the city, "with their built-in hostility toward the central city," who saw little political advantage in aiding Cleveland; the white newspapermen, who "indulged themselves in a form of steady, slow assassination"; and Ahmed Evans, the "stupid, phony so-called revolutionary" who "decided to shoot it out with the police one night in Glenville." In Stokes's estimation, many of his dreams for real reform died along with the police officers that night.[32]

More than just political forces lined up against Stokes and the city of Cleveland. Suburban growth in population and resources had left "the central city with its dwindling resources, its ever-diminishing tax base, its high concentration of the poor, the elderly and the politically impotent," Stokes wrote. "As mayor you are in control of territorial boundaries, but you have nothing with which to sustain yourself. You cannot look to the people in the central city, for they have more needs than they have resources." Stokes had few allies and few options. "You cannot look to the people in the suburbs, because that is why they are out there," he wrote. "You cannot look to the state, because the legislature is controlled by a suburban-rural coalition." Only the federal government could "reach to suburbs, make them part of a health or transportation or air-and-water-pollution control system, make them help support the city."[33]

Promises offered a thorough explanation for why his administration left only a modest record of accomplishment and why Stokes decided not to seek a third term. "In 1967 it still seemed that the cities could be turned around; three years later the economic tide had turned and we were headed for even more problems than before," he wrote. And on cities more generally: "Our lack of resources, the high crime rate, the seemingly inexorable slide into decay and deterioration, the continued desertion of the cities by even the marginally affluent, the increasing unemployment and labor problems—all these things were making cities virtually unmanageable. I could see that, for at least the time being, during a disastrous economic slump that was eroding our already pitiful tax base, the managers of cities could barely hold their ground."[34]

The book says little about the crisis in the urban environment that had consumed so much of his time and energy. The Cuyahoga fire warrants no mention. But Stokes relayed a story from June 1969 that conveys a great deal about Cleveland's predicament and its long road to recovery. Stokes describes the "damnedest period" in his life, which began with the death of Donald Waight, the young white man stabbed by a black man down the hill from Stokes's home. Incensed, many of the neighborhood's white residents took to the streets. Stokes drove to the scene to beg for calm, and after a tense confrontation with the dead man's father, the mayor climbed into his car and headed home up Woodland Avenue. There he found his darkened house encircled by police cars and officers carrying shotguns. They had been given word that the crowd of angry white residents was marching up the hill. An officer asked the mayor to join his family inside, keep the lights off, and get on the floor. His wife, Shirley, six months pregnant, lay on the floor upstairs with their two frightened and confused children. Stokes sat downstairs in the dark, listening to the screech of walkie-talkies outside and the ruckus of the approaching crowd—"a committee of my neighbors," Stokes called them—numbering as many as two hundred. The police used tear gas to halt the crowd. "The yard is filled with police to protect me," Stokes wrote later, "not from some foreign enemy but from a mob of people who live twenty blocks away from me." That night, sitting besieged in his own house, Stokes had no illusions about the power he held as the black mayor of a white city. Here was a city badly in need of change, and here was the man who might force it through, both of them trapped and powerless.[35]

Epilogue

WHAT BECAME
OF CLEVELAND

In May 2012, we explored the ground floor of Cleveland's Key Tower, the fifty-seven-story, granite-clad skyscraper designed by Cesar Pelli. Standing on the northeast corner of Public Square, the postmodern tower is adjoined to the Romanesque building designed by Burnham and Root for the Society for Savings in the late 1880s, part of the nation's first wave of skyscrapers. Visitors can walk through the beautifully restored banking floor in the old building and wander into the Key Tower lobby, which contains little more than banks of high-speed elevators. When completed in 1991 for Society Bank, the skyscraper superseded Terminal Tower as Cleveland's tallest building. Even as its home city continued to shed residents, dropping another 11 percent of its population in the 1980s, Society had been on a spending spree, acquiring smaller banks around the state, including Central National Bank in 1985. Society built the tower to house its new headquarters and to proclaim its growing prominence in the region. The tower gained its current name just three years after it opened, when Society merged with Key, in the ever-shifting world of banking.

The Key Tower and its lobby, with its large glass walls that allow the interior to connect visually with the green of Public Square to the south and the well-kept open mall to the east, serve as object lessons in the disconnect between downtown development and the broader health of American cities. Office space in central business districts expanded dramatically in the 1980s, even in cities that continued to fare poorly overall. But we didn't come to the Key Tower merely for a reminder of the continued importance of the financial sector in the service city. Rather, we were on our way up to Squire Sanders, a global law firm with roots in Cleveland and offices on the forty-ninth floor. We had come to interview Louis Stokes, who had joined the firm after his thirty years in Congress serving Cleveland's East Side and who was then nearing the end of his very successful career. He was gracious with his time and with his praise of his brother, about whom we spoke at length. "People come up to me and talk to me about Carl and what he meant to this city and let me know that their uncle played pool with Carl. But he's still revered in this city. I hear from white and black people in this city, people respect what he stood for, what he did, and what he meant to the city forty-four years ago." We talked, too, about Cleveland, as it was in 1969 and in 2012. "Well, of course, we've lost a lot of population. We're down under four hundred thousand now. And that's made a difference. And our school system reflects the fact that a lot of whites moved out of the city and left the schools like they are today, things of that sort," he said, fully cognizant that Cleveland was still struggling with serious problems a half century after it began to decline. But he added hopefully, "In spots we see gentrification, people, young people, particularly whites, coming back into the city. Which is always good, I think, because it points to a vibrancy and people feeling good about the city and that type of thing. So yeah, I think we're making progress. It's still a major city in our country, though we're far down from eighth now. But it's still a major city in this country, and a powerful city."[1]

As it happened, the Squire Sanders conference room in which we talked faced east, and that morning we had a clear view of many of the places about which we were writing. Closest was Erieview Tower and the attached two-story, glazed galleria mall that replaced the I. M. Pei–designed reflecting pool and plaza. Constructed in 1987, the mall has never worked well, except as home to a food court that serves lunch to office workers. Indeed, Pei's vision isn't much in evidence in the old Erieview urban renewal zone; little of what he planned came to fruition. Pei's handiwork was still visible that morning, however, for we could see his pyramidal Rock and Roll Hall of Fame building on the lake, completed in 1995 as part of the tourist infrastructure the city has built around its major-league sports venues. Farther down the lakeshore, we could see the 55th Street Marina, still the amenity that Stokes said it would be when he celebrated its completion in 1969. But in 2012 the city no longer managed the marina. The state had been operating several city parks, including Edgewater and Gordon, since 1978, when the city was too broke to keep them maintained. The state hadn't done a very good job either, and so Cleveland Metroparks, which has operated the suburban park system since 1917, took over management of what had been Lakefront State Park in 2013. To see the marina from the tower, we had to look over the site of the old Muny Light plant, which is no longer producing smoke (or power), and even its stacks have been removed. Although we couldn't see it from our vantage point, part of the old plant features a giant mural of swimming whales, creatures not found in Lake Erie, of course, but nice scenery for commuters on Interstate 90.

That morning we could also see in the distance the cluster of buildings that constitute Cleveland's other node of economic development: University Circle. Here Cleveland Clinic, University Hospitals, Case Western Reserve University, and several other affiliated and related institutions have made this area a center of employment and investment. As most of the city declined, this area grew because of its connection to two economic sectors critical to service city economies: health care and higher education. Case Western has a lovely urban campus that blends with cultural icons, such as the art museum and the orchestra's Severance Hall. Improvements around Case have been matched by those around Cleveland State University on the edge of downtown, another area of development success. All these new structures—skyscrapers downtown, tourist attractions, expanded hospitals, and improved university campuses—speak to the transition that began in the 1960s: the rebuilding of Cleveland as a service city.

Altogether our view that morning was spectacular, but our easterly window prevented us from seeing many of Cleveland's interesting sights. The steel mills to the south, for instance, were producing once again after decades of corporate transitions and sometimes lengthy shutdowns. Owned and operated by ArcelorMittal, a global company based in Luxembourg, Cleveland's massive mills are an awesome sight, even in their current diminished capacity, and they are a reminder that the transition did not make this a truly "postindustrial" city. We also could not see the gleaming white, twenty-two-story Carl B. Stokes Federal Courthouse, completed in 2002, a much-delayed, over-budget, but attractive addition to the Cleveland skyline. The courthouse is just one of the many ways in which Stokes's legacy has been built into the landscape.

We couldn't see the West Side, which was still solidly middle class in the 1960s but today looks every bit as troubled as the East Side did fifty years ago. This conclusion, which we derived by making explorations in car and on foot, is a reminder of what you can't see from the forty-ninth floor of a skyscraper no matter which way you face: poverty. Nearly 30 percent of Cleveland's residents live below the poverty line, making it one of the poorest cities in America. As poverty spread through the city, so did the abandonment of housing and the demolition of unused buildings. Almost all the city's neighborhoods contain empty lots, the starkest evidence of population decline. There are signs of hope in the neighborhoods, of course, even in the historically troubled Hough, which has seen some redevelopment, some clusters of infill construction, even some suburban-style homes. Still, empty lots abound. By 2010, Hough had fewer than 13,000 residents, down from its mid-1950s peak of more than 80,000. Just as significant, segregation persists here and around metropolitan Cleveland—one of the most segregated cities in America. Hough is nearly 95 percent black. The city is now majority African American. Many of its suburbs, especially distant suburbs like Chagrin Falls, Mentor, and Medina, are nearly all white. From the Key Tower we couldn't see the streets where the Glenville Shootout took place, but we've walked them, and they are so pocked with empty lots that only a student of the event would notice that all the buildings involved in the shootout have disappeared. Ironically, nearby Murray Hill, the city's Little Italy, the contested and violently defended neighborhood, is a rare bright spot inside the city limits. Its lively restaurants and residential development give little sense that this is a city that is still losing population.

Social problems are difficult to discern from seven hundred feet above the city. So too are ecological problems. We could see Lake Erie, which didn't die, and is in fact healthier than it was fifty years ago. But pollution and algal blooms still threaten the lake. Combined sewer overflows remain a concern after all these years, while mercury pollution from coal burning has become a more acute problem. Although some fish populations have improved, there are zebra mussels and other invasive species to contend with; perhaps most ominously, the lake's declining water level, which may be related to climate change, is a new cause for concern.

We also couldn't see the river, snaking through its deep valley below downtown. The landscape of the valley remains largely industrial: gravel yards, old warehouses, and abandoned factory sites line the river. But there are signs of transformation. In 2007, a shopping center called Steelyard Commons opened on the site of a former steel finishing mill, with restaurants and big-box stores such as Target, Walmart, and Staples that residents used to go to the suburbs to find. Near the mouth of the river, below the bluff from downtown, the fortunes of the area popularly known as the Flats have waxed and waned since it became a hotspot in 1980s. More apartments and condos and renewed interest from developers are bringing new life to this area and the nearby warehouse district, making this one of the few neighborhoods in the city that has actually gained population in recent years, part of the national trend of growth in the urban core.

Despite the few bright spots in Cleveland, and many more bright spots in a resurgent urban America, it is hard to avoid the conclusion that Carl Stokes was right forty-five years ago as he expressed skepticism on the eve of the first Earth Day. "I am fearful that the priorities on air and water pollution may be at the expense of what the priorities of the country ought to be: proper housing, adequate food and clothing," he said while governing a city that he knew had intractable environmental and social problems.[2] Then again, maybe it wasn't the nation's priorities that ensured the diminishment of pollution and the persistence of poverty. Perhaps the latter problem is simply more difficult to solve. Reflecting on the long battles to control air and water pollution, with their many technological hurdles and huge costs, we shouldn't underestimate how difficult creating a cleaner urban America really was. But the most difficult hurdles were not technological or economic—they were political. This was true for social problems as much as environmental problems, but the latter obviously spanned political boundaries. Air pollution wafted into the suburbs; water pollution flowed out into Lake Erie. As the Earth Day letters remind us, industrial pollution, certainly more intense and harmful in some neighborhoods, mattered all across the metropolis. Although it was a slow and arduous process, municipalities and counties gradually gave up authority to regional and federal regulatory agencies, including the Cleveland Regional Sewer District (now called the Northeast Ohio Regional Sewer District) and the Environmental Protection Agency. Unfortunately, many Americans continued to think that urban blight, and the poverty that went with it, could and should be contained. The "little kingdoms" of the suburbs continued to resist policies that might ease metropolitan poverty, and so instead it persisted and even deepened.

All this is not to say that the Stokes administration, and those that followed, accomplished nothing for Cleveland. Investments in the service city mattered, though some of them not right away. Abandoned housing, brownfields, and factory shells still dot the landscape, but the carcass of the past is clearly less burdensome to Cleveland than it was at the beginning of the transition. Perhaps more onerous to those who are constantly at work creating a new Cleveland are the memories of the urban crisis. The race riots, the "mistake on the lake," the city defaulting on its debts in 1978, even Mayor Ralph Perk's hair catching fire at a ribbon-cutting ceremony in 1972—all this still weighs on the city and holds it back.

Of all the tales of decline and crisis, though, none holds as much power as the burning river. In 1980, Jim Toman and Dan Cook addressed the city's collective funk in the preface to a book on the Terminal Tower and the city's glory years, noting that as a result of the Cuyahoga fire and other incidents, "Clevelanders seem to suffer from a type of urban insecurity."[3] In 1989, city officials opted not to participate in an event marking the twentieth anniversary of the fire, a river cruise led by the *Anthony J. Celebrezze*, the fireboat that doused the fire. Even as some Clevelanders began to take ownership of the fire through remembrance, Dale R. Finley, president of the Convention and Visitors Bureau of Greater Cleveland, lamented the continued attention: "I just wonder how long do we have to go before we don't have to continually bring up that there was a brief fire on a river 20 years ago?"[4]

We might ask a similar question. Of all the environmental, economic, and social problems facing Carl Stokes, why has the relatively modest fire become the most remembered? Ben Stefanski, reflecting back with some bemusement, recognized that "it was just a little fire. It was put out, didn't do much damage, and that was it. But then it took on a life of its own. This fire is like folklore."[5] The story that people began to tell about the fire was simple, with a straightforward message: a river in the one of the country's biggest cities gradually got more and more polluted, until one morning it caught fire and shocked the nation, waking everyone up to an environmental crisis. Lost in this and most other retellings of the Cuyahoga fire is the deeper history of the polluted river and the many previous fires. Lost too is the broader context of the fire—the crisis in the urban environment, with its smoke, rats, decay, and concentrated poverty.

Even if the growing Cuyahoga folklore ignored the larger story of polluted America, the 1969 fire represented a real transition—not concerning the river's ability to burn but having to do with Americans' understanding of ecology, their tolerance of pollution, and their attribution of deeper meaning to a burning river. Indeed, the growing awareness of the ecological connectedness of all places, especially bodies of water, gave the image of the burning river resonance. In October 1997, Adam Werbach, the then twenty-four-year-old president of the Sierra Club, was asked on CNN to explain why the 1969 fire was so important. "I mean a river lighting on fire was almost biblical," said Werbach, who was not yet born when the fire occurred. "And it energized American action, because people understood that that should not be happening." That understanding of the fire evolved quickly after June 1969.[6]

Despite the many delays in pollution abatement, the 1969 fire was the last on the Cuyahoga. This fact surely points to progress on the river—at least ecological progress. The closing of coking plants at the steel mills, the removal of the Sohio refinery, the decrease in chemical and paint manufacturing, and the general decrease in industry all contributed to the improvement in the river. As Cleveland's economic crisis deepened, at least this aspect of its environmental crisis eased. By the early 1990s, fish had returned to the once-lifeless stretch of the Cuyahoga in Cleveland. Scullers sliced its waters, and bars and restaurants replaced the warehouses and freight docks along its shores near downtown, in the Flats. Just as the river had been a symbol of what was wrong with the environment in the late 1960s and early 1970s, now it represented how much things had improved. In 1998, President Bill Clinton even included the Cuyahoga in his new program to support "American Heritage" rivers, in recognition of the historical importance of rivers and their need for additional environmental attention. The press announcement introducing the first fourteen Heritage Rivers, including the Hudson, Mississippi, Potomac, and Rio Grande, summarized the importance of the comparatively small Cuyahoga: "Once so polluted it caught on fire, the 100-mile-long Cuyahoga became a stark symbol of the plight of America's rivers and a rallying point for passage of the Clean Water Act, one of the nation's landmark environmental laws."[7] If a river had to be known for its fire, then at least the fire could serve as a rallying point.

As time goes on, the people of Cleveland are less sensitive about the fire and the pollution that once made their river a fire hazard. Burning River Pale Ale, brewed just up the hill from the river on the West Side, has proved popular in the city and beyond, its bottles and cartons decorated with flames on the water that add a glow to a rose-tinted skyline. Key Tower and Terminal Tower are framed by two of the many drawbridges in the Flats. Adding to the romance of the scene, brilliant stars shine down on the seemingly fortunate city. Great Lakes Brewing Company co-owner Patrick Conway said the company chose the name because it was "cheeky and irreverent" and because the image has staying power. "Everyone who comes through the city, who passes through our doors, all want to know, 'Is this the city where the river burned?'" Conway said in an interview in 2008. "Everybody knows about it universally. So it's not going away, so we decided to make some lemonade out of that."[8]

The brewery has made environmental stewardship a part of its brand, and in 2001 it held its first Burning River Festival, a chance to promote its beer and draw attention to the Cuyahoga and Lake Erie and their continued environmental problems. Proceeds from the annual festival go to the Burning River Foundation, which makes grants to local environmental organizations. The festival, held in recent years at the former U.S. Coast Guard station on Whisky Island at the river's mouth, includes a ceremonial lighting of floating pyres to commemorate the efforts to clean up the region's waterways since the Cuyahoga fire in 1969. At first a small event, drawing just a few hundred people, the Burning River Festival has grown into one of Cleveland's favorite summer gatherings, with local food vendors, bands, and, of course, plenty of beer. The event has garnered corporate sponsors beyond the brewery, including PNC Bank and Squire Sanders, which are eager to attach their names to the environmental cause.

As it gathered momentum, the Burning River Festival also gained the support of David Beach's EcoCity Cleveland, the organization dedicated to bioregionalism and sustainability. In 2007, EcoCity merged with the Natural History Museum, creating the Center for Regional Sustainability, which now goes by the name GreenCityBlueLake. Still guided by Beach's vision of an eco-city, GreenCityBlueLake is a clearinghouse for all news environmental, a cheerleader for improved public policy, and an active participant in the city's effort to follow through on the Sustainable Cleveland 2019 plan. Significantly, Cleveland set 2019 as a milestone in the drive toward sustainability because it will mark the fiftieth anniversary of the river fire, a year when, according to the plan, the city hopes to "inspire the world with its transformation to a bright green city on a blue lake." Launched by a gathering of political, environmental, and business leaders in 2009, the Sustainable Cleveland program has mostly served to publicize the goals of sustainability, and some progress has been made, such as making the city more bike-friendly and building support for regional wind power generation. So, for these and many other reasons, including improved air and water quality, the anniversary of the fire may bring reflection on how far Cleveland has come from the depths of its crisis in the urban environment. And rightly so. But clearly Cleveland, like all of urban America, is only beginning its transformation to a sustainable city where the production and consumption of energy, food, and other resources puts less of a strain on the natural and social environment. As we work to accelerate the transition to sustainability, surely we can learn much from critical reflection on the events and structures that slowed progress during urban America's last, long transition.[9]

Notes

Introduction: The Crisis in the Urban Environment

1. Carl B. Stokes, "Address to the Capital Press Club, Washington D.C. Shoreham Hotel, June 1, 1968," Carl B. Stokes Papers (hereafter CSP), container 60, folder 1128, Western Reserve Historical Society (hereafter WRHS).

2. Mabel Walker, "The American City Is Obsolescent," *Vital Speeches of the Day* 13 (1946–1947), 697–99.

3. John Skow, "The Question in the Ghetto: Can Cleveland Escape Burning?" *Saturday Evening Post*, July 29, 1967, 38–49.

4. Remarks by Mayor Carl B. Stokes, City Club, July 24, 1970, CSP, container 52, folder 970, WRHS.

5. Remarks by Carl B. Stokes, For Time Capsule to Be Placed in the Cornerstone of Central National Bank Building, June 13, 1969, CSP, container 51, folder 963, WRHS.

6. Carl B. Stokes, "Issues and Prospects in a Regional City," Address by Stokes for Colorado Municipal League Conference, Colorado Springs, June 10, 1971, CSP, container 60, folder 1137, WRHS.

7. "Pollution: A Fight to Stay Alive!" (Petitions April 1970), CSP, container 75, folder 1442, WRHS.

1. What Will Become of Cleveland?

1. Hodge School Letters, April 22, 1970, CSP, container 75, folder 1438, WRHS.

2. *Cleveland Press*, April 20, 1970.

3. Andrea Rady to Carl Stokes, April 22, 1970, CSP, container 75, folder 1438, WRHS.

4. Robert L. Tasse to Carl Stokes, April 22, 1970, CSP, container 75, folder 1438, WRHS.

5. Shannon Havranek to Carl Stokes, n.d. [April 1970], CSP, container 75, folder 1438, WRHS.

6. Rady to Stokes, April 22, 1970.

7. "Text of Inaugural Address by Mayor Carl B. Stokes, Cleveland, Ohio—November 13, 1967," CSP, container 60, folder 1125, WRHS.

8. Carl B. Stokes, *Promises of Power: A Political Autobiography* (New York: Simon and Schuster, 1973), 93, 94.

9. "Text of Inaugural Address by Mayor Carl B. Stokes."

10. "A Program for Progress," Carl B. Stokes Papers Series II (hereafter CSP II), container 1, folder 20, WRHS. This brochure also quotes the newspaper endorsements. Stokes before the American Institute of Architects at the Hollendon Hotel, September 20, 1967, CSP, container 60, folder 1125, WRHS.

11. Debbie Mohorcic to Carl Stokes, April 22, 1970, CSP, container 75, folder 1438, WRHS.

12. Pat Pivonka to Carl Stokes, April 22, 1970, CSP, container 75, folder 1438, WRHS.

13. Barb Gray to Carl Stokes, April 22, 1970; Jill Jaffe to Carl Stokes, April 22, 1970, CSP, container 75, folder 1438, WRHS.

14. Craig Miller to Carl Stokes, April 22, 1970; Claudia Mendat to Carl Stokes, April 23, 1970, CSP, container 75, folder 1438, WRHS.

15. Mendat to Stokes, April 23, 1970; Finis Dunaway, "Gas Masks, Pogo, and the Ecological Indian: Earth Day and the Visual Politics of American Environmentalism," *American Quarterly*, March 2008, 67–99. Bob Adelberger to Carl Stokes, April 22, 1970, CSP, container 75, folder 1438, WRHS.

16. Tasse to Stokes, April 22, 1970.

17. Nancy Danker to Carl Stokes, April 22, 1970; Loren Clark to Carl Stokes, April 23, 1970, CSP, container 75, folder 1438, WRHS.

18. Ralph Simpson to Carl Stokes (n.d. but included with February 1970 letters), CSP, container 75, folder 1434; Richard Dusky to Carl Stokes (n.d.), CSP, container 75, folder 1434, WRHS.

19. Shelley Stelmach to Carl Stokes, April 22, 1970, CSP, container 75, folder 1438, WRHS.

20. Jeffrey K. Hadden, Louis H. Masotti, and Victor Thiessen, "The Making of the Negro Mayors 1967," *Trans-Action*, Jan.–Feb. 1968, 30.

21. *New York Times*, February 25, 1968.

22. "Program for Progress."

23. Louis Stokes, interviewed by Richard and David Stradling, May 25, 2012, Cleveland.

24. *Plain Dealer*, September 7, 1968.

25. Interview with Dr. E. Frank Ellis, Director of the Health Department, July 1971, CSP II, container 3, folder 51, WRHS.

26. *Plain Dealer*, May 2, 1968.

27. Louis Rodriguez to Carl Stokes, April 22, 1970; Mark Hudak to Carl Stokes, April 22, 1970, CSP, container 75, folder 1438, WRHS.

28. Melissa Stevens to Carl Stokes, April 22, 1970, CSP, container 75, folder 1438, WRHS.

29. Daniel E. Morgan Science Class to Carl Stokes, April 23, 1970, CSP, container 75, folder 1438, WRHS.

30. Daniel E. Morgan Science Class to Stokes, April 23, 1970.

31. Stokes, *Promises of Power*, 23.

32. Dorothy Cassidy to Carl Stokes, July 23, 1968, CSP, container 83, folder 1637, WRHS.

33. *Plain Dealer*, May 2, 1968.

34. Carl B. Stokes, "Rebuilding the Cities," *The Humanist* 29 (March–April 1969), 7, 9.

35. Anonymous to Carl Stokes (n.d.), CSP, container 8, folder 126, WRHS.

36. An old tax payer to Carl Stokes, December 14, 1968, CSP, container 8, folder 126, WRHS.

37. Danker to Stokes, April 22, 1970; Glenn Gray to Stokes, April 22, 1970, CSP, container 75, folder 1438, WRHS; Martin Luther King Jr. used the phrase "fierce urgency of now" in his "I Have a Dream" speech in 1963.

38. Bernard N. Sroka to Stokes, June 13[?], 1970, CSP, container 75, folder 1440, WRHS.

39. Carl B. Stokes to Bernard Sroka, August 12, 1970, CSP, container 11, folder 171, WRHS.

2. *Hough and the Urban Crisis*

1. Carl B. Stokes, *Promises of Power: A Political Autobiography* (New York: Simon and Schuster, 1973), 23–25.

2. "Remarks by Mayor Carl B. Stokes, Kick-off of Rat Control Program," June 2, 1969, CSP, container 51, folder 963, WRHS.

3. Interview with Ben Stefanski, Director of Public Utilities, July 1971, CSP II, container 3, folder 49, WRHS.

4. Gary V. Bound to Carl Stokes, July 3, 1969, CSP, container 11, folder 308, WRHS.

5. Kenneth B. Clark, *Dark Ghetto: Dilemmas of Social Power* (New York: Harper and Row, 1965), xv, 29.

6. Bound to Stokes, July 3, 1969.

7. Stokes to Bound, July 16, 1969, CSP, container 17, folder 308; news release, April 17, 1969, CSP, container 51, folder 962, WRHS.

8. City of Cleveland Neighborhood Fact Sheet, http://planning.city.cleveland.oh.us/census/factsheets/spa19.html.

9. Marvin B. Sussman and R. Clyde White, *Hough, Cleveland, Ohio: A Study of Social Life and Change* (Cleveland: Press of Western Reserve University, 1959), 2, 84.

10. Sussman and White, *Hough, Cleveland, Ohio*, 83.

11. Mildred Chadsey, "An Investigation of Housing Conditions of Cleveland's Working-men" (Cleveland: Department of Public Welfare, 1914), 11, 12, 14, 16, http://digitalcase.case.edu:9000/fedora/get/ksl:chainv00/divinv00.pdf.

12. Sussman and White, *Hough, Cleveland, Ohio*, 90.

13. Chadsey, "Investigation of Housing Conditions," 5.

14. Walter Williams, "Cleveland's Crisis Ghetto," *Trans-action*, September 1967, 33–42.

15. John Skow, "Can Cleveland Escape Burning?" *Saturday Evening Post*, July 29, 1967, 38–49.

16. Paul Hofmann, "Cleveland's Ghetto," *New York Times*, June 4, 1967.

17. David E. Lantz, *The Brown Rat in the United States* (Washington, D.C.: Government Printing Office, 1909), 9, 32. Although Americans associate it with early modern Europe, the plague was still raging in India in the early 1900s, and as Lantz wrote, it threatened to become pandemic yet again. In fact, seventy-seven people had died of the disease in San Francisco the year before. In response, that city attempted to destroy its rat population, removing hundreds of thousands of them through traps and poison. Lantz understood, though, that rats had kept pace with "the advance of civilization" and that the war against the vermin promised to be "never-ending."

18. "Grant Request for Establishment of an Environmental Improvement and Rat Control Program," 9, CSP II, container 3, folder 58, WRHS.

19. Lyndon B. Johnson, "Special Message to the Congress: America's Unfinished Business, Urban and Rural Poverty" (March 14, 1967), American Presidency Project, http://www.presidency.ucsb.edu/ws/print.php?pid=28133.

20. The 1961 City Council resolution can be found as an appendix in U.S. Commission on Civil Rights, *Hearing before the United States Commission on Civil Rights: Hearing Held in Cleveland, Ohio, April 1–7, 1966* (Washington, D.C.: Government Printing Office, 1966), 674.

21. U.S. Commission on Civil Rights, *Hearing*, 12.

22. Robert E. Park, Ernest W. Burgess, and Roderick D. McKenzie, *The City* (Chicago, 1967 edition of 1925 original), 108.

23. U.S. Commission on Civil Rights, *Hearing*, 45.

24. The CDC report is included as an appendix in U.S. Commission on Civil Rights, *Hearing*, 657–71.

25. The follow-up CDC report can be found as an appendix in the U.S. Commission on Civil Rights, *Hearing*, 695–96.

26. Clark, *Dark Ghetto*, 56, 57.

27. Carl B. Stokes to Joanne Finley, January 24, 1968, CSP II, container 3, folder 58, WRHS.

28. "Grant Request for Establishment of an Environmental Improvement and Rat Control Program," 6–8.

29. Bailus Walker, interviewed by Richard Stradling, December 12, 2011, Washington, D.C.

30. Bailus Walker, "Health Hazards Associated with Urbanization and Overpopulation," *Journal of the National Medical Association*, July 1970, 260.

31. "Housing and Urban Development Legislation of 1968," Hearings before the Senate Subcommittee on Housing and Urban Affairs of the Committee on Banking and Currency, 90th Congress, 2nd session, March 1968, 686.

32. Lyndon Johnson, *Special Message to the Congress on Urban Problems: "The Crisis of the Cities,"* February 22, 1968, The American Presidency Project, http://www.presidency.ucsb.edu/ws/print.php?pid=29386.

33. Robert A. Beauregard, *Voices of Decline: The Postwar Fate of U.S. Cities* (Cambridge, Mass.: Blackwell, 1993), 86–87. Beauregard (111) claims that in the postwar era commentators began to more fully distinguish slums (residential and in need of demolition) from blight (an economic characteristic of areas around downtown that needed clearance for new development).

34. "Housing and Urban Development Legislation of 1968," 701–2; PATH Citizens Advisory Committee, *Plan of Action for Tomorrow's Housing in Greater Cleveland* (Cleveland: Greater Cleveland Associated Foundation, 1967), 7–8.

35. From the 1957 enabling law found (along with dozens of CRC publications) at http://www.law.umaryland.edu/Marshall/usccr/chrolist.html#1957.

36. *Plain Dealer*, August 14, 1965.

37. *Plain Dealer*, April 5, 1966.

38. Notebooks, Paul Alden Younger Papers, container 1, folder 1, WRHS; U.S. Commission on Civil Rights, *Hearing*, 18–33.

39. U.S. Commission on Civil Rights, *Hearing*, 107–11.

40. U.S. Commission on Civil Rights, *Hearing*, 144.

41. U.S. Commission on Civil Rights, *Hearing*, 230–36.

42. U.S. Commission on Civil Rights, *Hearing*, 632–34.

43. Paul Younger, United States Civil Rights Commission, Ohio Sub-Committee, "Report of Findings," April 28, 1966, Paul Alden Younger Papers, container 1, folder 2, WRHS.

44. Paul Unger to Paul Younger, February 23, 1967, Paul Alden Younger Papers, container 1, folder 6, WRHS.

45. "Federal Role in Urban Affairs," Hearings before the Subcommittee on Executive Reorganization of the Committee on Government Operations, U.S. Senate, 89th Congress, 2nd session, August 24, 25, 26, 1966, Part 4, 975.

46. *Cleveland Press*, January 7, 1966.

47. *Cleveland Press*, July 19, 20, 1966.

48. CAY Trustees to Locher, July 22, 1966; "Statement and Recommendations by Hough Citizens," July 21, 1966, Ralph Sidney Locher Papers, container 8, folder 9, WRHS.

49. *Cleveland Press* as found in "Federal Role in Urban Affairs," Part 4, 959–60.

50. "Federal Role in Urban Affairs," Part 4, 943.

51. "Federal Role in Urban Affairs," Part 4, 943.

52. "Federal Role in Urban Affairs," Part 4, 946.

53. "Federal Role in Urban Affairs," Part 4, 951–52.

54. "Federal Role in Urban Affairs," Part 4, 954–55.

55. "Federal Role in Urban Affairs," Part 4, 950–55.

56. "Federal Role in Urban Affairs," Part 4, 981, 987.

57. Cleveland Citizens Committee on Hough Disturbances, Testimony of August 22–25, 1966 (held at WRHS), 3.

58. Cleveland Citizens Committee on Hough Disturbances, 34.

59. Report as contained in "Federal Role in Urban Affairs," Part 4, 1039–49.

60. Frederick Graves, "How Cities Can Avoid Another Long Hot Summer," *Jet*, May 18, 1967, 14–21.

61. Skow, "Can Cleveland Escape Burning?" 38–49.

62. John Skow, "Cleveland: The Flicker of Fear," *Saturday Evening Post*, September 7, 1968, 24.

63. *Plain Dealer*, June 4, 1969.

64. *Cleveland Press*, June 9, 10, 11, 13, 1969.

65. Statement before the House Select Committee on Crime, Washington, D.C., July 28, 1969, 6, CSP, container 51, folder 964, WRHS.

66. Clyde Fehn, *Second Evaluation of Rat Control Project* (Cleveland: Department of Public Health and Welfare, Environmental Health Services, 1970).

67. Cleveland City Planning Commission, Neighborhood Fact Sheet: Hough, http://planning. city.cleveland.oh.us/census/factsheets/spa28.pdf; Bailus Walker Jr., "Environmental Management in Four Urban Centers of the United States" (Ph.D. diss., University of Minnesota, 1975), 116. The city lost more than 43,000 housing units in the 1960s and 1970s, the vast majority of them in the black neighborhoods of the East Side.

68. *New York Times*, May 15, 1972; Cleveland City Planning Commission, "Housing Abandonment in Cleveland" (October 1972). On arson in Cleveland in the 1970s, see Daniel Kerr, *Derelict Paradise: Homelessness and Urban Development in Cleveland, Ohio* (Boston: University of Massachusetts Press, 2011), 185–90.

3. Downtown and the Limits of Urban Renewal

1. Remarks by Carl B. Stokes, For Time Capsule to Be Placed in the Cornerstone of Central National Bank Building, June 13, 1969, CSP, container 51, folder 963, WRHS.

2. Remarks by John A. Gelbach, President, Society Corporation Records, container 38, folder 453, WRHS.

3. F. J. Blake to E. L. Carpenter, April 23, 1969, Society Corporation Records, container 38, folder 45, WHRS; *Plain Dealer*, September 9, 1966; *Cleveland Press*, March 24, 1970.

4. Pamphlet marking groundbreaking, September 18, 1967, Society Corporation Records, container 38, folder 452, WRHS; Central National Bank of Cleveland, *1969 Annual Report*.

5. I. M. Pei and Associates, *Erieview, Cleveland, Ohio: An Urban Renewal Plan for Downtown Cleveland* (New York: I. M. Pei, 1961).

6. *New York Times*, November 23, 1973.

7. "Statement and Recommendations by Hough Citizens," July 21, 1966, Ralph Sidney Locher Papers, container 8, folder 9, WRHS.

8. Cleveland Advertising Club, *Report on Urban Renewal in Cleveland* (September 1955), 2.

9. "Urban Renewal," Hearings before the Subcommittee on Housing of the Committee on Banking and Currency, House of Representatives, 88th Congress, 1st session, October 22, 23, and 24,1963, Part 1, 174.

10. "Urban Renewal," Part 1, 174, 180.

11. "Talk by State Representative Carl Stokes at Open-Air Meeting on Urban Renewal Site at East 75th Street and Woodland Avenue," August 27, 1967, CSP, container 60, folder 1125, WRHS.

12. "Talk by Stokes, Candidate for Democratic Nomination for Mayor, to the Cleveland Club," September 7, 1967, CSP, container 60, folder 1125, WRHS.

13. I. M. Pei and Associates, *Erieview*, 8.

14. Oliver Zunz, *Making America Corporate, 1870–1920* (Chicago: University of Chicago Press, 1990), 124.

15. *New York Times*, November 23, 1973.

16. George Salapa to Carl Stokes, June 6, 1969, CSP, container 17, folder 306, WRHS.

17. Sanford C. Frumker to Carl Stokes, May 29, 1969, CSP, container 17, folder 306, WRHS.

18. Charles Abrams, *The City Is the Frontier* (New York: Harper and Row, 1965), 308–9.

19. Cleveland City Planning Commission, *Downtown Cleveland 1975: The Downtown General Plan* (1959), 6.

20. Cleveland City Planning Commission, *Downtown Cleveland 1975*, 34.

21. Cleveland City Planning Commission, *Cleveland Today . . . Tomorrow: The General Plan of Cleveland* (1950), 22–23, 10.

22. Cleveland City Planning Commission, *Downtown Cleveland 1975*, 3.

23. "Remarks by Stokes upon the 115th Anniversary of the Birth of Tom L. Johnson," July 18, 1969, CSP, container 51, folder 964, WRHS.

24. *Call and Post*, July 20, 1968, as quoted in Leonard N. Moore, *Carl B. Stokes and the Rise of Black Political Power* (Urbana: University of Illinois Press, 2002), 103.

25. "Remarks by Mayor Carl B. Stokes," Lee-Seville Housing Rally on the Mall, June 9, 1969, CSP, container 51, folder 963, WRHS.

26. *Plain Dealer*, June 26, 1967.

27. "Talk by Mayor Ray T. Miller, Mayor of Cleveland," July 6, 1933, Ernest J. Bohn Papers, box 7, folder 15, Kelvin Smith Library Special Collections, Case Western Reserve University.

28. Grisanti v. City of Cleveland 179 N.E.2d 812 (1962).

29. "Urban Renewal in the District of Columbia," Hearings before the Subcommittee on the District of Columbia, House of Representatives, 88th Congress, 1st session, June 21, July 26, August 14, 1963, Part 4, 1618; "Urban Renewal," Part 1, 180.

30. "Summary Analysis of Progress on '16 Point Immediate Action Program,' University-Euclid Renewal Project, Cleveland, Ohio, as of December 1966"; "Statement by Mayor Carl B. Stokes, News Conference, 9:30 a.m., Dec. 15, 1967," CSP II, container 3, folder 88, WRHS.

31. *Plain Dealer*, July 7, 1970.

32. "Perspective," *Clevelander* 47 (July 1970), 10.

33. Greater Cleveland Growth Association, "The Outlook for Greater Cleveland in 1990," Society Corporation Records, container 38, folder 453, WRHS.

34. *Plain Dealer*, May 25, 1990.

4. Policy and the Polluted City

1. "Remarks by Mayor Carl B. Stokes at Dedication of E. 55th Street Marina," June 17, 1969, CSP, container 85, folder 1682, WRHS.

2. Willie L. Morrow to Stokes, June 14, 1969, CSP, container 17, folder 307, WRHS.

3. *Cleveland Press*, August 7, 1968.

4. *Plain Dealer*, August 10, 1968.

5. Hon. Carl B. Stokes Testimony, "Public Works Appropriations for 1970 for Water and Power Resources Development," *Hearing before a Subcommittee of the Committee on Appropriations* (House), 91st Congress, 1st session, June 5, 1969, Part 5, 995.

6. Stokes Testimony, "Public Works Appropriations for 1970," 995–96.

7. Interview with Ben Stefanski, July 1971, CSP II, container 3, folder 49, WRHS.

8. *Plain Dealer*, July 18, 1969.

9. Annette Koman to Carl Stokes (received August 14, 1969); Edward Martin to Annette Koman, August 22, 1969, CSP, container 85, folder 1683, WRHS.

10. JoAnne Olszewski to Carl Stokes, June 1, 1968, CSP, container 38, folder 709, WRHS.

11. William A. Strong letters, variously addressed and dated, June 1937; Arch C. Klumph to Ernest J. Bohn, July 16, 1937, Ernest J. Bohn Papers, box 12, folder 39, Kelvin Smith Library Special Collections, Case Western Reserve University.

12. Joseph Swatek to Thomas Burke, December 26, 1946; January 25, 1947; February 20, 1947, Thomas A. Burke Jr. Papers, container 1, folder 1, WRHS.

13. Joseph Swatek to Thomas Burke, May 2, 1947, Burke Papers, container 1, folder 1, WRHS.

14. Robert Crosser to Thomas Burke, March 24, 1952; Burke to Crosser, March 31, 1952, Burke Papers, container 1, folder 3, WRHS. Officer Schroeder's reports from June 1944 can be found in the Burke Papers, container 1, folder 1, WRHS.

15. "Petition for Writ of Mandamus" (filed May 26, 1965), Bar Realty Corporation v. Ralph Locher, Cuyahoga County Court of Common Pleas, Case No. 813769.

16. *Plain Dealer*, May 22, 1964; Betty Klaric, interviewed by Richard Stradling, May 27, 2008, Mayfield Heights, Ohio.

17. U.S. Department of Health, Education and Welfare, *Proceedings, Conference in the Matter of Pollution of Lake Erie and Its Tributaries, Cleveland, August 3–6, 1965* (Washington, D.C.: U.S. Department of Health, Education and Welfare, 1965), 4:1065, 1066, 1071.

18. "Joint Answer of Ralph S. Locher, et al." (filed September 10, 1965), Bar Realty Corporation v. Ralph Locher, Cuyahoga County Court of Common Pleas, Case No. 813769; *Plain Dealer*, August 24, 1965.

19. "Memorandum of Opinion" (August 10, 1970); "Judgment" (August 28, 1970), Bar Realty Corporation v. Ralph Locher, Cuyahoga County Court of Common Pleas, Case No. 813769.

20. The State, Ex Rel. Bar Realty Corp., et al., Appellees, v. Locher, Mayor, et al., Appellants, 30 Ohio St.2d 190; 283 N.E.2d 164 (1972).

21. "Federal Water Pollution Control Act Amendments—1969," Hearings before the Committee on Public Works, House of Representatives, 91st Congress, 1st session, 1969, 70–76.

22. "Federal Water Pollution Control Act Amendments—1969," 149, 151, 155.

23. *Plain Dealer*, November 4, 1966.

24. *Plain Dealer*, August 23, 1966.

25. *Plain Dealer*, February 25, 1961; May 1, 1966.

26. *Plain Dealer*, April 10, 1969.

27. Bob Bauerlein to John C. Little, October 7 and October 17, 1969, CSP, container 11, folder 176, WRHS.

28. *Pollution of Lake Erie and Its Tributaries*, 4:800.

29. "Separating Storm and Sanitary Sewers in Urban Renewal," Report No. 1648, House of Representatives, 89th Congress, 2nd session, 1966, 13.

30. *Pollution of Lake Erie and Its Tributaries*, 4:825–27.

31. Statement by Mayor Carl B. Stokes, April 10, 1969, CSP, container 51, folder 962, WRHS.

32. *Plain Dealer*, June 29, 1969.

33. "Statement by Bailus Walker, Jr., . . . Before the Public Hearing . . . May 23, 1969," CSP, container 51, folder 962, WRHS.

34. *Cleveland Press*, May 23, 1969; Richard L. DeChant, "Remarks to the Air and Water Pollution Committee of Cleveland City Council," CSP, container 54, folder 1014, WRHS.

35. "Statement of R. Thomas Schoonmaker," June 13, 1969, CSP, container 54, folder 1014, WRHS.

36. "Freeway—Airport-in-Lake Plan Unveiled," *Plain Dealer*, June 24, 1966.

37. Havens and Emerson, *Feasibility of a Stabilization-Retention Basin in Lake Erie at Cleveland, Ohio* (May 1968), iv, 5, 46.

38. Havens and Emerson, *Feasibility of a Stabilization-Retention Basin*, 4.

39. *Cleveland Press*, November 4, 1968.

40. *Cleveland Press*, November 6, 1968.

41. L. Amory to Mr. Carl B. Stokes, March 5, 1969, CSP, container 8, folder 126, WRHS.

42. Clean Water Task Force, "Action Program," March 1969, 2, 4, CSP, container 86, folder 1692, WRHS.

43. "Statement by Mayor Carl B. Stokes," April 14, 1970, CSP II, container 2, folder 28, WRHS.

5. The Burning River

1. *Cleveland Press*, May 26, 1969 (Klaric Collection, Cleveland Public Library).

2. Betty Klaric, "Stokes Promises to Lead Pollution Fight," *Cleveland Press*, June 24, 1969.

3. Betty Klaric, interviewed by Richard Stradling, May 27, 2008, Mayfield Heights, Ohio.

4. *Plain Dealer*, June 23, 1969; *Cleveland Press*, June 23, 1969.

5. *Columbus Dispatch*, July 4, 1969.

6. *Plain Dealer*, June 24, 1969.

7. *Cleveland Press*, June 25, 1969.

8. "The Cities: The Price of Optimism," *Time*, August 1, 1969, 41.

9. *Audubon*, November 1969, back cover.

10. David Zwick, interviewed by Richard Stradling, March 11, 1999, by telephone.

11. "Pollution, Threat to Man's Only Home," *National Geographic*, December 1970, 5–7.

12. *Cleveland Daily Plain Dealer*, August 29, September 2, 1868; *Cleveland City Council Proceedings*, September 1, 1868, 303.

13. "A Great Oil Fire," *New York Times*, February 4, 6, 1883; *Plain Dealer*, May 2, 1912; *Cleveland Press*, May 2, 1912; *Plain Dealer*, May 3, 1912; "Oil Barge Explodes, 5 Dead," *New York Times*, May 2, 1912.

14. Standard Oil of Ohio, *Annual Report, 1966* (ProQuest Historical Annual Reports).

15. *Plain Dealer*, July 20, 1964.

16. "Long-Feared River Peril Happens—Cuyahoga Burns," *Cleveland Press*, February 7, 1936.

17. *Cleveland Press*, February 8, 9, 1948; "River Oil Fire Perils Clark Bridge," *Plain Dealer*, February 8, 1948.

18. *Plain Dealer*, August 11, December 18, 1948.

19. *Cleveland Press*, August 12, 1948.

20. *Cleveland Press*, March 17, 1941.

21. "Report of the Cleveland City Council Committee on Stream Pollution to the Council of the City of Cleveland, Ohio," October 10, 1946, 2, 24, 37.

22. "Report of the Cleveland City Council Committee on Stream Pollution," table 8.

23. *Cleveland Press*, February 20, 1948.

24. *Cleveland Press*, July 29, 1948.

25. *Plain Dealer*, April 8, 1960.

26. *Plain Dealer*, June 25, 1969.

27. John E. Richards to Carl Stokes, July 3, 1969, CSP, container 85, folder 1683, WRHS.

28. Edward J. Martin to James A. Rhodes, July 7, 1969, CSP, container 85, folder 1683, WRHS; *Cleveland Press*, July 8, 1969.

29. John E. Richards to Edwin [*sic*] Martin, July 14, 1969, CSP, container 85, folder 1683, WRHS.

30. "Water Pollution—1970," Hearings before the Subcommittee on Air and Water Pollution, U.S. Senate, 91st Congress, 2nd session, April 28, 1970, 412.

31. Rivers and Harbors and Flood Control Act of 1970, H.R. 19877, 91st Congress, 2nd session, *Congressional Record*, December 7, 1970, H 40150.

32. *Plain Dealer*, March 13, 1951; *Cleveland Press*, October 13, 1950, and May 6, 1952.

33. *Plain Dealer* November 2, 1952; "The Cities: The Price of Optimism," *Time*, August 1, 1969, 41.

34. *Cleveland Press*, November 4, 1952.

35. *Columbus Dispatch*, November 2, 1952; "Cleveland Recovering from Steel Strike Effects, FRB Reports," *Wall Street Journal*, November 4, 1952.

36. T. J. Ess, "Jones & Laughlin . . . Cleveland Works," reprinted from *Iron and Steel Engineer*, February 1959.

37. "42nd Annual Meeting of Shareholders, Jones & Laughlin Steel Corporation," Pittsburgh, April 30, 1964.

38. News release from Republic Steel, December 19, 1968, Steel Mill Water Pollution Control Files, 1963–1980, series 1785, container 4, folder 20, Ohio State Archives.

39. *Cleveland Press*, September 4, 1969.

40. "Statement by John R. Lowey before the Federal Water Pollution Control Administration Hearing," Pick-Carter Hotel, Cleveland, Ohio, October 7, 1969, Republic Steel Corporation Records, 1895–2001, container 232, folder 21, WRHS.

41. J. W. Mills to W. J. DeLancey, November 19, 1969, Republic Steel Corporation Records, container 236, folder 21, WRHS.

42. "Minutes of Meeting," March 14, 1969, Greater Cleveland Growth Association Records, container 184, folder 6, WRHS.

43. "Statement by Louis F. Birkel at the Ohio Water Pollution Control Board Hearing to Establish Water Quality Standards for the Cuyahoga, Rocky, Chagrin and Grand Rivers," Cleveland, Ohio, May 22, 1968, Republic Steel Corporation Records, container 236, folder 21, WRHS.

44. *Cleveland Press*, January 21, 1969.

45. *Plain Dealer*, August 17, 1969.

46. *Cleveland Press*, May 2, June 18, 1969.

47. *Cleveland Press*, July 17, 1969.

48. *Cleveland Press*, October 7, 1969.

49. Paul R. Pine to Board of Directors, August 21, 1963, Greater Cleveland Growth Association Records, container 138, folder 10, WRHS; *Cleveland Press*, March 2, 1970.

50. *Cleveland Press*, October 9, 1969.

6. From Earth Day to EcoCity

1. *Plain Dealer*, April 16, 1970; *Call and Post* April 25, 1970; *New York Times*, May 4, 1970. The phrasing used here comes from the *New York Times*.

2. *Call and Post*, April 25, 1970.

3. *Plain Dealer*, April 19, 1970.

4. *Cleveland Press*, April 23, 1970.

5. *Call and Post*, April 25, 1970.

6. Nathan Hare, "Black Ecology," *Black Scholar*, April 1970, 2–8.

7. *Call and Post*, May 2, 1970.

8. The Students of St. Peter High School (Pat Ryba) to Carl Stokes, November 30, 1970, CSP, container 11, folder 171, WRHS.

9. Carl B. Stokes to John W. Chambers, April 12, 1971, container 11, folder 171, WRHS.

10. *The Cuyahoga River Watershed: Proceedings of a Symposium held at Kent State University, Kent, Ohio, 1 November 1968* (Kent, Ohio: Kent State University, 1969), 4.

11. *Observer*, April 10, 1970.

12. *Plain Dealer*, October 11, 1971.

13. *New York Times*, October 2, 1966.

14. A. Q. Mowbray, *Road to Ruin* (Philadelphia: Lippincott, 1969), 61, 68.

15. Carl B. Stokes to Editor of the *Plain Dealer*, October 12, 1971, CSP, container 52, folder 982, WRHS.

16. Carl B. Stokes to Philip Richley, September 27, 1971, CSP II, container 2, folder 31, WRHS.

17. Statement on the planned march against the war in Vietnam, April 14, 1970, CSP, container 52, folder 969, WRHS.

18. Statement by Mayor Carl B. Stokes, May 5, 1970, container 52, folder 969, WRHS.

19. *Plain Dealer*, April 9, 1970.

20. Opening Remarks by Mayor Carl B. Stokes, "Crisis at Our Colleges: A Dialog with Mayor Stokes," TV 3, 9:30 P.M., Thursday, May 7, 1970, container 52, folder 969, WRHS.

21. Ruth Sicherman to Carl Stokes, August 29, 1971, CSP, container 11, folder 171, WRHS.

22. Carl B. Stokes to Hugh Corrigan, May 25, 1970; Robert Bauerlein to Ann Felber, May 26, 1970, CSP, container 11, folder 172, WRHS.

23. Ohio Constitutional Revision Commission Reports 1970–1977, 6:2856, www.lsc.state.oh.us/ocrc/.

24. Ohio Constitutional Revision Commission Reports, 6:2874.

25. Ohio Constitutional Revision Commission Reports, 6:2851.

26. *Plain Dealer*, June 24, 1972.

27. Three Rivers Watershed District, *Fourth Annual Report*, (February 15, 1970).

28. George F. Linn, Health Commissioner, Huron County, to John W. Cashman, Director, Ohio Department of Health, January 11, 1973, as found in Army Corps of Engineers, *Wastewater Management Study for Cleveland-Akron Metropolitan and Three Rivers Watershed Areas, Appendix II* (August 1973).

29. C. B. Roscoe, Director, Huron County Regional Planning Commission, to Col. Robert Moor, U.S. Army Corps, January 5, 1973, as found in Army Corps of Engineers, *Wastewater Management Study for Cleveland-Akron Metropolitan and Three Rivers Watershed Areas, Appendix VIII* (August 1973).

30. *EcoCity Cleveland*, April 1993, 1, 2.

31. Frank Ellis to Richard Greene, October 6, 1970, CSP, container 75, folder 1431, WRHS.

32. Carl B. Stokes, *Promises of Power: A Political Autobiography* (New York: Simon and Schuster, 1973), 116, 237, 147, 139.

33. Stokes, *Promises of Power*, 237.

34. Stokes, *Promises of Power*, 272.

35. Stokes, *Promises of Power*, 249.

Epilogue

1. Louis Stokes, interviewed by Richard and David Stradling, May 25, 2012, Cleveland.

2. *Plain Dealer*, April 16, 1970; *Call and Post*, April 25, 1970; *New York Times*, May 4, 1970. The phrasing used here comes from the *New York Times*.

3. Jim Toman and Dan Cook, *The Terminal Tower Complex* (Cleveland: Cleveland Landmarks Press, 1980).

4. Associated Press, June 18, 1989, LexisNexis.

5. Ben Stefanski, interviewed by Richard Stradling, April 26, 1999, Cleveland.

6. Adam Werbach, CNN Morning News, October 17, 1997, transcript 97101703V09, LexisNexis.

7. http://clinton2.nara.gov/CEQ/Rivers/.

8. Patrick Conway, interviewed by Richard Stradling, May 26, 2008, Cleveland.

9. http://www.gcbl.org/files/resources/sc2019executivesummary9sep10.pdf.

Bibliographic Essay

PRIMARY SOURCES

We were fortunate to have access to an embarrassment of primary resources concerning Cleveland in the late 1960s and early 1970s. We conducted a series of interviews with some of the key figures in this story, including Louis Stokes (Cleveland, May 25, 2012); Bailus Walker (Washington, D.C., December 12, 2011); Patrick Conway (Cleveland, May 26, 2008); Betty Klaric (Mayfield Heights, Ohio, May 27, 2008); Steve Tuckerman (Cleveland, April 12, 1999); Ben Stefanski (Cleveland, April 26, 1999); and David Zwick (telephone, March 11, 1999). These interviews provided access to issues not covered in the written record, but the written record is remarkably complete. The Western Reserve Historical Society holds the manuscript collections that made this work possible. Most important are the two collections concerning Carl Stokes (Carl B. Stokes Papers, MS 4370; Carl B. Stokes Papers Series II, MS 4800), which contain extensive records from his administration and political campaigns. Photographs from the Stokes administration can be found in Carl Stokes Photographs, 1968–1971, PG 429. We also accessed other useful collections at the Western Reserve Historical Society, including the Paul Alden Younger Papers, MS 3869; Republic Steel Corporation Records, 1895–2001, MS 4949; Society Corporation Records, MS 4319; Thomas A. Burke Papers, MS 4035; Ralph Sidney Locher Papers, MS 3337; Charles Beard Papers, MS 4802; Casimir Bielin Papers, MS 4074; William Ganson Rose Papers, MS 3365; and Greater Cleveland Growth Association Records, MS 3471. At Case Western Reserve's Kelvin Smith Library Special Collections we consulted the Ernest J. Bohn Papers for documents related to planning, though mostly from an earlier period. The papers from the Ohio Water Pollution Control Board, series 1785 and series 2398, and the Ohio League of Women Voters, MS 354, held at the Ohio Historical Society in Columbus, also proved useful.

In addition to manuscript collections, we read the local newspapers. The Cleveland Public Library makes available the historical *Plain Dealer*, which is word-searchable and therefore extremely useful. We also made several visits to the massive *Cleveland Press* clippings files at Cleveland State University, and we consulted the Cleveland Public Library's Betty Klaric clippings file, which is now on microfiche and offers a tight focus on environmental reporting. In addition, we had access to the electronic files of the *Call and Post*, Cleveland's weekly African American newspaper, and ProQuest's historical *New York Times*.

We have listed other, more narrowly useful primary sources by chapter below.

Secondary Sources

The details of this book have come almost exclusively from primary sources, but our interpretation and presentation are derived from the secondary literature in urban and environmental history. What follows is not a comprehensive list of secondary works in these expansive fields. Rather, it includes those works that have been most important to our thinking and to which we owe the greatest intellectual debts.

Urban History

Dozens of important books have addressed the urban crisis. Among the most important is Thomas Sugrue, *The Origins of the Urban Crisis: Race and Inequality in Postwar Detroit* (Princeton: Princeton University Press, 1996), which traces Detroit's decline to the shrinking of industrial employment beginning in the 1950s and discrimination in employment and housing that adversely affected African Americans throughout the postwar period. In *White Flight: Atlanta and the Making of Modern Conservatism* (Princeton: Princeton University Press, 2005), Kevin M. Kruse offers a detailed and convincing portrait of how whites resisted integration by essentially ceding the city and its services to African Americans, retreating to racially exclusive suburbs and private services (including schools), and then developing an anti-government, anti-tax philosophy. Unsurprisingly, this set of actions contributed to the impoverishment of Atlanta. Our thinking has also been shaped by Amanda I. Seligman's *Block by Block: Neighborhoods and Public Policy on Chicago's*

222

West Side (Chicago: University of Chicago Press, 2005), which describes an urban crisis consisting of two conjoined threats—environmental decay and racial succession. Seligman emphasizes the latter, which whites struggled to resist in the late 1950s and early 1960s, but she also describes programs to stem physical deterioration in neighborhoods threatened by blight and desegregation. Nancy Kleniewski, writing from a different perspective and for a different purpose, makes a convincing argument that urban renewal sped the physical transformation of industrial cities into corporate cities, a process that heightened inequality in cities. See "From Industrial to Corporate City: The Role of Urban Renewal," in *Marxism and the Metropolis: New Perspectives in Urban Political Economy*, edited by William K. Tabb and Larry Sawers (New York: Oxford University Press, 1984). For the longer story of the rise and fall of an American industrial city, see S. Paul O'Hara's *Gary: The Most American of All American Cities* (Bloomington: Indiana University Press, 2010), which describes that city's fate as the consequence of neoliberal policies, automation, and the mobility of capital.

Students of the postwar period should consult John C. Teaford, *The Rough Road to Renaissance: Urban Revitalization in America, 1940–1985* (Baltimore: Johns Hopkins University Press, 1990), which offers a detailed account of how municipal governments responded to deterioration, providing evidence and examples from around the nation. For a readable survey of government's longer effort to reduce poverty, see James T. Patterson's *America's Struggle against Poverty in the Twentieth Century* (Cambridge, Mass.: Harvard University Press, 2000). Robert A. Beauregard's *Voices of Decline: The Postwar Fate of U.S. Cities* (Cambridge, Mass.: Blackwell, 1993) discusses the gathering urban crisis and subsequent recovery, focusing on the discourse concerning the fate of American cities. Elihu Rubin's wonderful study of Boston, *Insuring the City: The Prudential Center and the Postwar Urban Landscape* (New Haven: Yale University Press, 2012), provides a useful treatment of the role of the insurance industry in the evolving service city, an analysis of postwar architecture, and a biography of Charles Luckman, all embedded in a broader discussion of urban redevelopment. See also the work of Wendell Pritchett, including "Which Urban Crisis? Regionalism, Race, and Urban Policy, 1960–1974," *Journal of Urban History*, January 2008, 266–86.

For an analysis of demographic changes in postwar American cities, see Arnold R. Hirsch's classic *Making the Second Ghetto: Race and Housing in Chicago, 1940–1960* (Cambridge: Cambridge University Press, 1983), and also on Chicago, see Beryl Satter's very moving *Family Properties: Race, Real Estate, and the Exploitation of Black Urban America* (New York:

Metropolitan Books, 2009), which describes in great detail how blacks over-paid for real estate and the consequences of this exploitation for entire neighborhoods. June Manning Thomas's *Redevelopment and Race: Planning a Finer City in Postwar Detroit* (Baltimore: Johns Hopkins University Press, 1997) focuses on the work of planners and concludes that the city didn't have the tools or staff necessary to prevent deterioration. Students of urban renewal will want to read Christopher Klemek's *The Transatlantic Collapse of Urban Renewal: Postwar Urbanism from New York to Berlin* (Chicago: University of Chicago Press, 2011). For a fine case study of a very different kind of city negotiating the rapid changes brought on by the civil rights movement and the persistence of liberal policies in the late 1960s and early 1970s, see Kent B. Germany's *New Orleans after the Promises: Poverty, Citizenship, and the Search for the Great Society* (Athens: University of Georgia Press, 2007).

We also learned from a variety of urban histories that are tangential to the story we've told. These include Douglas W. Rae, *City: Urbanism and Its End* (New Haven: Yale University Press, 2003), and Robert M. Fogelson, *Downtown: Its Rise and Fall, 1880–1950* (New Haven: Yale University Press, 2001), which concerns an earlier period but contains considerable insight on how downtowns grow and function. See also Alison Isenberg's readable and insightful *Downtown, America: A History of the Place and the People Who Made It* (Chicago: University of Chicago Press, 2005), which emphasizes the role of retail in the history of "Main Street." See also Fogelson's brief and useful *Bourgeois Nightmares: Suburbia, 1870–1930* (New Haven: Yale University Press, 2005), which describes the evolution of middle-class fears of urban mixing of people and land use. All students of urban history will want to read Max Page's wonderful work on the power of capitalism to reshape a city: *The Creative Destruction of Manhattan, 1900–1940* (New Haven: Yale University Press, 1999). For an analysis of the role of automobiles in reshaping downtowns, see John Jakle and Keith Sculle, *Lots of Parking: Land Use in a Car Culture* (Charlottesville: University of Virginia Press, 2005). We have also been influenced by the work of two exceptional doctoral students working on postwar cities at the University of Cincinnati: Robert Gioielli, whose revised dissertation has been published as *Environmental Activism and the Urban Crisis: Baltimore, St. Louis, and Chicago* (Philadelphia: Temple University Press, 2014); and Aaron Cowan, who completed his dissertation, "A Nice Place to Visit: Tourism, Urban Revitalization, and the Transformation of Postwar American Cities," in 2007.

A number of works allowed us to understand how contemporary scholars defined and grappled with these problems. For the most complete contemporaneous study of ghettos, see Kenneth B. Clark's classic *Dark Ghetto: Dilemmas of Social Power* (New York: Harper and Row, 1965), which became influential because Clark wonderfully balanced an insider's perspective with scholarly remove—and did so in engaging prose. On the War on Poverty, see Daniel Patrick Moynihan's *Maximum Feasible Misunderstanding: Community Action in the War on Poverty* (New York: Free Press, 1969). Anyone studying urban growth should know the work of two important twentieth-century thinkers: Lewis Mumford and Jane Jacobs. Mumford wrote extensively about how cities grew, describing phases in urban development. In *The Culture of Cities* (New York: Harcourt, Brace, 1938), Mumford imagined more healthful, moral, and well-planned cities. He favored redevelopment, the remaking of cities through decentralization and mobility. Jane Jacobs wrote the classic response to the modernist attack on urban density and diversity: *The Death and Life of Great American Cities* (New York: Vintage Books, 1961). For a prescient—and brief—description of the urban metamorphosis, see Mabel Walker, "The American City Is Obsolescent," *Vital Speeches of the Day* 13 (1946–47), 697–99.

One of the earliest and most complete critiques of urban renewal came from Martin Anderson. First published in 1964 and reissued in a mass market paperback three years later, *The Federal Bulldozer* (New York: McGraw-Hill, 1967) was an important part of the national discussion of urban renewal's problems. Anderson argued that since urban renewal seemed unlikely to actually renew any cities it should be discontinued, which would save money and heartache. Engaging Anderson in this debate was the housing expert Charles Abrams, who answered with *The City Is the Frontier* (New York: Harper and Row, 1965). After a clear-headed treatment of urban decline, Abrams described the opportunities and responsibilities for government in reshaping American cities. Unlike Anderson, Abrams still found great potential in urban renewal, hoping it would lead to central cities that could compete with their suburbs. Among other things, Abrams argued that cities should reclaim their natural features, such as riverfronts, and enhance their walkability.

Political scientist John Mollenkopf wrote an important body of work on cities going through the "postindustrial revolution." His most complete discussion of "progrowth coalitions" and postwar urban politics appears in *The Contested City* (Princeton: Princeton University Press, 1983), in which he describes the postindustrial physical transition as a rejection of the industrial city. Students of urban development will also learn much from John R. Logan and Harvey L. Molotch, *Urban Fortunes: The Political Economy of Place* (Berkeley: University of California Press, 1987). Ironically, Molotch developed his Marxian theory, casting cities as "growth machines" fueled by production and rent, just when both of these factors were losing their power to organize urban space. We learned a great deal about the difficulty of municipal governance in this period from John V. Lindsay's *The City* (New York: Norton, 1969), in which he describes managing New York in the late 1960s. (On New York, see also Vincent J. Cannato's thorough *The Ungovernable City: John Lindsay and His Struggle to Save New York* [New York: Basic Books, 2001].) We also learned a great deal from the political scientist Robert A. Dahl, whose description of pluralistic governance in cities still strikes us as useful. Both of us read Dahl's case study of New Haven, *Who Governs? Democracy and Power in an American City* (New Haven: Yale University Press, 1961), as undergraduate students in the 1980s.

On perceptions of the urban environment, see Yi-Fu Tuan's classic *Topophilia: A Study of Environmental Perception, Attitudes, and Values* (Englewood Cliffs, N.J.: Prentice-Hall, 1974). Kevin Lynch's *What Time Is This Place?* (Cambridge, Mass.: MIT Press, 1972) is a stimulating rumination on the relationship between places and our sense of time which provides a useful way of thinking about rapid change in cities and the historic preservation impulse it inspired in the early 1970s. His earlier work, *The Image of the City* (Cambridge, Mass.: Technology Press and Harvard University Press, 1960), also provides useful tools for thinking about the city.

Readers might find some value in John A. Jakle and David Wilson's *Derelict Landscapes: The Wasting of America's Built Environment* (Savage, Md.: Rowman and Littlefield, 1992), although we were troubled by the authors' assumptions of the disunity between the built and natural environment and the unity of "Americans," a group we find too disparate to draw many conclusions about. The economist Edward Glaeser, in *Triumph of the City: How Our Greatest Invention Makes Us Richer, Smarter, Greener, Healthier, and Happier* (New York: Penguin Press, 2011), makes a confounding assertion: "The folly of building-centric urban renewal reminds us that cities aren't structures; cities are people" (9). Our understanding is that cities are both people *and* structures, and both matter a great deal to urban success. Ironically, Glaeser spends much of his book describing urban structure—skyscrapers and sprawl—a reminder that cities actually *are* structures in which people live, work, and recreate.

ENVIRONMENTALISM AND ECOLOGY

A vast and rapidly growing literature describes the environmental movement. In *Crabgrass Crucible: Suburban Nature and the Rise of Environmentalism in*

Twentieth-Century America (Chapel Hill: University of North Carolina Press, 2012), Christopher C. Sellers writes convincingly about the development of environmentalism on Long Island and in suburban Los Angeles, but we would argue for the polygenesis of environmental philosophies and the political movement in the 1960s. Surely the many urban residents fighting pollution and other environmental problems deserve attention from scholars trying to understand the growth of environmental activism. Adam Rome's influential *The Bulldozer in the Countryside: Suburban Sprawl and the Rise of American Environmentalism* (Cambridge: Cambridge University Press, 2001) also argues for the suburban origins of environmentalism, describing the many consequences of sprawling development as impetus for action. Rome and Sellers describe essential aspects of the movement, but a focus on the suburbs leaves out important parts of the complex story of environmental activism.

Three books on quite different topics describe the spread of ecological thinking in American culture, via the popularization of science by activist scientists and via the counterculture. Michael Egan's *Barry Commoner and the Science of Survival: The Remaking of American Environmentalism* (Cambridge, Mass.: MIT Press, 2007) is especially useful in detailing the connection between science and environmental activism. Frank Zelco's *Make It a Green Peace! The Rise of Countercultural Environmentalism* (New York: Oxford University Press, 2013) explores the international dimension of the movement and the cultural relevance of lay ecology. See also Andrew Kirk's *Counterculture Green: The Whole Earth Catalog and American Environmentalism* (Lawrence: University Press of Kansas, 2007) for a valuable discussion of the cultural contributions to the movement.

Other important books describe aspects of the environmental movement that are quite distant to what we've explored, but they offer valuable context for our story. Among the best are Thomas Robertson, *The Malthusian Moment: Global Population Growth and the Birth of American Environmentalism* (New Brunswick, N.J.: Rutgers University Press, 2012), and Chad Montrie, *To Save the Land and People: A History of Opposition to Surface Coal Mining in Appalachia* (Chapel Hill: University of North Carolina Press, 2003).

Those interested in learning more about urban environmental history will want to seek out the work of Martin Melosi and Joel Tarr. Both have long lists of publications, but we suggest beginning with Melosi's encyclopedic *The Sanitary City: Urban Infrastructure in America from Colonial Times to the Present* (Baltimore: Johns Hopkins University Press, 2000) and Tarr's collection of essays, *The Search for the Ultimate Sink: Urban Pollution in*

Historical Perspective (Akron, Ohio: University of Akron Press, 1996). One of the best urban environmental histories is an early contribution: Andrew Hurley's *Environmental Inequalities: Class, Race, and Industrial Pollution in Gary, Indiana, 1945–1980* (Chapel Hill: University of North Carolina Press, 1995), which is a must-read for those interested in the role of race in determining exposure to pollution. See also Harold Platt's important comparative study: *Shock Cities: The Environmental Transformation and Reform of Manchester and Chicago* (Chicago: University of Chicago Press, 2005). Other scholars working on environmental issues in cities include Jeffrey Craig Sanders, whose book *Seattle and the Roots of Urban Sustainability: Inventing Ecotopia* (Pittsburgh: University of Pittsburgh Press, 2010) deserves more attention. Another book on Seattle, the influential *Emerald City: An Environmental History of Seattle* (New Haven: Yale University Press, 2007), by Matthew Klingle, covers the broader sweep of the city.

Those seeking a succinct survey of environmentalism should consult Hal K. Rothman's *The Greening of a Nation? Environmentalism in the United States since 1945* (Fort Worth, Tex.: Harcourt Brace College Publishers, 1998). Readers might also find value in Frederick Buell's *From Apocalypse to Way of Life: Environmental Crisis in the American Century* (New York: Routledge, 2003), which is essentially an analysis of environmentalist literature in the relevant period.

On the history of ecology, see Sharon E. Kingsland, *The Evolution of American Ecology, 1890–2000* (Baltimore: Johns Hopkins University Press, 2005), a remarkably helpful guide to the development of the scientific field. Unfortunately, Kingsland is less interested in the popularization of ecological ideas, and so many of the most visible scientists (Barry Commoner, for instance) play little role here. See also Donald Worster's seminal *Nature's Economy: A History of Ecological Ideas* (New York: Cambridge University Press, 1977), which is concerned almost entirely with the development of ecology before World War II, but Worster was writing in "the Age of Ecology," and he gives hints about the growing influences of ecological ideas in postwar American culture.

On the use of ecological metaphors to understand cities, start with the classic: Robert E. Park, Ernest W. Burgess, and Roderick D. McKenzie, *The City* (Chicago: University of Chicago Press, 1925), reprinted in 1967 and still alive with ideas useful for those studying the urban crisis. See also Mabel L. Walker, *Urban Blight and Slums: Economic and Legal Factors in Their Origin, Reclamation, and Prevention* (Cambridge, Mass.: Harvard University Press, 1938)—a great big book that reveals how serious these issues had become during the Great Depression. Wendell E. Pritchett also tackled the issue of blight in "The 'Public Menace' of Blight: Urban Renewal and the Private Uses of Eminent Domain," *Yale Law and Policy Review*, Winter 2003, 1–52. His wonderful article is packed with information about the role of blight in expanding the use of eminent domain in urban policy. For more on the power of ecological metaphors in American cities, see Jennifer S. Light, *The Nature of Cities: Ecological Visions and the American Urban Professions, 1920–1960* (Baltimore: Johns Hopkins University Press, 2009). For an early articulation of urban ecology, see Forest Stearns and Tom Montag, eds., *The Urban Ecosystem: A Holistic Approach* (Stroudsburg, Pa.: Dowden, Hutchinson and Ross, 1974), which provides a general and theoretical introduction to the topic.

CLEVELAND AND CARL B. STOKES

Cleveland has a rich history, but not an especially rich historiography. We regularly consulted two excellent online sources: Cleveland State University Libraries' "Cleveland Memory" website (www.clevelandmemory.org), useful for most topics covered in this book, and "The Encyclopedia of Cleveland History" (http://ech.cwru.edu/), the product of a collaboration between Case Western Reserve University and the Western Reserve Historical Society. Those interested in a comprehensive history of Cleveland should see William Ganson Rose's encyclopedic *Cleveland: The Making of a City* (Cleveland: World Publishing, 1950), which follows the city's history through the late 1940s. (The final chronological chapter, "Greatness Achieved, 1940–," gives no sense of the depths of the problems that were just around the bend.) For a more accessible narrative, see Carol Poh Miller and Robert A. Wheeler, *Cleveland: A Concise History, 1796–1996* (Bloomington: Indiana University Press, 1997).

We made ample use of Carl B. Stokes's own words, published in *Promises of Power: A Political Autobiography* (New York: Simon and Schuster, 1973). Stokes has also been the subject of several book-length treatments, most importantly Leonard N. Moore's fine political biography: *Carl B. Stokes and the Rise of Black Political Power* (Urbana: University of Illinois Press, 2003). Charles H. Levine's *Racial Conflict and the American Mayor: Power, Polarization, and Performance* (Lexington, Mass.: Lexington Books, 1974) is a less useful account of Cleveland's electoral politics and the inability of Stokes to build a lasting coalition during his two terms. For a contemporary summary of the Stokes era, see Estelle Zannes, *Checkmate in Cleveland: The Rhetoric of Confrontation during the Stokes Years* (Cleveland: Press of Case

Western Reserve University, 1972), which is a rambling narrative based on news reports and interviews focused on issues of race (and sideshow politics) and more concerned with the campaigns than actual policy or governance. For a better contemporary book, see Kenneth G. Weinberg's *Black Victory: Carl Stokes and the Winning of Cleveland* (Chicago: Quadrangle Books, 1968), which is a celebratory but useful political biography of Stokes through his 1967 election. For another, brief celebratory summary of the Stokes administration, see *The Stokes Years* (Cleveland, 1971), produced by Stokes's staff to tout his accomplishments in office. For Norman Krumholz's personal reflection on the development of "equity planning" in Cleveland, during the Stokes administration and beyond, see Krumholz and John Forester, *Making Equity Planning Work: Leadership in the Public Sector* (Philadelphia: Temple University Press, 1990), which includes a useful chapter on highway planning.

Given his important role in our story, we also consulted the doctoral work of Bailus Walker Jr. His "Environmental Management in Four Urban Centers of the United States" (Ph.D. diss., University of Minnesota, 1975) relies on a mix of public documents and personal experience to describe environmental health policy making and implementation in Cleveland and three other cities for which he worked: Dayton, Newark, and Washington, D.C. We found this work remarkably useful. The contemporary study of the Glenville Shootout, Louis H. Masotti and Jerome R. Corsi's *Shoot-Out in Cleveland: Black Militants and the Police: July 23, 1968* (New York: Bantam Books, 1969), is both riveting and indispensable in understanding Cleveland in the late 1960s.

Of the secondary literature less directly related to our work, we found most useful Andrew Wiese's *Places of Their Own: African-American Suburbanization in the Twentieth Century* (Chicago: University of Chicago Press, 2004). It includes discussion of a distant Cleveland suburb, Chagrin Falls, which attracted African American residents, and East Cleveland, the first large suburb to turn majority black just outside the city. Students of Cleveland history will also want to read *Cleveland: A Tradition of Reform*, edited by David D. Van Tassel and John J. Grabowski (Kent, Ohio: Kent State University Press, 1986), a collection of essays that describe areas of reform activism, largely in the pre–World War II era. On earlier periods, see Ronald R. Weiner, *Lake Effects: A History of Urban Policy Making in Cleveland, 1825–1929* (Columbus: Ohio State University Press, 2005). Weiner describes a series of regimes—shifting coalitions—that led Cleveland, but he notes that the city was never entirely in control of its fate, regardless of who held influence. On deeper roots of housing concerns, see John Grabowski, "A Social Settlement in a Neighborhood in Transition: Hiram House, Cleveland, Ohio, 1896–1926"

(Ph.D. diss., Case Western Reserve University, 1977). With *Derelict Paradise: Homelessness and Urban Development in Cleveland, Ohio* (Amherst: University of Massachusetts Press, 2011), Daniel Kerr offers a long history of planning and policy failures related to housing and homelessness. The book includes useful discussions of Cleveland's ghettos and the Hough and Glenville rebellions. See also Jennifer Frost, *"An Interracial Movement of the Poor": Community Organizing and the New Left in the 1960s* (New York: New York University Press, 2001), which includes considerable discussion of Students for a Democratic Society activism in Cleveland, especially a project on the near West Side. On the influence of race on disinvestment, see Townsand Price-Spratlen and Avery M. Guest, "Race and Population Change: A Longitudinal Look at Cleveland Neighborhoods," *Sociological Forum* 17 (March 2002), 105–36. Very interested readers might find of use Diana Tittle's *Rebuilding Cleveland: The Cleveland Foundation and Its Evolving Urban Strategy* (Columbus: Ohio State University Press, 1992), although it presents a jumble of organizations and programs with little context or consequence.

1. What Will Become of Cleveland?

Adam Rome's *The Genius of Earth Day: How a 1970 Teach-In Unexpectedly Made the First Green Generation* (New York: Hill and Wang, 2013) argues convincingly that Earth Day played a critical role in creating a more powerful and organized environmental movement. Rome's book provides excellent context for our narrower story of Earth Day. See also Garrett De Bell, ed., *The Environmental Handbook* (New York: Ballantine Books, 1970), published in preparation for Earth Day, and *Earth Day—the Beginning: A Guide for Survival Compiled and Edited by the National Staff of Environmental Action* (New York: Bantam Books, 1970), which is a compendium of some of the materials produced for the first Earth Day. On the diversity of the African American response to Earth Day, see Sylvia Hood Washington, "Ball of Confusion: Public Health, African Americans, and Earth Day 1970," in *Natural Protest: Essays on the History of American Environmentalism*, edited by Michael Egan and Jeff Crane (New York: Routledge, 2009).

2. Hough and the Urban Crisis

Government documents contain valuable information concerning federal study of ghettos and renewal efforts. Especially valuable is the *Hearing before the United States Commission on Civil Rights: Hearing Held in Cleveland, Ohio, April 1–7, 1966* (Washington, D.C.: Government Printing Office, 1966), which includes all the testimony heard during the commission's visit that spring and some additional supporting documents. Congressional hearings are also useful. See "Urban Renewal," Hearings before the Subcommittee on Housing of the Committee on Banking and Currency, House of Representatives, 88th Congress, 1st session, October 22, 23, 24, 1963, and "Federal Role in Urban Affairs," Hearings before the Subcommittee on Executive Reorganization of the Committee on Government Operations, U.S. Senate, 89th Congress, 2nd session, August 24, 25, 26, 1966.

For understanding Hough in particular, other contemporary studies proved useful, including the United States Bureau of the Census, *Special Census of Cleveland, Ohio: April 1, 1965* (Washington, D.C.: Government Printing Office, 1966), which gives demographic details at mid-decade, and Marvin B. Sussman and R. Clyde White, *Hough, Cleveland, Ohio: A Study of Social Life and Change* (Cleveland: Press of the Western Reserve University, 1959), a fine sociological study of a neighborhood at the tipping point. For housing data, see also work published by the National Urban League: *The National Survey of Housing Abandonment* (New York: National Urban League, 1971), and Cleveland City Planning Commission, "Housing Abandonment in Cleveland" (October 1971).

For background on the rat problem, see David E. Lantz, *The Brown Rat in the United States* (Washington, D.C.: Government Printing Office, 1909), which is a surprisingly entertaining and informative pamphlet published by the Department of Agriculture's Biological Survey. See also Malcolm McLaughlin, "The Pied Piper of the Ghetto: Lyndon Johnson, Environmental Justice, and the Politics of Rat Control," *Journal of Urban History*, July 2011, 541–61, a scholarly study of urban rats in the 1960s. McLaughlin makes the important argument that we should be more concerned with the environmental sequelae of the processes that created the urban crisis.

We also made use of some national publications addressing urban disorder. The most valuable were two *Saturday Evening Post* essays by John Skow: "Can Cleveland Escape Burning?" (July 29, 1967) and "Cleveland: The Flicker of Fear" (September 7, 1968). See also Frederick Graves, "How Cities Can Avoid Another Long Hot Summer," *Jet*, May 18, 1967, 14–21. For an insider's perspective on one federal program, see Charles M. Haar, *Between the Idea and the Reality: A Study in the Origin, Fate, and Legacy of the Model Cities Program* (Boston: Little, Brown, 1975).

Useful secondary sources on Cleveland's ghettos and renewal efforts include Todd M. Michney, "Race, Violence, and Urban Territoriality: Cleveland's Little Italy and the 1966 Hough Uprising," *Journal of Urban History*, March 2006, 404–28, and William D. Jenkins, "Before Downtown: Cleveland, Ohio, and Urban Renewal, 1949–1958," *Journal of Urban History*, May 2001, 471–96, which argues that Cleveland, under the leadership of Ernest Bohn, used urban renewal in an attempt to revive failing neighborhoods before turning to downtown renewal. J. Mark Souther has published an excellent study of urban renewal on Cleveland's East Side: "Acropolis of the Middle-West: Decay, Renewal, and Boosterism in Cleveland's University Circle," *Journal of Planning History*, February 2011, 30–58. Those interested in learning more about Hough should also read Karen Ferguson, "Organizing the Ghetto: The Ford Foundation, CORE, and White Power in the Black Power Era, 1967–1969," *Journal of Urban History*, November 2007, 67–100. Daniel Kerr's essay, "Who Burned Cleveland, Ohio? The Forgotten Fires of the 1970s," found in Greg Bankoff, Uwe Lubken, and Jordan Sand's collection, *Flammable Cities: Urban Conflagration and the Making of the Modern World* (Madison: University of Wisconsin Press, 2012), tells the story backward, suggesting that neighborhood abandonment *follows* burning, an interpretation we don't support.

3. Downtown and the Limits of Urban Renewal

Like all large cities, Cleveland has produced a string of planning documents. We used three from the Cleveland City Planning Commission: *Cleveland Today... Tomorrow: The General Plan of Cleveland* (1950); *Downtown Cleveland 1975: The Downtown General Plan* (1959); and *The Urban Renewal Plan University-Euclid Urban Renewal Project No. 1, Ohio R-44* (1961). The Cleveland Advertising Club published an overview of Cleveland's extensive renewal plans: *Report on Urban Renewal in Cleveland* (September 1955). Also of great interest is the plan created by I. M. Pei & Associates: *Erieview, Cleveland, Ohio: An Urban Renewal Plan for Downtown Cleveland* (New York: I. M. Pei, 1961). The critical perspective on Erieview can be found in the court records: Grisanti v. City of Cleveland 179 N.E.2d 798 (1962) and Grisanti v. City of Cleveland 181 N.E.2d 299 (1962). See also the informative "Premature Approval of Large-Scale Demolition for Erieview Urban Renewal Project 1, Cleveland, Ohio," produced by the General Accounting Office and contained within "Urban Renewal in the District of Columbia," Hearings before the Subcommittee on the District of Columbia, House of Representatives, 88th Congress, 1st session, June 21, July 26, August 14, 1963, Part 4.

Given our interest in the Central National Bank, we read Rose Marie Jollie's *On the Grow with Cleveland: A Brief History of Cleveland and the Central National Bank of Cleveland* (Cleveland: Central National Bank, 1965). As one would expect from a corporate history, this isn't terribly insightful, but it provides the basic narrative of the bank's growth.

For secondary literature on planning in Cleveland, consult Walter C. Leedy Jr., "Cleveland's Struggle for Self-Identity: Aesthetics, Economics, and Politics," in *Modern Architecture in America: Visions and Revisions*, edited by Richard Guy Wilson and Sidney K. Robinson (Ames: Iowa State University Press, 1991), a valuable piece on the Group Plan's origins and evolution. Just as valuable: Thomas S. Hines, *Burnham of Chicago: Architect and Planner* (New York: Oxford University Press, 1974), which contains a chapter exploring Burnham's engagement in the Group Plan. We also read Holly M. Rarick, *Progressive Vision: The Planning of Downtown Cleveland, 1903–1930* (Cleveland: Cleveland Museum of Art, 1986), an informative and richly illustrated book that accompanied an exhibition at the museum. For a discussion of Terminal Tower, illustrated with wonderful images, see John J. Grabowski and Walter C. Leedy Jr., *The Terminal Tower, Tower City Center: A Historical Perspective* (Cleveland: Western Reserve Historical Society, 1990). For a more critical perspective on planning, see Kenneth Kolson, *Big Plans: The Allure and Folly of Urban Design* (Baltimore: Johns Hopkins University Press, 2001).

For a valuable discussion of skyscraper development in the two most important cities, see Carol Willis, *Form Follows Finance: Skyscrapers and Skylines in New York and Chicago* (New York: Princeton Architectural Press, 1995). Willis argues that historians have overlooked the speculative nature of skyscrapers, that they grew not so much as an expression of corporate power but as money-making real estate investments. See also Oliver Zunz's *Making America Corporate, 1870–1920* (Chicago: University of Chicago Press, 1990), which describes the development of skyscrapers in the context of the growth of corporate culture. Helen B. Lybarger, *History of the Cleveland Restoration Society* (Cleveland: Cleveland Restoration Society, 1982), is brief but helpful.

4. POLICY AND THE POLLUTED CITY

Government publications, and studies conducted at the behest of government, provide rich detail on pollution and pollution control. Of particular value are the studies of the engineering firm Havens and Emerson: *Master Plan for Pollution Abatement, Cleveland, Ohio* (June 1968) and *Feasibility of a Stabilization-Retention Basin in Lake Erie at Cleveland, Ohio* (May 1968). We also consulted the many conference proceedings published as the federal government attempted to get a handle on Great Lakes pollution. Most important: U.S. Department of Health, Education and Welfare, *Proceedings, Conference in the Matter of Pollution of Lake Erie and Its Tributaries, Cleveland, August 3–6, 1965* (Washington, D.C.: U.S. Department of Health, Education and Welfare, 1965). Official documents regarding air pollution are more scarce, but interested readers might find useful the Air Conservation Committee's "Summary Report" published in 1970 and held at the Cleveland Public Library.

In the secondary literature, the Lake Erie story has been well told in a variety of ways. Dave Dempsey offers a very readable, broad context for the Great Lakes story. See *On the Brink: The Great Lakes in the 21st Century* (East Lansing: Michigan State University Press, 2004). In *Lake Erie Rehabilitated: Controlling Cultural Eutrophication, 1960s–1990s* (Akron, Ohio: University of Akron Press, 2000), William McGucken offers a detailed history of the effort to improve water quality in Lake Erie, focusing primarily on the development of scientific knowledge and policy formation. Terence Kehoe offers a similarly detailed recitation of the politics surrounding pollution control, focusing on the shift to federal involvement. Kehoe's *Cleaning Up the Great Lakes: From Cooperation to Confrontation* (DeKalb: Northern Illinois University Press, 1997), relies heavily on the many conferences on water quality in the 1960s while setting the narrative in the context of the growing environmental movement. To read the story from the perspective of middle-class environmental activists, see Terrianne K. Schulte, "Grassroots at the Water's Edge: The League of Women Voters and the Struggle to Save Lake Erie, 1956–1970" (Ph.D. diss., State University of New York at Buffalo, 2006).

For an analysis of water pollution control more generally, told from the perspective of Washington, see Paul Charles Milazzo, *Unlikely Environmentalists: Congress and Clean Water, 1945–1972* (Lawrence: University Press of Kansas, 2006), which argues that Congress deserves considerable credit for passing sweeping environmental legislation. For context on the air pollution problem, see especially Scott Hamilton Dewey's *Don't Breathe the Air: Air Pollution and U.S. Environmental Politics, 1945–1970* (College Station: Texas A&M University Press, 2000), and for the earlier period, see David Stradling, *Smokestacks and Progressives: Environmentalists, Engineers, and*

Air Quality in America, 1881–1951 (Baltimore: Johns Hopkins University Press, 1999).

5. THE BURNING RIVER

We consulted several government documents that concerned the Cuyahoga. Most important are "Report of the Cleveland City Council Committee on Stream Pollution to the Council of the City of Cleveland, Ohio," October 10, 1946, and "Water Pollution—1970," Hearings before the Subcommittee on Air and Water Pollution, United States Senate, 91st Congress, 2nd session, April 28, 29, 30, May 1, 6, 1970. The limnologist John H. Hartig's *Burning Rivers: Revival of Four Urban-Industrial Rivers That Caught on Fire* (Burlington, Ontario: Ecovision World Monograph Series, 2010) provides some historical context concerning pollution on the Buffalo, Cuyahoga, Rouge, and Chicago rivers but is most useful in providing descriptions of recent recoveries.

For an introduction to the growing literature on the relationship between rivers and cities, see Stephane Castonguay and Matthew Evenden, eds., *Urban Rivers: Remaking Rivers, Cities, and Space in Europe and North America* (Pittsburgh: University of Pittsburgh Press, 2012). For an introduction to the wonderful work being done on rivers more generally, see the essays in Christof Mauch and Thomas Zeller, eds., *Rivers in History: Perspectives on Waterways in Europe and North America* (Pittsburgh: University of Pittsburgh Press, 2008).

6. FROM EARTH DAY TO ECOCITY

Cleveland State University Libraries' "Cleveland Memory" (www.cleveland memory.org), useful for most topics covered in this book, is especially valuable on highways. It allows access to the series of route location studies issued in the 1960s by the engineering firm Howard, Needles, Tammen & Bergendoff, including the unbuilt Central, Bedford, Heights, Lee, and Clark freeways, all planned for East Side Cleveland and neighboring suburbs. For context on the anti-highway movement, see A. Q. Mowbray's jeremiad *Road to Ruin* (Philadelphia: Lippincott, 1969), which decries national highway policy and uses the Clark and Lee freeways in Cleveland as an example. For the national context of the freeway revolt, see Robert Gioielli, " 'We Must Destroy You to Save You': Highway Construction and the City as a Modern Commons," *Radical History Review*, Winter 2011, 62–82, and Mark Rose and Raymond Mohl, *Interstate: Highway Policy and Politics since 1939* (Knoxville: University of Tennessee Press, 2012).

On watershed management and Three Rivers planning, see the good summary in Daniel A. Mazmanian and Jeanne Nienaber, *Can Organizations Change? Environmental Protection, Citizen Participation, and the Corps of Engineers* (Washington, D.C.: Brookings Institution, 1979), which is a useful study of how the Army Corps altered its culture in response to public demands for environmental accountability. The corps' planning documents are available and contain correspondence with citizens and organizations. See *Wastewater Management Study for Cleveland-Akron Metropolitan and Three Rivers Watershed Areas Summary Report* (August 1973), especially Appendixes II and VIII. Ohio Department of Natural Resources also published a massive study, *Northeast Ohio Water Plan, Main Report, 1972*, although only the most ardent student would find it useful. See also Daniel Schneider's surprisingly interesting history of sewage treatment: *Hybrid Nature: Sewage Treatment and the Contradictions of the Industrial Ecosystem* (Cambridge, Mass.: MIT Press, 2011).

On the issue of regional or watershed governance, see the Ohio Constitutional Revision Commission Reports 1970–1977, Local Government Committee (available at www.lsc.state.oh.us/ocrc/); U.S. Department of Health, Education and Welfare, *Report for Consultation on the Greater Metropolitan Cleveland Intrastate Air Quality Control Region*, February 1969 (also available through www.epa.gov/nscep/index.html); and *The Cuyahoga River Watershed: Proceedings of a Symposium held at Kent State University, Kent, Ohio, 1 November 1968* (Kent, Ohio: Kent State University, 1969). David C. Sweet, Kathryn Wertheim Hexter, and David Beach, eds., *The New American City Faces Its Regional Future: A Cleveland Perspective* (Athens: Ohio University Press, 1999), contains the substance of a conference held at Cleveland State in 1996 and includes several interesting pieces on the difficulty of regional thinking and action.

On urban sustainability, see *EcoCity Cleveland: Ideas and Tools for a Sustainable Bioregion*. Issues can be found at GreenCityBlueLake's website: www.gcbl.org/research/ecocity-cleveland-journal-1993-2001. Cleveland's sustainability document can be found at http://www.gcbl.org/projects/sustainable-cleveland-2019. Scholars from a variety of fields have created a large, mostly theoretical literature on sustainability. Readers may find useful Joan Fitzgerald, *Emerald Cities: Urban Sustainability and Economic Development* (New York: Oxford University Press, 2010), and James S. Russell, *The Agile City: Building Well-Being and Wealth in an Era of Climate Change* (Washington, D.C.: Island Press, 2011).

Index

Note: Page numbers in italics refer to figures.

INDEX

INDEX

INDEX

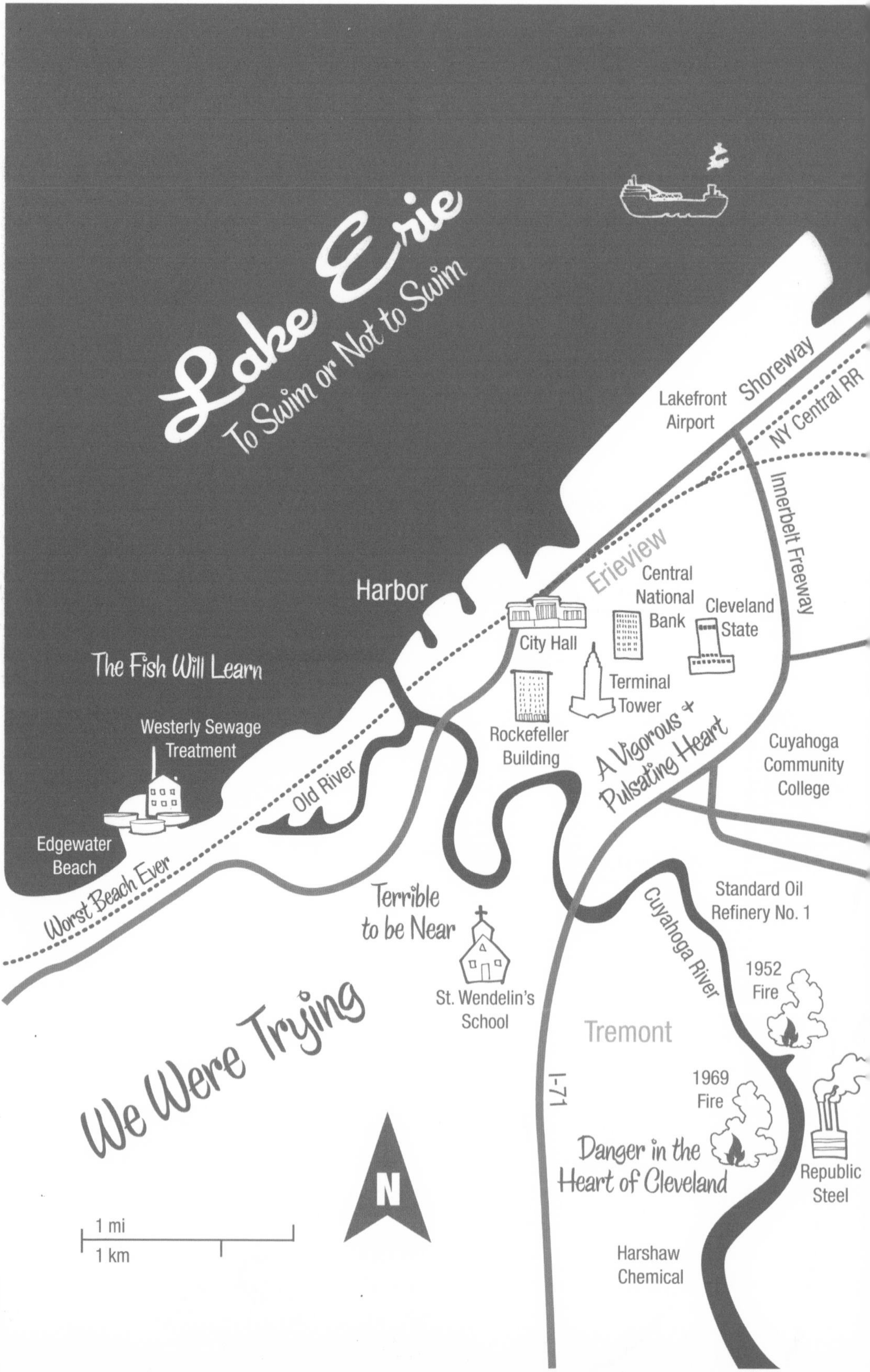

Lake Erie
To Swim or Not to Swim
Shoreway
Lakefront Airport
NY Central RR
Innerbelt Freeway
Erieview
Harbor
Central National Bank
Cleveland State
City Hall
Terminal Tower
Rockefeller Building
A Vigorous + Pulsating Heart
Cuyahoga Community College
The Fish Will Learn
Westerly Sewage Treatment
Old River
Edgewater Beach
Worst Beach Ever
Terrible to be Near
St. Wendelin's School
Standard Oil Refinery No. 1
Cuyahoga River
1952 Fire
Tremont
I-71
1969 Fire
Danger in the Heart of Cleveland
Republic Steel
We Were Trying
N
1 mi
1 km
Harshaw Chemical